Haunted Liverpool 29

Tom Slemen

The Tom Slemen Press

Copyright © 2018 Tom Slemen

All rights reserved.

ISBN-10: 1718881452
ISBN-13: **978-1718881457**

For

Nigel Peever, best narrator in the business.

CONTENTS

A Love that Never Dies	1
The League of Blondes	6
The People of the Cards	11
Weird Family Omen	16
Tit-Willow	22
Ghosts without a History	26
Captain Starlight	59
Shanghaied by a Ghost	66
The Mystery of Elva	71
You Are Everything	88
The Sinister Marriage Wrecker	96
A Tale of Two Witches	104
Time Twins	119
Vampires on Lower Lane?	123

Jack in the Box	142
The Mystery of Mersey Hafen	153
Voices on a Bus	164
Approaching Shadows	168
Strange Warning	177
The Vamps	183
The Carbon Copy People	189
Vanishing Debra	213
Marjorie	224
Snippy	229
The Shapeshifters	245
Right Into Tomorrow Today	270
The Warning Emojis	285
The Reader	290
Vampire Cult	295
The Thing Under the Royal Court Theatre	311

Tattoo Jack	320
Glimpses of Strange Futures	335
The Encourager	364
The Strange World of Warning Dreams	370
The Grave Worms	379
Bogeyman from Above	387
Mr Forgettable	391

A LOVE THAT NEVER DIES

It was a Saturday afternoon, Christmas Eve, 2011. He stood in the packed railway carriage heading for Bromborough Rake when his eyes chanced to meet her face – and at first Jon Trent thought she was someone famous because she looked so familiar, but then he realised she was not someone off the television or out of some film – she was someone out of *his* life yet he simply couldn't place her, and he was going to be forthright and ask her who she was, but the train decelerated and she walked away from him, ready to exit. 'Excuse me,' he said, but she didn't hear him. The train stopped with a slight inertial jolt, and people crowded around her before the doors slid apart. They all poured out at Port Sunlight, and Jon watched her through the window, walking away, her back straight as a plank, and she had an elegant and confident way of walking, he thought. He watched her until she was out of view and the train moved off, heading south. All through the remainder of that Christmas Eve he thought about her at his terraced home on Beechwood Road, and try as he may, he could not drive her face from his mind. Who on earth was she? How could he know her yet not recall seeing her anywhere? Had she been some model in a magazine? No. Some girl he'd gone to school with? No, she seemed to be about 26 and he was 36. Was she someone he'd met on holiday? No – he most certainly had not met a girl as beautiful as her on his recent holiday to Malta. He sat down in his gaming chair with a glass of wine and entered a meditative state as he recalled the mysterious lady. What had she been wearing? A woollen roll-neck jumper, skinny jeans and Keds. She'd held a River Island carrier bag and some other bags. He muttered to himself: 'Come on; *where* have you seen her before?'

He racked his memory trying to unravel the mystery of that eerily familiar girl but it was no use – she simply couldn't be placed. Jon found his mobile and called his best mate Charlie Vincent and told him about the girl on the tip of his memory and Charlie said: 'What it is mate is this: they all look the same nowadays, these birds, especially blondes – like clones they are.'

'She was a brunette,' Jon told him.

Charlie yawned. 'Whatever. They all dress the same – that's why you think you've seen her before.'

'No, she was like no girl I've ever seen before,' Jon confessed.

'Oh I'm going before you make me throw up,' said Charlie, and hung up.

This was Jon's first Christmas alone since the split with his girlfriend Joely, yet he did not feel at all sad nor did he wallow in self-pity because he was too preoccupied by the mystifying girl he'd seen on the train. Christmas came and went, and at 5:10pm on

Wednesday 18 January, he boarded the train at Lime Street to take him home after work – and she was standing in the crowded carriage. Jon felt his heart go into freefall for a moment as he noticed her. This time she turned to look at him – and her large green eyes widened – as if she knew him. She was looking at him the way he had looked at her on Christmas Eve. He smiled. She blinked, looked away – and then slowly turned to look at him again. Jon and the woman said simultaneously to each other: 'How do I know you?' then started to laugh. Jon told the girl – who gave her name as Saffron – that he couldn't place her, and that since he'd seen her on the train three weeks before, he had been driven to distraction trying to identify her. Saffron said that was odd because she somehow knew his face and yet she couldn't work out why. When Saffron got off the train at Port Sunlight, Jon disembarked too for some reason – even though his stop was Bromborough Rake, further down the line. He stood there for a moment on the platform looking awkwardly at the highly recognisable face of a woman he felt he'd known all of his life, and she hesitated, half turning away, ready to walk on, when he said, 'Saffron, you might think this really cheeky of me, but I *have* to see you again.'

'She returned a quizzical look, fidgeted with the long thin strap of her handbag, and then, with a coy smile she asked: 'Why?'

'It's bizarre,' he confessed, 'but I feel as if I've always known you.'

Under normal circumstances, Saffron would have just laughed off such a random request for a date from a man she didn't know – but she felt that these were *not* normal circumstances, as she too felt as if Jon was somehow well-known to her. She seemed stuck for words as Jon looked on and people passed them going to and from the train. 'Look, Jon, I really don't know what to say, but well, I hardly know you, and you seem like – well – '

'I'm sorry,' Jon closed his eyes and nodded his head, 'it is ridiculous, but I mean maybe we could swap numbers – or is that crazy too?'

Saffron chuckled, raised her eyebrows and shrugged.

'No, you're right, it *is* crazy,' Jon looked at the floor, then slowly turned and saw the train leave.

'Jon, you *are* crazy but so am I,' she said to his back.

He turned around and saw that her mobile was already in her hand.

Jon and Saffron swapped numbers and within days they met up for a coffee - and then they started to see one another, and the mystery of the way they seemed familiar to one another deepened over the coming weeks. Saffron said she'd had recurring dreams of being with a man who looked just like Jon for years, and the couple found they shared so many tastes in books, art and music. They visited a seaside fortune teller in Blackpool one day, and she told Jon and Saffron they were both "old souls" who had shared many previous lives.

This suggestion seemed to strike some chord deep in the psyches of the couple. Had they known one another in some previous reincarnation? Jon eventually visited a clinical hypnotherapist in Liverpool, and he was 'regressed' to what seemed to be a life in 18th century France. He was an aristocrat during the Revolution – and Saffron was his wife. They both died on the guillotine. Saffron was regressed, and although she did not know the facts about Jon's regression (because he had decided to divulge nothing in case the hypnotist was a fraud), she too recalled her life as a well-to-do lady during the French Revolution, and remembered fainting as she was taken to the guillotine. Around this time, something bizarre took place; Saffron started to talk in her sleep – in a French accent – even though she only knew basic French phrases of the sort tourists pick up from guidebooks and YouTube tutorials. Jon managed to record some of the French sleep talk and it was clear that Saffron was having a fluent full-blown in-depth conversation with someone in the French language. The hypnotherapist eventually determined that Jon and Saffron had shared four other lives stretching back into medieval times. The couple were later married, and they remain inseparable. They really do seem to be what we now class as "Soulmates" - and one wonders – will they meet again in some future existence?

THE LEAGUE OF BLONDES

For legal reasons I've had to change some of the names and places in this story, but the rest, as far as I know, is a true and very strange account. In July 1977, a 45-year-old out of work actor named Mark Pritchard bumped into an old friend named Clive Scott in the Bowring Park pub, Court Hey. During the conversation over a pint, Mark told his friend that work had dried up and that he was even prepared to have a go at window cleaning when Clive said: "Well, if you're serious, I've got a set of old ladders in my garden shed you can have.'

'You're on,' Mark told Clive and accompanied him to his house on Huyton's Mayfair Avenue. The shed had been broken into and the ladders and most of the garden tools had been stolen, but Mark calmed his friend down and pitched an idea to him. 'I'll pay rent on your shed – a tenner a week.'

'You want to live in my shed?' a bewildered Clive asked.

'Not live – work," Mark replied, his eyes scanning the interior of the large green shed. 'I'm going to have a go at making chairs and cupboards, you know, carpentry and all that. Here's the deposit.' He gave

Clive a tenner.

'My Karen won't like it – ' Clive began to say, but Mark smiled and nodded and said, 'She'll be alright.'

Well, Mark had a rudimentary knowledge of electrical engineering, and so he illegally tapped into an electricity supply – possibly from a nearby lamp post, and he also tapped the cable running to a public telephone box. He fitted a neon light to the ceiling of the hut and upon an old green baize card table he placed an unwanted telephone he'd acquired from his aunt. Then Mark visited the local church hall where a duplicating machine could be hired for 50p an hour and he produced hundreds of sheets advertising his 'new company' Pritchard Investigations – yes, Mark had set himself up as a private investigator; £10 a day plus expenses. Those sheets went everywhere: the windows of filling stations, post offices, libraries, social clubs and supermarket bulletin boards and so on, but Mark Pritchard had to answer the phone right away if it rang – because it would also be ringing in the local public phone box!

He got two cases in one day – a woman who suspected that her poodle had been kidnapped and the manager of a supermarket who believed a staff member was stealing boxes of frozen foods. Both cases were satisfactorily solved within a week, despite Karen Scott threatening to evict Mark. He bought Karen a bouquet of roses and a box of Matchmakers and she left him alone for a while – under the condition he would find a proper office when his earnings became stable.

Then came the strange case; a rich 50-year-old company director named Roland Olliston said a person or persons unknown were out to kill him. They'd tampered with the brakes of his Mercedes, made silent calls to him and his wife in the dead of night, and on one occasion he'd been sent a doll that contained an incendiary device which had destroyed his living room. On Valentine's Day seven months back, Roland had received a card saying he'd been targeted by "The League of Blondes" but had thrown the card away, thinking someone was just playing a silly prank. Mark said he'd visit Roland for more information but the promising client insisted on visiting Mark, and he was very surprised to see that the office was a garden shed. Mark had to say his usual office was being refurbished. There were obvious questions to be asked. 'Mr Olliston, do you know of any former female employees – any previous old flame for that matter – who might be behind these attempts on your life?' Mark enquired.

'I'm a one-woman man, Pritchard – I don't have affairs, and all of my previous secretaries have left the firm under amicable conditions. But of course, some secretaries did make passes, but I made it clear I wasn't interested and I even had a photograph of my wife on the desk to underline my loyalty.'

'Whoever it is,' said Mark, 'they seem very determined to cause harm – fixing brakes, sending fire-bombs to you; call me sexist but I don't associate all that with a woman.'

'Don't underestimate a woman scorned, Pritchard,' said Roland, lighting a cigarette. 'Who on earth is this League of Blondes? I need you to find out. A thousand for you if you do.'

Mark worked overtime on this one, and he traced

previous secretaries who had worked for Olliston – and noted they were all blonde. Then Mark started to receive warnings from a woman over the phone. This woman said that Roland Olliston was getting his just desserts. Karen Scott, the wife of Mark's friend Clive, began to have terrible nightmares about women dressed in black who warned her to have nothing to do with Mark Pritchard. Still, Mark delved into the case, and he suspected that witchcraft was being used against him and his client. Then Roland's wife visited Mark and told him to drop the case. She said that she'd hired a 'proper private eye' to look into the matter and he had discovered the sordid truth. Her husband had a habit of hiring young blonde secretaries, and then he'd wine and dine them, take them to a hotel, where they'd book in as a married couple. Once Roland had his way with the secretary, he'd fire her – and move on to the next victim. He often compared these young women to cars and joked about getting a new model once he'd had enough of the last one. According to Mrs Olliston, Roland could not accept ageing and had to periodically prove to himself that he could still pull "dolly birds". One secretary he had dumped had committed suicide because she had loved Roland, but he hadn't shown an iota of concern at her death. One of the 'conquests' was an accomplished witch, and she had formed a coven made up from the discarded secretaries and taught them potent black magic. And the League of Blondes was born.

So, Mark abandoned the case, and a month later he read in the papers about the curious death of Roland Olliston. He had been found dead from heart failure under a hedge in his garden, his eyes bulging in terror at something. Mark wondered if the League of Blondes had finally ended the life of the lecherous businessman with their potent black magic. Hell hath no fury like a woman scorned, but a whole coven of scorned women would result in devilry that could kill a legion of men. I wonder if there are similar Leagues of wronged women resorting to supernatural payback today...

THE PEOPLE OF THE CARDS

I've had to change a few names in this strange story, but beyond that, I am reporting events exactly as they were related to me. Her name was Christina Wedlake, the pretty 26-year-old fiancée of a fairly well-known television actor we shall call Graham Pye. In the autumn of 1977, Graham and Christina moved into a small cottage in Frankby, and on the day after the housewarming party, Graham was off to Sussex to shoot scenes for a TV drama for three days. Most of the year, Graham was away, filming on location, and Christina was looking for any work at all to fill the void created by Graham's periodic absences, and she'd recently been interviewed at a local café where a waitress was needed. She was now waiting to hear if she'd landed the job. On this grey Monday afternoon of 31 October, Christina found herself feeling quite depressed as she sat alone in the cottage, pining for Graham. The telephone rang and she eagerly answered it. The voice she heard cheered her up immediately; it was Graham, doing his usual Inspector Clouseau impersonation. 'Who is this?' she asked, knowing very well it was her fiancé, and Graham replied, 'Jacques – Jacques Clouseau speaking on zee fern.'

'I might be able to get home a day early,' said

Graham in his real voice, 'the weather's been too bad to film some scenes.'

Christina was so glad to hear this, and after the conversation ended, she went for a spin in her Triumph Herald to the church of St John the Divine, to visit the grave of an uncle in the cemetery. On the top step of a plinth supporting a towering Celtic cross in the cemetery, Christina noticed a purple box about five inches long, three inches wide, with a depth of some two inches to it. She looked about, and seeing no one was around, she picked up the box and saw that it contained vintage, velvet-backed playing cards. Who would leave cards in such a hallowed place? She wondered, and walked off with them – and she had the eerie feeling someone was watching her. She went for a drive to West Kirby, then headed back to the cottage. She felt so down eating alone, and so she kept the sorrow at bay with wine, and around 10pm she dozed off on the sofa. She awoke at midnight, put on her nightgown and went to bed, but couldn't get back to sleep. After much tossing and turning she finally got up around 3am, and she recalled the pack of cards she'd found, so she picked them up, shuffled them, and sat at the table in the kitchen playing Patience. She started to have romantic thoughts about Graham, and thinking it might be a good idea to marry Graham at the church of St John the Divine, she started to fantasise about the big day - but her pleasant reverie was suddenly shattered by a heavy knocking at the oak door of the cottage. Christina tiptoed to the door and nervously asked, 'Who's that?'

'Jacques!' came the reply.

Christina excitedly slid the bolt off and unlocked the

door, thinking it was Graham doing his Inspector Clouseau impersonation. She imagined he'd got away from filming early and had driven home through the night just to be with her – how romantic!

But when the door was swung open, the young lady saw it was a strangely-dressed man with seven other people standing behind him, and their attire was also outlandish.

'Hello there, mademoiselle, I am Jacques the Knave,' said the man who had knocked, and he wore the exact same style of hat and gaudy clothing as the Jacks on the playing cards. The "Knave" had a prominent broken nose and facially he reminded Christina of the French actor Jean Paul Belmondo. Then it hit her – Graham knew some oddball thespians – had he arranged for a motley crew of actors to pay her a visit as some Halloween prank? The other figures included two stout and stern looking Kings, a Queen with a very pale face and a pair of sad bloodshot eyes, another Knave (with black bushy eyebrows that met in the middle), a sinister-looking joker who continually sniggered at her, and an abnormally tall figure in a medieval-looking outfit of black velvet with a silver spade symbol emblazoned on his chest. His face was pale and elongated and he had piercing eyes like black buttons. Christina just knew he represented the traditional death card – the Ace of Spades. 'Is Graham behind all this?' Christina asked, and gave a nervous laugh, and she hoped to God that her fiancé *was* behind this peculiar charade – or she had just let a group of unhinged-looking strangers into her home.

Jacques seized her, kissed her hard, and tried to rip off her night gown. She screamed and tore herself from his icy-handed embrace. 'Pute ingrate!' he roared at her – the words sounded like the French for "ungrateful whore".

'You shall be our new Queen!' said the square-shouldered King in an accent with traces of French, and he thrust a piebald costume of many colours with a ruffled collar at Christina, but she ran out of the cottage screaming. One of her slippers came off about twenty yards from the cottage, and she hesitated and was about to go back for it but she saw the sinister costumed intruders running after her. Christina screamed and continued to run. She heard voices, sometimes in French and sometimes in English, shouting out very offensive words at her, and at one point she looked back and saw the knave Jacques who had tried to assault her with a dagger in his hand, and he was running far ahead of the rest of the band of costumed maniacs. Christina lost her freakish pursuers at one point and hid behind the hedge of a garden, where she remained, trembling with fear and the cold. Around 3.40am she heard the measured tread of someone coming her way and grabbed a chunk of sandstone from a rockery, ready to strike whoever it was, but it turned out be a policeman on his beat on Hill Bark Road.

He didn't believe Christina's story – no one did – and those cards were nowhere to be found when she returned to the cottage a mile away - but Graham was convinced *something* strange had happened to terrify his fiancée – but he thought a bunch of drunken revellers on their way back from some fancy dress party had called on Christina – probably because they'd seen the light on in the cottage. Christina said she felt there was something supernatural about the visitants, and she recalled how Jacques – who had been dressed as a knave – looked exactly like one of the Knave cards in that mysterious deck of vintage cards. Christina believed that somehow, those figures were connected to the cards and that they wanted to dress her up as one of the Queens and force her to join them. After that night, whenever Graham was away shooting scenes on location, Christina stayed with her mother over in Liverpool, and in the end, the couple moved to Heswall and were married. Just what happened in the early hours of that Halloween morning in 1977, is, like the vanishing deck of cards, an insoluble mystery.

WEIRD FAMILY OMEN

In my last book, *Haunted Liverpool 28*, I compiled a large chapter about Liverpool's cursed families – a collection of what are known as generational curses – curses that may stretch over generations, lasting for decades, or even centuries. The bloodlines of many families - local and global - really do seem to carry these long-lasting jinxes, and the curses have been cast by witches and also by everyday people who were wrongfully defamed, tricked out of money or even fatally wounded by the ancestor of the 'damned' family. There are countless reasons why one would curse an entire lineage, but sometimes the origins of a family curse have been long forgotten, and that is the case in the following story. A 17-year-old Childwall girl named Debbie was chillingly introduced to her family's curse in a very sinister way. She had finished some early Christmas shopping one dark afternoon in the late November of 1966, and as she passed the Wizard's Den joke shop on Moorfields, she noticed a small man (about three and a half feet in height) in a tweed trilby and mustard-coloured mackintosh – and he had a ghastly grey skull-like face. She went cold when she saw him, and he began to follow her. No one else seemed fazed by the man's creepy-looking face, and Debbie started to wonder if he was some figment of her imagination. She saw that he cast a shadow, and he was real enough to make a sound as he walked along closely behind her, so why didn't anyone cast even a cursory glance at him?

Debbie reached a crowd at the bus stop, and seconds later a 79 bus arrived and she was so scared of that little weird man catching up with her, she pushed through people and quickly boarded the vehicle. She sat at a window seat and looked for the uncanny dwarf, and at first she could not see him, and then with a start she saw the top of his trilby just visible below the window, and he seemed to be queuing to get on the bus, but the conductor suddenly shouted, 'We're full! No more! That's it!' And people trying to get on the bus groaned but the conductor told them: 'Sorry, were packed like sardines here! There'll be another bus in a few minutes, cheerio!'

The bus engine laboured as the vehicle heaved up the incline of Brownlow Hill, and Debbie just felt so glad that the repugnant little man had not been able to get on the Number 79. But then, a terrible sense of foreboding welled up in the teenager's mind; Debbie became convinced that the vehicle was going to crash and that she'd be killed. She had an urge to get off at each stop, but told herself she was being silly. As the bus went up Wavertree Road, Debbie suddenly became thoroughly sure that she was going to die on the bus and she became hysterical and cried for the driver to stop to let her off. She argued with the conductor, but the driver stopped the bus at the Durning Road junction and roared at the girl: "Get off then you frigging lunatic!"

At that moment a fully-laden coal lorry with faulty brakes came thundering down Durning Road, and it went through a red light and hurtled onwards down Tunnel Road. If the bus hadn't stopped to let Debbie off, the lorry would have ploughed into it with many resulting fatalities. It would have been complete carnage on Wavertree Road.

Debbie told her parents what had happened and her Nan, Maureen, said there was an old curse on the family (which was of Irish descent), and as a consequence of this curse, every now and then a weird little man with a skeletal face was seen – a warning of impending death, but if death could be avoided 3 times, he'd go away for 30 years.

'What a load of tripe,' said Debbie's father, 'Uncle Eamon said he met him when he was a kid, and because he had nightmares he ran away instead of going with the rest of the family on the *Titanic!* Fairy stories!'

'It was true!' Maureen snapped at Debbie's dad and waved her finger at him, 'And he described him just as our Deborah just did: a little pipsqueak of a man with a face of bone with sockets and staring eyes! You'll know it if you see him!'

'Hey, don't be wishin' him on me!' Debbie's father seemed spooked by his mother's suggestion, and he hid behind a broadsheet *Echo* and tried to ignore her.

'Ooh, it goes right through me just imagining his horrible face and beady eyes,' Debbie's mother said, and shuddered as she poured her daughter a cup of tea.

'It's been some bleedin' kid wearing a horror mask from the Wizard's Den!' Debbie's father said from behind the newspaper. 'That's where she saw him, wasn't it - outside the Wizard's Den? You're all letting superstition run away with you! It's 1966, not 1066!'

'Dad it was *not* a mask, he had a real horrible...' Debbie couldn't finish the sentence because she started to cry. Her mother stopped stirring her cup of tea and threw her arms around her. 'Aww, come on love,' she told her daughter, 'whatever it was, he can't harm you – Our Lord wouldn't let him, and you can have my St Christopher medal!'

'I was wondering when he'd appear again only the other day,' said Nanny Maureen, and she held her palms towards the glowing coals of the fading fire in the grate.

'Shurrup Mam,' Debbie's father muttered, and shook his newspaper. 'You'll kick Debbie off again.'

Maureen continued anyway. Maybe she was oblivious to the upset she was causing, or maybe she just couldn't help it and was letting her infamous tongue run away with itself. 'Yeah, I was only talking about *him* to Patricia Byrne the other day; her family's cursed on her husband's side by a banshee...'

'Mam!' the head of Debbie's father popped up from behind the *Liverpool Echo* and his raised eyebrows were somewhere under his overhanging quiff. 'Mam! Will you let it go now, please?'

Debbie left the table and went upstairs, sniffling as her mother tutted at Nanny Maureen.

'Oh, stop telling me to shut up!' Maureen told her son, who was now watching the back of his daughter vanish through the doorway of the living room. 'This is Great Britain, not China – we have free speech here!' Maureen ranted on, and she started to cough because of her bronchitis.

About three days after this, Debbie bit into a fruit

cake and got a sharp pain in her first premolar on the left side. She looked at the tooth with her compact mirror and to her horror she noticed a tiny hole. She panicked and started to sweat. She brushed her teeth, thinking the hole was just a seed from the cake – but it was still there when she looked in the mirror again. She went to the dentist and made an appointment, and days later, she returned to the dentist – and that little man with the gruesome face of a skull was standing on the steps of the building. Debbie did a u-turn and went home. She told her mum and Nan who she had seen and her father accused her of making the story up to get out of going the dentist. In those days it was easier to change dentists, and Debbie ended going up to one in Knotty Ash, and she later heard something which chilled her to the bone. At her usual dentist, on the day she was supposed to go and get a filling, a woman with a heart complaint died in the dentist's chair, possibly from the effects of the anaesthetic gas. The woman had been a very nervous patient and although she was only getting a filling, she had been given gas because she was terrified of needles and could not have her mouth numbed by cocaine. Debbie was convinced that she was supposed to die in the dentist's chair that day and recalled the grinning face of that ominous pygmy.

Months went by, and the omen of death was not seen, but when Debbie visited a relative in Manchester, she was invited to a Spring wedding in Birmingham, but she saw the macabre little man at the train station – so she refused to get on the train and pretended she was ill – and that train crashed at Stechford, killing 9 passengers. After that, Debbie never saw the diminutive man with the hideous face again. The thirty years elapsed, and during that time, Debbie was married twice and had five children, but when she got to the age of forty-seven, she was convinced the grisly little man would come on the scene again, but so far, Debbie has not encountered him, although she occasionally has nightmares about the little omen of death with the face of a skull...

TIT-WILLOW

David Thornwynn, who had just turned 18, and his 16-year-old girlfriend Jennete Besty, went to see a play called *The Closing Door* at Liverpool Playhouse on Williamson Square one warm May evening in 1964. As David and Jennete arrived at the Playhouse they saw a scruffy busker sitting on the floor near the entrance with a massive head of curly hair and a bushy beard, and as he strummed on his small guitar he sang: 'On a tree by a river a little tom-tit sang "Willow, titwillow, titwillow..."'

David sniggered at the man, and Jennete giggled with her hand to her mouth. 'I've seen *The Mikado* many times and that has to be the worst version of *Tit-Willow*!' David laughed.

The busker's voice faltered, and he stopped strumming. He looked down at the body of the little child-sized acoustic guitar with a sullen expression in his eyes.

The couple enjoyed the evening play, and afterwards they went to a milk bar, talked about places they could go on a date next weekend, and then David walked Jennete home. It was a lovely warm evening, and the young couple enjoyed these walks home at the end of their dates, holding hands and simply enjoying the feelings young love brings. The young lovers stopped several times under a waxing gibbous moon that night to kiss and whisper sweet nothings to one another, and it was David's idea to take a shortcut through a moonlit Sefton Park at midnight to reach Jennete's home on Templemore Avenue, Mossley Hill. At the back of David's mind, he kept thinking of the day when he'd make love to his girlfriend. He had mentioned it once and she had told him they'd 'do it' when she had an engagement ring. David started to believe that he could somehow seduce Jennete on this perfect feverish night, perhaps beneath the shade of one of the beech trees in the park. He had read that moonlight affected girls, making them nymphomaniacs.

'I know you said we should wait until after I buy you a ring, Jennete, but – ' David started to say, when his girlfriend stopped dead. She was looking straight ahead.

'David, who's that? Look!' she whispered, and nodded to someone further down the path. It was a bizarre sight. Standing there in the moonlight was a man with some sort of white hood with a beak protruding from it. He was standing stock-still near to the bronze base of the Eros statue. He was tall and stocky, and wore a check shirt, black elbow-length gloves and jeans. He was not facing the couple – his 'beak' was pointed to their left, at right angles to their intended path.

'David, let's go back,' Jennete said, for she sensed that the man was unbalanced, and she tugged at her boyfriend's arm, but David thought he'd look cowardly to Jennete if he turned around and went back, and so, letting his pride get the better of him, he said, 'Take no notice – ignore him. I'll punch him if he tries anything.'

Then the man with the weird mask turned to them and they saw he was wielding what seemed to be a medieval mace. It was a short piece of wood, about two feet in length, and attached to it was a chain, and at the end of this chain there was a black metal ball with spikes sticking out in all directions like the plumed seeds of a dandelion. It looked like one vicious weapon.

'*Willow, titwillow, titwillow,*' sang the man in the beaked mask – and the couple recognised that voice; it was that busker they'd seen outside the Playhouse. David halted, and in a monotone voice the weird man said: 'I have a gun; stay there.'

Jennete started to shake, and David said, 'What do you want?'

'You will sing that song – both of you – or you won't ever go home again,' said the man in the bizarre bird mask. He lifted the archaic weapon above his head, ready to strike, and he made the couple sing the old Gilbert and Sullivan song, and Jennete was in tears as she sang.

'You're tone deaf!' the menacing stranger told David, 'Once again – or else!'

David broke wind as his bowels turned to water – he was so afraid – he really did expect the iron spiked ball of that mace to come crashing through his skull. He wanted to run, but his legs felt as if they were numb through the fear he was feeling.

As David was singing, the man pointed the gun at Jennete's head and with his other gloved hand he waved the mace in the air as if he was a conductor waving a baton.

Minutes later the unhinged man suddenly said, 'Okay, enough! Walk away and don't look back or you'll be very sorry. I might still have to shoot both of you anyway.'

The couple held onto one another with squeezing interlocked hands and walked away, and David glanced back - and saw no one. The parents of Jennete thought the man had been some warped joker, but David and his girlfriend were sure the masked man had been that busker they'd skitted at, and they never saw him again, although one summer's night, a few years after this terrifying incident, David was sitting in bed one warm night at his home on Booker Avenue with the bedroom window open, when he heard someone walk by, and they were whistling that song from *The Mikado*: *Tit Willow*. David immediately turned off his bedside lamp and gingerly peeped out the window, and he saw the tall and stocky silhouette of the whistler walking into the distance – but whether it was that psychopathic man in the weird mask – or whether it was simply some Gilbert and Sullivan fan – is not known.

GHOSTS WITHOUT A HISTORY

I have some weird supernatural entities documented in my files, and a bundle of them are labelled 'Ghosts without a history' – as they have no known back-story which explains the haunting, and these types of apparitions are the most annoying ones to me because I like to know about the incidents which lead to a ghost becoming bound to a certain place. Here are just a few of these baffling ghosts with no back story. I'll start over in Birkenhead, on a wintry morning in 2010...

She saw his left shoe first, protruding from around the corner of the Cock and Pullet pub, and what a strange shoe it was: long and black and pointed like a medieval crakow – like something out of that old period comedy TV series *Blackadder*, Lilli thought, and then she saw his pale face barely visible in the shade of the black hood as he peeped around the corner at her and Becci – two 21-year-old students walking back to their digs (on Ridley Street) from a party on Wirral's Storeton Road. There was ice as hard as glass layering the pavements of Woodchurch Road upon this glacial morning in December 2010, and snow was starting to fall again, and being 6:30am the sun had not yet risen, so only the dismal amber glow of a nearby sodium street lamp threw some feeble illumination on the grey streetscape. But that black hooded figure with the pointed shoes stood out stark as he peeped at the students from the alleyway at the side of the pub, and what made the entity seem even more scary was his abnormal height, for the girls estimated he must have been between ten and twelve feet in height. The tallest man in medical history – Robert Pershing Wadlow – was just 8 feet and 11 inches tall in comparison. I asked the girls if the giant of Woodchurch Road had perhaps been two hoaxers, one sitting on the shoulders of the other under that elongated funereal habit – but my suggestion was quickly dismissed by the students. 'No, it was a real person, a giant, and he moved naturally,' Becci recalled, with goosebumps rising on her arms, 'and, [she added] it was a freezing, bitterly cold morning – not the weather for arsing about pulling silly pranks.'

The towering hooded man stepped out from behind that corner, and Lilli and Becci turned, ready to run, but were both wearing heels and the ice-slicked pavement made a rapid retreat impossible. Lilli fell, grazing her knee, and then Becci almost slipped and landed on her palms, hurting her wrist. Somehow the students managed to hold onto one another as they got to their feet, and Becci took off her shoes and ran barefoot with her soles almost sticking to the cruel stinging ice. She stopped at one point and turned, then dragged Lilli – who had fallen again – up Woodchurch Road. Becci saw the Brobdingnagian bogeyman walking slowly and silently towards her and Lilli, and he was bent over, as if he was stooping to get a better look at them. Somehow the students managed to run along the skating-rink sidewalks of Woodchurch Road until they saw that their menacing monastic pursuer had vanished. The girls returned to the scene of the party on Storeton Road, half a mile away, where a few revellers were still drinking, and of course, no one believed the seemingly far-fetched story of the students, who were now gulping down scotch to steady their nerves and fire up the circulation after their chilling ordeal. I mentioned the 'giant monk' in black on a radio programme not long afterwards and received intriguing calls and emails from people ranging from milkmen and policemen to postmen and even a former prostitute who had plied her trade on the peripheries of Oxton, and they had all allegedly seen an entity which tallied very close to the description given by the students, although the height given by witnesses varied between 7 and 10 feet, and the earliest report dated from 1967. I delved into the history of the pub – the Cock and Pullet – where the students had first seen the überlanky monk, peeping around the corner – but I could find no religious orders associated with the drinking establishment, which was originally called the Royal Oak (after a massive oak tree that stood in front of the pub in the middle of Woodchurch Road). A former policemen told me how, one snowy morning in January 1970 at around 1.30am, he and a colleague were on the beat on Bessborough Road when they saw a very tall shadowy figure on Derwent Road, about sixty yards away. The weird gangling lurker was apparently looking through one of the dimly-lit bay windows of a terraced house on the corner of Bentley Road. The policemen sensed that the peeping Tom was unearthly, but crept up on it, and when they were within about 15 yards of him, they saw that the prowler had on a long black robe and his face was hidden by a hood of the sort you associate with monks. The thing turned towards the policemen, apparently startled, and flitted away from them 'as if he was on wheels' recalled one of the constables. It turned the corner into Normanston Road, and when the policemen gingerly turned that same corner seconds later, they saw no one about. They split up and walked on opposite sides of Normanston Road, shining their torches down the eleven alleyways of the road as well as every nook and cranny. The hyper-agile 'monk' was nowhere to be seen – and what the thing was remains a mystery. These apparitions can lay dormant for years, and then they usually start to walk again, and I will not be in the least bit surprised if the mysterious monk of Woodchurch Road starts doing the rounds again in the near future.

We now move across the Mersey, to a bizarre paranormal entity which haunted a couple in Walton in 2015, and like the giant monk of Woodchurch Road, this menacing being was never identified. The couple – Kian (aged 22) and Emmie (aged 19), decided to rent a 3-bedroom semi on Walton's Crescent Road, as Emmie's family only lived nearby on Stalmine Road, and she knew the area well enough to know that Crescent Road wasn't a bad area of Walton. Kian was originally from Dublin and had settled in Liverpool after staying with his brother at his flat in the city centre for a year. Kian had now landed a job with an insurance firm and had recently bought his first car. Emmie worked at a local supermarket, stacking shelves and occasionally she was put on duty behind the counter of the supermarket's customer services counter. It wasn't a very fulfilling job, and Emmie – who was into crafting and scrapbooking – harboured dreams of getting a degree in art so she could design her own greeting cards. The couple moved into the house on Crescent Road and Emmie's brothers and her parents helped her and Kian to move in. In the evening, Emmie was in the kitchen, boiling a kettle to make two Pot Noodles for her and Kian when the landline – an old push-button BT telephone – started to ring. Kian answered and the line was dead. He then looked down and saw that the phone was not even plugged into its wall socket – so how on earth had the thing rung? Emmie came into the lounge and asked who it was, and Kian said, 'There was no one there, and you won't believe this Emmie, but the phone isn't even plugged in.'

'Ooh,' Emmie replied, and she wiggled the fingers of her hands in the air as if she was playing an invisible piano and jokingly said, 'don't tell me this place is haunted, ha!' The reality and the implications of what Kian had just told her had not sunk in yet.

She went back into the kitchen, brought in the Pot Noodles and forks and then went back to get two bottles of Stella Artois.

The telephone rang again, and this time Emmie dashed from the kitchen to answer the 'call'. She picked up the handset and nearly dropped it when loud, echoing laughter erupted from the earpiece. It sounded like young laughter, Emmie thought, like that of a boy of about ten or twelve years of age.

'What the – ' Kian clearly heard the weird laughter and rose from the sofa and walked to his partner, who was holding the handset away from her face as if there was a spider on it. The echoing laughter faded. Kian took the telephone from his trembling girlfriend and he replaced the handset and then he wound the two metres of grey mounting cord around the phone.

'What's going on?' an anxious Emmie asked, looking up at her tall boyfriend's anxious face. 'Is this place haunted?' She always looked to him for answers.

Kian shook his head. 'I think someone's playing games with us.' He took the phone into the kitchen and he put it in a cupboard next to the cooker. He seemed to be in a daze, as if he wasn't sure what he was doing. He closed the door and when he reached the lounge, the phone he had put away started to ring a few times, startling him and Emmie.

'That's not someone playing games,' said Emmie, looking at the cupboard where the unplugged telephone had rung, 'that's a ghost.'

'Don't talk daft, Emmie,' Kian told her with a forced smile, 'it's someone messing about. Probably got a remote control thingy in the phone. The laughter we heard sounded like a kid; it'll be some lad messing about.'

Emmie had only known Kian a year and yet she knew he had always avoided the subject of the supernatural and seemed to be very superstitious, and she loved him, so she didn't push him into explaining just how anyone – especially a child – could make a disconnected telephone ring. They sat down and ate their Pot Noodles – mostly in silence - and then, to make conversation in the tense atmosphere, Emmie asked Kian when he was going to mount the TV on the wall, and in an uncharacteristically flat few words he said he'd do it in the morning. He seemed quite on edge since that incident with the phone. That night, the couple clung on to one another in bed, expecting something to happen, and Emmie felt a strong presence in the bedroom, and kept her eyes closed. At around 4am she walked into the door as she hurried to the toilet with her eyelids almost closed, but thankfully that night, nothing further happened. Emmie never mentioned the weird landline incident over breakfast, and then at 8.15am the couple left their house in Kian's new car. He dropped Emmie off at the supermarket and he drove on to the city centre to his own workplace. They arrived home within minutes of one another in the evening at around 6pm, and Emmie now felt that the presence was back – and it was strongest in the lounge, but she said nothing to Kian. He seemed a bit spooked by something too, and he suggested eating out. Emmie put her make-up on in a rush (whereas she usually took at least half an hour) and then Kian drove her to Bella Italia. Emmie sensed Kian just wanted to get out of that house, and thought that this was not a good start to living in a new home. The couple had their meal, and then they picked up a few bottles of wine and went home, and Kian ended up having the TV on (which had not been mounted on the wall and was leaning against the mock fireplace), as well as the radio, and every light on the house was on. Emmie got a bit tipsy and told Kian, 'Don't be scared love, nothing will harm you – I love you too much.'

Kian rolled his eyes and then he shook his head and turned away from her. 'Stop going on about *that*, will you? There's nothing – no ghost – in this house.'

He sulked for the rest of the evening and then they went to bed around one in the morning. Every time

Emmie tried to put her arm around Kian in the bed, he pulled away or said, 'Stop it. I'm alright.'

Emmie turned away and tears flowed from her eyes. She saw the mascara stains on the new pillow, even though the room was only faintly lit by a streetlamp's light filtering through the drawn curtains. She reached out for her iPhone on the box of unpacked books at the side of the bed and checked for text messages. There were none. She then heard Kian snore lightly. He'd gone out like a light after that wine. Emmie decided to text her best friend Beka, to tell her about Kian's crabby behaviour when she felt his foot touch her calf, and she smiled; he'd obviously pretended to be asleep with that snoring sound. Emmie turned to Kian, and she felt that foot of his travel up to her crotch. He was still making that snoring sound – taking the joke a bit *too* far. Emmie felt something wasn't quite right, and she lifted the sheets and by the light of the iPhone's screen, she saw a small greyish head with two eyeless sockets and a wide smiling mouth, and she recoiled in shock upon finding this thing in the bed. She thought she felt small cold hands on her thigh before she threw herself backwards out of the bed, knocking her back on the box of books. She got up and cried out Kian's name as she flew to the light switch, and she heard him swear. He sat up, looked at her with screwed-up eyes, and then he looked down at the blankets – and Emmie could see movement under those blankets, on the side of the bed she had just vacated. Kian swore, and leaped out of the bed, but he did not pull back the sheets. He seemed terrified of whatever was moving under them. Kian walked to the bedroom door, bumping into

Emmie, and he said, 'I've had enough of this – we're leaving here tomorrow!'

Emmie summoned up courage from nowhere and she went over to the bed, and despite Kian's pleas for her to come back, she threw back the blankets – and saw that there was nothing there. She told him she had seen a small grey head, like that of a child, and described the empty eye sockets and the ghastly smiling lips, and Kian kept telling her to shut up. They got dressed and sat in the lounge, and Kian said he was going to kill the estate agent. 'He must have known about this. They know the history of places, it's their job!' He pounded his fist in his palm.

'We can stay in our house till we get a place, Kian,' Emmie told him.

'All that rigmarole to get this place as well – credit checks and that deposit!' Kian seethed. 'If he doesn't reimburse us I'll go to the papers and report them!'

'We'll get the deposit back and the month's rent we paid in hand love, me dad's good at dealing with estate agents – he'll be in their office tomorrow when I tell him about this.'

'I sensed there was something in here when I first set foot in the door,' Kian confessed, 'but I didn't say anything because I know you loved this place.'

'I'll make us some coffee, Kian, we'll be okay, love,' Emmie replied, and she switched on the kitchen light.

She saw something in the sink there. At first she thought it was a worm on the rim of the sink the way it squirmed about. It was a finger - a small finger, like the tiny finger of a child, only it looked grey. Kian was still talking about the estate agent, and he hadn't yet noticed that Emmie was standing there in shock, gazing at the sink.

'Holy shit,' she suddenly said. Four fingers of a right hand curled over the rim of the sink and then a little left hand rose out from the sink as far as the wrist, and it was making a V gesture to Emmie. She heard a faint chuckle come from the direction of the sink.

Kian looked up after his little rant and he could plainly see his girlfriend was transfixed by something. He got up off the sofa and slowly walked to her, knowing she'd seen something paranormal. He saw the little grey hands in the sink, and he reflexively pulled Emmie out of the kitchen and slammed the kitchen door shut before retreating backwards. That kitchen door had a panel of shatterproof frosted glass in it, and Kian and Emmie saw something grey and spindly climb quickly out the sink through that panel. It was fuzzy because of the frosted glass, but they could see it was skeletal. Its face pressed against the panel and the terrified couple could see those eyeless sockets, a triangular hollow where the nose should have been, and that dark crescent of a mouth.

'Oh God! Help us!' Kian shouted, and he turned and looked at the bunch of keys – the house keys and the car keys – lying on the coffee table. He rushed over to the keys and in a panic he unlocked the door, pushed Emmie out into the cold night, and he forgot to disable the house alarm, and so a siren started screaming as the couple hurried to the car in the driveway. Kian hesitated and said he'd better go back and switch off the alarm but Emmie swore and told him to leave it and get to her parents' house. Kian drove just 150 yards down Birchdale Road to Stalmine Road. Emmie's mum answered her daughter's frantic knocking, and when she heard about the strange goings-on, she told her daughter and Kian they could stay as long as it took to find a new place. Emmie moved back into her old room, and her father and Kian brought the new double bed from the troubled dwelling on Crescent Road to the house. The couple eventually got their deposit back – and the month's rent they had paid in advance, but only after threatening to go to the *Liverpool Echo*. A year after this, a woman told Emmie's mother that a family who had moved into the haunted house on Crescent Road had been plagued with all sorts of strange goings-on, including the materialisation of a boy who appeared to be hanging from the ceiling with a wire around his neck in the bedroom. The 17-year-old daughter of the family said she had awakened at 4am to see the small suspended figure rotating in front of the window as he laughed, and the laughter was described as echoing. Nothing more is known about this haunting. There have been no murders - of children or adults - committed there and at the time of writing, a family is living in the house in question, but for how long?

Orwell Road in the Kirkdale area of Liverpool has been the scene of some strange goings-on over the years. In July and August 2017, several local people reported seeing a glowing female figure in the entry facing New Yungs Fish and Chips Shop. Most of the sightings were in the evening, and some believed that the dazzling female apparition was a vision of the Blessed Virgin Mary, as the 'vision' wore a blue mantle and a white headscarf similar to the Muslim hijab – items traditionally associated with Marian visions. Just why a vision – be it of the Virgin Mary or just a ghostly woman – should appear at the mouth of an alleyway on Orwell Road, is not known. Around a dozen people of all ages, ranging from a 13-year-old girl to a 69-year-old man, saw the bright manifestation, which was consistently described as having its palms pressed together as if it was in prayer. Each encounter seems to have lasted for no more than ten seconds, after which the figure vanished, leaving an after-image on the retina of the witness, thus proving that it had been a real entity and not an imagined one.

Moving back further in time, to the 1960s, Orwell Street was again the backdrop to another supernatural phenomenon. Around 1964, there was a boarded-up dwelling on this street of terraced houses which was haunted a group of ghostly children. A milkman making deliveries on Orwell Road is said to have heard ghostly laughter at around half-past five in the morning, and he would always hurry past the empty house because the eerie laughter and whispers of the unseen children scared him. A woman named Carol, who lived on Orwell Road during this time told me how, one summer evening at around 10pm, her mother stood on her doorstep and shouted for her two sons, aged ten and twelve, to come home, because she thought she could hear them laughing in the vacant house. Someone had opened the door to the empty dwelling and a few kids had started going into the unoccupied house. Carol – aged 6 at the time - appeared behind her mother in the hallway and tugged at her skirt. 'Mum, the boys are upstairs in their room,' the girl told her mother. Carol's mum, however, was sure she could hear her lads messing about in the empty house, and she went over there, pushed the creaky green door of the uninhabited house open, and gingerly ventured inside. She called her two sons by their names, and the familiar voices of two boys simultaneously declared, 'We're not going home!'

Carol then heard her mother scream and run out of the house. She grabbed Carol by the arm and dragged her home. Carol heard her mother tell her father that she had seen a gang of ghostly children in the house, and all of their faces looked pale and ghastly. Carol's older brothers came bounding down the stairs and asked what the matter was, as they had heard their mother screaming, but their father ordered them back to bed.

Other people I have spoken to who were children at the time of the Orwell Street haunting have told me how, when they went on errands, they would either run past the haunted house or even cross the road to avoid going past the deserted abode. Just whose ghosts haunted that house remains unknown. A priest allegedly blessed the empty house and a family later moved into it, and there were no further reports of any strange goings-on. The ghostly children of Orwell Road are an excellent example of ghosts without a historical cause. There were no fires or murders involving the death of any children at that troubled house in the past, so what are we to make of the haunting? I remain baffled.

In the many years I've spent investigating the supernatural, I have found that on the whole, you are more likely to find ghosts in modern settings rather than a graveyard. Flaybrick Cemetery is something of an exception, though. Visitors to the Birkenhead cemetery have often heard a growling noise, and heavy footsteps plodding behind them when they walk through the place. Some visitors to the cemetery have even seen what looks like a tall, hairy hunched werewolf-like figure skulking among the graves. In Victorian times, there was a gravestone with the curious inscription: 'Here lies one who was half man, half beast'. The stone seems to have been removed by someone in the 1960s, but what was it referring to?

The most active ghost in Flaybrick Cemetery is alleged to be the so-called Clown Woman, and she has been seen since around Edwardian times, but no one knows who she is. I have scoured burial registers, cemetery receipt books and various archives and cannot find a reference to a clown buried in the cemetery, but this entity continues to be seen even today. The first report I have comes from June 1937. The body of Charles Fry of Leamington Road, Wallasey, was due to be interred at Flaybrick Cemetery, and quite a crowd of mourners attended because Fry had perished in the prestigious Isle of Man Air Race the week before when his plane crashed into a house at Hanworth. One of the female mourners at the graveside noticed that the old coffin at the bottom of the newly-excavated hole bore the rusted name plate of Fry's uncle, and she cried out: 'This is not the right grave! This is not the family grave!'

The mourners had to wait for almost two hours while the gravediggers were taken to another plot where the Fry family grave was located, and they began to dig – and a very strange woman, dressed in the costume of a Pierrot clown came upon the scene, laughing and joking about the blunder made by the cemetery staff. On a hot June day in broad daylight, over fifty mourners saw this strange woman in her white clown outfit, and some chased her away, thinking she was a lunatic, but they soon realised she was a ghost when she vanished, only to reappear behind various gravestones and tombs. She pulled faces at the unnerved mourners and even threw water urns and flowers from graves at them. The older of the two gravediggers toiling away with shovels told his nervous young colleague that the weird prankster was the ghost of a female clown. He had last seen her in the cemetery in 1910.

In May 1996, a newspaper reporter and a photographer were travelling up Boundary Road, which runs past the western side of Flaybrick Cemetery, on their way to Flaybrick Reservoir, where thousands of gallons were leaking through the reservoir's old sandstone wall. It was a newsworthy story, and the reporter was to meet a representative of North West Water for an interview, but as he drove past Flaybrick Cemetery, a figure in a strange one-piece white suit jumped out into the road into the path of the car. The reporter almost crashed as he swerved to avoid the suicidal person, and then the photographer noticed that the jaywalker was a woman dressed as a clown. She ran back towards the six-foot-high cemetery wall, which was topped with railings – and cleared it in one leap. At this point an old man coming from the allotments to the right of the car told the reporter and photographer that they had just seen the "Clown Woman". 'Is she insane? What's she dressed like that for?' the reporter asked.

'She's dead. She's a ghostie,' said the elderly man,

and walked off.

Some who have encountered the ghost say she occasionally plays a tiny guitar, possibly a ukulele, and people have heard spooky music being plucked and strummed by the eerie clown all hours at night, when the cemetery is closed. In 1995, a gang of teenagers climbed over the wall of the cemetery one summer night at around 11pm and played hide and seek. One of the trespassers, a girl of 14, hid behind a large upright marble cross, when she suddenly noticed something on the moonlit grass – the shadow of someone creeping up on her. She turned and saw it was a woman, about 5 feet 7 in height, and she had on a baggy white silk one-piece suit with large furry pink pom pom buttons, and her face was covered in thick white make-up. On her head she wore a white cap of some sort. She swore at the girl and said, 'Get away from my grave!'

The teen screamed, tried to run, but fell. She felt gloved hands around her throat, and then the hands began to throttle her and shake her so her head repeatedly hit the ground. She somehow broke loose, and ran past her friends, too scared to even utter a warning. She then heard her friends cry out as the ghost attacked them, and all of the teens climbed over the wall and ran off down Tollemache Road. The Clown Woman still prowls, and hopefully I might discover her identity one day.

Here's another ghost that I'm having a hard time explaining. The story of this haunting started one gloriously sunny St Patrick's Day in 1965, as Paddy Brennan and Billy Clarke – both aged forty - were singing the Righteous Brothers' *You've Lost that Lovin'*

Feeling in harmony as they shifted the timber at the building site in Halewood. Paddy stopped singing when he spotted something glinting in the soil excavated for the footings of the houses that were going up. He let go of his end of the beam and Billy swore and watched the Dubliner go and pick up something from the soil and clay. It was a golden circle with a cross of Jerusalem in it and a bail loop at the top.

'Will you look at that? A gold pendant,' said Paddy, and he polished it with his hanky and Billy said they should split whatever it was worth, but Paddy said: 'I found it, it's mine.'

'Work it up you then!' Billy whined, and went off in a huff and sulked until he returned for elevenses (as Paddy had chocolate digestives). Paddy took out the gold pendant and looked at it in his rough palm. He smiled and said: 'Look, Billy, I'll get the thing valued, and if it's worth a good few bob, I promise you I'll give you a percentage. What do you take me for?'

'Nah, you found it, you keep whatever it's worth,' said Billy, and he put a whole chocolate biscuit into his mouth and then drank from the chipped enamelled cup before he couldn't even chew the digestive.

'Maybe we should go over this ground with a rake,' mused the Irishman, eyeing the ploughed-up soil. 'You know what they say, Billy, where there's one there's more. We could be walking on a fortune here.'

That afternoon, 16-year-old apprentice plumber Charlie Dunn came running past Paddy and Billy, tripped, and fell. Paddy helped him up, and Charlie said a man in a suit of armour had just tried to kill him with a big sword.

'A what?' Paddy asked, and he saw the lad's bulging eyes were full of fear.

'A knight! A knight in armour with a big massive sword! I'm going home!' Charlie babbled, getting to his feet. He ran off the building site and kept looking back with an expression of wide-eyed horror. Paddy peeped around the corner of a hut, expecting to see the knight Charlie had described, but he saw nothing out of place – just a few bricklayers on the far side of the site having a smoke on their break. Paddy told Billy what the boy had said, and Billy smiled and replied: 'God, that is some bleedin' excuse to swing the lead, the lazy sod! Been watching too much *Ivanhoe* he has.'

The two men then lifted a beam, one at each end of it, when Paddy heard a metallic clanking sound.

'What was that?' Paddy asked, and his eyes swivelled towards the hut. He thought the clatter of metal had come from behind that hut.

'What was what?' Billy impatiently inquired, and he blew air up from his lips to knock his overhanging quiff out of his eyes.

'That!' exclaimed Paddy. 'Listen!'

At first, Billy thought it was a robot coming around the corner of the hut. It was a knight in full armour with a huge helmet which resembled a bucket with two slits for eyes – and it was wielding a massive wide-bladed sword! The muffled voice of this knight sounded as if he was speaking in a Mancurian and Scottish accent, and Paddy and Billy could not understand a word he was saying as he swung the sword at them. The tip of that blade missed Billy's head by just a few inches and he fell backwards, grabbed a plank, and thrust it at the armoured psycho, and the sword's blade flashed through the plank as if it was balsa. Paddy's fear unleashed tremendous strength and he rammed the six-foot-long beam into the breastplate of the knight, but the wood didn't even dent the plate of well-tempered steel. The impact sent the end of the beam Paddy was holding into his belly, winding the Irishman. At this point Paddy saw the circle with the Cross of Jerusalem emblem on the breastplate of the knight, emblazoned in gold, and remembered the gold pendant he had found earlier. He turned and ran with Billy, but the knight chased them off the site.

'Charlie *was* telling the truth!' Billy shouted to Paddy, and gasped for breath as he ran along.

Paddy fell over, and in a small act of rage in the middle of this nightmare, he pulled up a sod of grass and threw it at the knight.

'Oh, that's going to stop it, isn't it you stupid peasant!' Billy cried at his friend. The stitch in his side was agonising now, and he looked up and down a road, wishing a car or wagon would approach so he could flag it down.

'You do better then, you fat windbag!' cussed the Irishman, and he suddenly had a thought. He took the gold pendant out of his trouser pocket and with great reluctance, Paddy threw it at the knight – and it vanished instantly. Billy continued his staggering run as Paddy stood there, astounded by the vanishing act of the deadly knight.

'Billy!' Paddy shouted twice, but Billy was now crawling away on all fours, unaware that the medieval menace had gone. 'Billy you shithouse! It's gone!'

Billy turned, and slowly got up as he looked past

Paddy to where he expected the unearthly pursuer to be. He approached Paddy with a stumbling gait, his face twisted in pain as he held the palm of his hand over that stitch in his side. 'Where did it go?' he asked.

Paddy stooped at the spot where the knight had disappeared, hoping to find that gold pendant, but it was nowhere to be seen.

The foreman, a huge Scotsman named Hughie, came on the scene and said, 'Hey you two! Back to work! I saw yous tryin' to skive off!'

'Listen here jock,' said Paddy, 'you're not going to believe what just happened to us two...'

'Aye, you were caught trying to piss off early, that's what happened pal!' the foreman butted in, and he beckoned them back towards the building site with a windmilling of his right arm. 'Come on! Back to work!'

'I've got a good mind to hand my cards in,' carped Paddy, 'this place is haunted!'

'Paddy, don't even bother trying to explain to Hughie,' advised Billy, 'you might as well talk to these planks. There's nothing there with him, just drinking and money. I just hope that thing doesn't come back.'

'I don't think it will,' said Paddy, 'I think he got a cob on with us because that gold pendant belonged to him.'

Paddy and Billy never saw that ghostly knight again during the time they spent on the site after that day, which was about two months. Paddy stuck to his belief - that some Norman knight from the days of ancient Halewood had returned from beyond to claim that gold cross; and if this was the case, he must have treasured that pendant, and I wonder what the gold cross meant to that forgotten warrior. Yet another case of a ghost whose history is unknown.

In February 1996, a family from Bebington moved into a house on Highfield Road, Rock Ferry. It was a rented abode, and the rent was quite cheap, because – according to the landlord - a railway track ran parallel to Highfield Road and passed the bottom of the back garden. The family didn't mind this at all, and soon settled into the old Victorian house. James and Sarah, the couple who had rented the house, had four children – Tom, aged 15, Barry aged 13, Stephen, aged 10, and 8-year-old Polly. Polly said she didn't like the house, and told her mother there was 'something dark about it' but her mother said she was just being silly and that she'd soon get used to her new home. Sarah was very green-fingered and made plans to transform the overgrown wilderness of the back garden into a colourful sanctum of flowers, and her Liverpudlian husband, a bricklayer by trade, repaired the crumbled wall of the front garden. Polly was given the attic as a type of playroom, because no one could find a use for the room, and it had a large old-fashioned radiator in it. By Wednesday 7 February, the playroom had been papered and carpeted, and the mound of toys belonging to Polly was put up there. Polly's best friend, Zoe, came and visited and she said there was something 'spooky' about the playroom and the house too, and this upset Polly. At 8.30pm that night, Polly went to bed complaining of a sore throat, and at 9.30pm, just as James and Sarah were settling down to watch *Hetty Wainthropp Investigates* on BBC1, they heard Polly scream. They ran upstairs and burst into her bedroom, and found their daughter hiding under the blankets, trembling. She said an old man – described as being bald with glasses, a white beard and moustache – had shaken her awake and asked, 'Why is Goldilocks sleeping in my bed?' And he was smiling as he said this. Polly had flaxen blonde hair and her mother had often jokingly called her Goldilocks in their old home in Bebington, but she had never used the affectionate nickname in the present house. 'It's okay, love,' Polly's father told his daughter, 'you've had a nightmare, that's all.' Sarah felt Polly's forehead – she did not seem to have a temperature with the sore throat. 'He was a ghost,' Polly insisted, 'he vanished,' she said, and her large blue eyes darted about as if she was looking for him. The parents sat with the girl for a quarter of an hour, and Polly's big brother Tom came into the room and assured her he was only next door, and that he'd be in like a flash if she shouted for him. The girl reluctantly tried to get back to sleep, and everyone left her room.

James was watching *Sportsnight* (a popular midweek sports 'magazine' programme) on the telly at around 10.45pm, and Sarah was taking a pizza out of the oven, when they heard Polly scream again, and this time the child came running down the stairs. She said that the bearded old man had returned, and this time he had three horrible dolls with him – dolls that could move and talk, and one of them had brandished a little hatchet. Polly became hysterical and said she wanted to go back to her old home, and then Tom and his two brothers came downstairs, and to his mother, Tom said, 'We heard a man's voice.'

James went up to Polly's bedroom and saw that the mattress had been pulled from the bed and the pillows had been put on top of the wardrobe. There was also an aroma of pipe tobacco hanging in the air, and yet James and his wife were non-smokers. Polly said the old man had told her: 'I killed three girls like you a long time ago, and they are my dolls now. Do *you* want to be my doll?'

The three dolls the man had brought with him then climbed on the bed. One was dressed like a sailor, one said her name was Miss Flitch, a teacher, and she struck Polly's hand with a cane. The third doll had a striped blazer, and his stringy hair was combed over his head. He held a hatchet and in a plummy well-spoken voice he said: 'I could kill you quite quickly Polly – you wouldn't even know you were dead.'

'She would know,' said the sailor doll, 'because she wouldn't be able to go back to her mammy and daddy.'

Polly had then thrown herself out the bed and screamed as she escaped from the room. Polly slept in her parent's room after that night, and the family heard what sounded like 1920s music coming from the attic each evening. The family finally moved out when a neighbour told them the house was a 'hard-to-let' because it was said to be haunted by the man who had killed a child named Nellie Clarke in the 1920s. Nellie Clarke was an 11-year-old child who had been raped and strangled, literally just across the road from the haunted house one wintry night in January 1925 whilst running an errand. She had called at a nearby house as she fled from her killer, and had shouted through the letterbox 'Help! Father Christmas is after me! Let me in!' But by the time the door was answered, Nellie had gone. Her body was later found propped up against a telegraph pole in an alleyway off Spenser Avenue. The killer was never caught. Polly had described that bald bearded ghost as looking like Father Christmas, which means it's possible that the man haunting that house on Highfield Road might be the ghost of a serial child killer, but no one's sure. The bearded phantom and his sinister dolls is yet another case of a haunting which is lacking in background information. I will continue to look into the case though, and hope that someone, somewhere knows something about the whys and wherefores of this intriguing and frightening case.

We know flit across the Mersey to the scene of another ghost with a blank biography, and this one is still being reported.

At the risk of seeming sadistic, I must admit that, for me, there is nothing more satisfying than a sceptic being half scared to death by a ghost. A case in point is a hackney cab driver named Graham who once emailed me and asked why, despite living for forty-five years, he had never seen a single ghost. I told him it was all down to chance, like seeing a shooting star, but Graham simply didn't believe in ghosts. Then, one sunny afternoon in May 2010, his cab company despatched Graham to pick up a woman named Jeanie from Ford Cemetery, Bootle, where she had spent half an hour tending to her uncle's grave. Graham was driving into the cemetery when a man in a top hat and a long black coat stepped in front of the cab. The oddly-dressed man was facing away from Graham, and he stood there, still as a statue. Graham wound down his window and shouted, 'Oi! You're in my way!' but the figure didn't even react. Graham assumed it was just someone larking about, dressed as a Victorian, perhaps trying to scare mourners. He beeped his horn, and the figure slowly turned – and Graham saw that the man in the dated clothes had no face. Where the face would have been there was just a convex, flesh-coloured surface as smooth as an egg. Graham let out a profanity in shock, and then he saw a mouth open wide in the surface of that blank face, and the thing let out a ghastly noise, as if it was clearing its throat. Gripped by panic, Graham reversed out of the cemetery for seventy yards and almost backed into an oncoming van on Gorsey Lane. He saw that faceless man in Ford Cemetery flit at high speed towards the gravestones and vanish. Graham waited there until another car ventured into the cemetery and he followed it in and eventually picked up Jeanie. He was so scared by the close encounter, Graham forgot to turn on his meter. He talked incessantly about the ghost to his colleagues, and eventually contacted me. I told him that he had met just one of the five ghosts that haunt that cemetery. The faceless man's identity is unknown, but there is a much scarier apparition, and this is the phantom of a former circus clown suspected of being a serial child killer in Edwardian times, and one of his alleged victims, 7-year-old Madge Kirby, murdered in 1908, happens to rest in Ford Cemetery. Graham became fixated with the idea of videoing the faceless ghost, but he was eventually told to stay away from the cemetery by police after local residents complained of seeing him prowling around in the place of the dead with a video camera almost every day. The faceless apparition continues to haunt Ford Cemetery, and as recently as June 2017 two elderly brothers visiting the grave of their uncle were startled when the ghost approached them. The brothers, sensing that the faceless man was something evil, turned and walked back out of the cemetery and onto Gorsey Lane, where the entity followed them. The supernatural relic from the Victorian or Edwardian era then proceeded to follow the two brothers across a road until it vanished on Kirkstone Road West. I have other reports of the faceless man going back to the 1950s, but they throw no light on the ghost's identity. If he is haunting the place of his own burial, he must have been of the Catholic faith, as Ford is a Catholic cemetery, but he would be one of 300,000 people buried at the cemetery, and that, along with his missing face, may prevent the mystifying haunter from ever being identified.

At dusk, Tranmere's Agnes Road is a sleepy little row of two-dozen houses, terraced, detached and semidetached, nestling among a row of young horse chestnut trees adjoining the verdant spaces of Mersey Park. However, behind the respectable facade of this pleasant suburban road, a supernatural terror lurks in one of the houses, and it is a haunting which has left an unfathomable mystery in its wake that remains unsolved to this day. This certainly is a glaring case of a ghost with no history. The house in question was, like most of the terraced houses on Agnes Road, built in 1945, and in the early 1970s a couple in their twenties – Keith and Heidi – moved into the house. Keith was a taxi driver and Heidi had just started as a secretary in a local school. It was summer when the couple moved into the house, and Keith called on a friend named Roger to get the back garden into shape, as the grass was overgrown and there was a rampant growth of weeds that needed to be tackled. At 11am, Roger arrived at the house in his old green Morris

Minor on a Saturday morning with shears, a machete and a petrol-driven lawnmower, and Heidi continually supplied him with ice-cold Robinson's barley water and sandwiches as he worked, stripped to the waist under a blistering sun. 'You've got some piss-the-beds in here, haven't you?' Roger told Heidi as she brought him a choc-ice during one break in the attack on the weeds.

'Sorry?' she was baffled by the question.

'Dandelions,' explained Roger, 'we used to call them that when we were kids. I think it's because the leaves are diuretics or something if you eat them.'

'Oh,' said Heidi, squinting in the harsh sunlight, 'we use to blow on them to tell the time.'

'Yeah, that goes back to an old Anglo-Saxon custom – ' Roger began, tearing the matte foil off the choc-ice, but before he could continue his talk of plant lore, Heidi heard the letterbox flap clank and the thud of something in the hallway, so she went to see what it was. It was just that legal form of litter - junk mail. She went back into the kitchen but saw that Roger had gone to the bottom of the back garden. She went to watch the telly in the lounge and lit a cigarette. Around twenty minutes later, as Heidi was watching an inane Abbot and Costello film on the television, Roger ran into the lounge and declared that he had just seen a ghost. 'Hurry up! Before she goes!' he told Heidi, and then he ran through the kitchen and into the garden, but when Heidi got out there, Roger said, 'She's gone. She was dressed all in black, and she had a sort of sticky-out dress on. Her face looked white as chalk, and her hair was jet black and done up in a bun.'

'Oh great, that's all we need in a new home – a

ghost,' said Heidi, with a little icy shudder down her back on such a hot August day.

'I'm serious Heidi,' said Roger, staring at the spot at the end of the garden where he'd seen the ghost appear, 'I'm not pulling your leg or anything.'

'I know, Roger, I believe you,' said Heidi, 'and your arms have gone all goosepimply,' she observed, a sure sign that Roger had been spooked by something.

'She was bending down, as if she was picking something up or searching for something near that tree stump,' Roger recalled, stooping slightly as he showed Heidi how the ghost had bent over, and then he seemed to gather some courage and he walked off, wading through the long grass and dispersing the clock seed-heads of the dandelions and aggravating lethargic bees till he reached the spot. He looked back at Heidi, who was keeping at a safe distance, and he shouted: 'Just here she was!' He bent down and almost vanished into the jungle of weeds and grass, and then Heidi saw him throwing grass sods he'd uprooted in every direction. Roger then lifted something up – it looked like a box. He brought it over to Heidi. It was a small coffin. Heidi felt faint when she saw it. 'It looks like a baby's coffin!' she said, drawing back from the little casket, which was about two feet in length.

'Who'd bury a child in a garden?' Roger wondered, and he tried to wipe the encrusted soil from the small rusted plaque on the coffin lid, but instead he lost his grip on the box and he swore as it slipped from his hand and landed on the stony path. Upon impact the lid came off and something fell out as Heidi screamed. A strange-looking wooden doll in a dusty grey smock tumbled across the path towards Heidi's sandalled feet.

She was relieved it wasn't a corpse, but it was still a gruesome find. Roger crouched down and said, 'Look at that – what in God's name?'

The doll's head, which felt to Roger as if it was carved out of oak, had five little daggers of brass - each about 3 inches in length - inserted into it; one in each ear, one in each eye and one in the mouth. There was something ritualistic about them, Roger thought, and he gingerly took one of the daggers out then slid it back in.

'That is – ' Heidi struggled to find an adjective.

'Horrible,' said Roger, 'and weird.'

Under the ragged clothes, the doll was jointed with little interlocking rings like eye screws, and Roger was shocked to see that the person who had created this effigy had even carved out breasts with nipples and a vagina. He covered the doll with its frayed smock before Heidi saw the embarrassing details of the carving.

'Put it back where you found it,' Heidi told him, screwing her face up in disgust at the doll. 'Or burn it – it's making my skin crawl.'

'Nah, that looks real old that,' said Roger, putting the wooden body back in its coffin and holding the lid in place. 'I'll show it to George Hargreaves the antiques fellah down by me; see if it's worth anything.'

'I think that thing's unlucky, Roger, you'd be better burying it,' said Heidi, and she thought of the apparition Roger had seen stooped over the doll's grave. 'Please, Roger, get shut of it.'

Roger smiled, slowly closed his eyes and said: 'I'll get Hargreaves to have a look at it Heidi and then if it isn't worth a carrot I'll dump it.'

Roger mowed the back garden and then he said he'd be back on Sunday afternoon to clean up the garden with Keith. He kissed Heidi on the cheek, hugged her and whispered in her ear, 'Stop worrying about that doll, you big soft thing.' Roger then went out to the front of the house and put the doll in the boot of his car. He recalled he'd left the lawnmower in the garden and went back to get it, and once again he reassured Heidi that he'd get shut of the doll if it wasn't worth anything.

Heidi's husband Keith then returned home on a break from the cabs. Before Heidi could mention the ghost and the doll in the coffin, Keith said, 'You're not going to believe this; as I was pulling up outside, I saw a woman in black – all old fashioned clothes and that – and she was looking into Roger's car.'

'What?' gasped Heidi. Keith said this figure had vanished as he got out the car. Heidi told him that the same ghost had been seen in the back garden and she also told him about the doll with the daggers in its head that had been found in a coffin interred in their back garden. 'I told him to bury it, but he's taking it because he thinks it might be worth something,' Heidi whispered to her husband as Roger pulled the lawnmower from the far end of the back garden.

'Hey, give me a hand you lazy sod!' Roger shouted to Keith.

As Keith helped him carry the lawnmower out of the garden and through the kitchen and hallway, Roger kept telling him about the ghost and the doll and tried to get Keith to go and see the doll, but the cabby said he was scared of anything to do with the supernatural and he also said it'd ruin his tea, which he was about to have. Keith was glad Roger was taking the doll, as he felt the thing had something to do with witchcraft. However, as Roger drove home that day, he got the fright of his life when he saw the pale-faced woman in black hovering alongside the car. It was, without a shadow of a doubt, the ghost he'd seen in the back garden. She screeched at Roger and her head and arms somehow came into the car and made grabbing motions at him. Roger had a blood pressure problem and he saw floating spots and flashing blue lights in front of his eyes. His heart pounded with fear as he swerved the car around, almost hitting a motorcyclist. The apparition vanished, and he sped back to the house on Agnes Road. He hammered on the door, and when Keith answered, Roger almost knocked him over as he barged through the hallway with the coffin. Keith was furious, but Roger was so scared, he hardly spoke, and he placed the coffin in that hole by the stump of the tree, and then he began to throw the clods of uprooted grass on top of it. He then got to his feet a bit too fast, suffered a dizzy spell, and fell backwards, landing on his bottom. Heidi and Keith took him into the kitchen and gave him iced water and told him to breathe slowly. Roger jabbered about the woman in black hovering next to the car as he drove along, and he described her face as being white as snow, and her black eyeballs with light green irises.

Keith later drove his friend home, and Heidi, unwilling to stay in the house in case she saw that woman in the garden, came along with them. The couple didn't last long at their new house. Three days after the reburial of the doll, Keith and Heidi went to bed one evening around midnight, and just after Keith turned the bedside lamp out, he and his wife heard the faint strains of a woman singing somewhere. Keith could not identify the song, but Heidi could.

'It's *Hush Little Baby* - an old lullaby my mum used to sing to Paul [Heidi's younger brother] when he was a baby.'

'It'll be *her*,' said Keith in a low solemn voice that frightened Heidi. She knew who he was referring to.

'I think that song's American, though,' Whispered Heidi.

'Yes, I can hear the words now,' murmured Keith, embracing his wife. 'Just heard her say "Mama's gonna buy you a diamond ring". Maybe we should get out of here, eh love?' Keith asked, and he felt Heidi nod against his chest.

The couple stuck it out for a week, and Keith even wired up a microphone to his cassette tape recorder and managed to record the ghost singing. On this occasion he could not make head or tails of the song because it sounded like another language, but a neighbour he showed it to said it was an old Welsh lullaby called "Suo Gân". Heidi had to have company in the evenings because she was terrified of being on her own, and one night when Keith was at work on the cabs, Heidi had a friend named Leslie over, when they heard a woman crying. 'It's coming from out there,' Leslie said, nodding at the drawn curtains, and she went to open them.

'Leslie don't!' Heidi pleaded, 'It'll be her.'

Leslie couldn't help herself and she opened the curtains wide, and because it was night time without a moon in the sky, the young women could see nothing. The back garden was just a void of impenetrable blackness. Today, there'd be solar-powered lights out there, but in the 1970s there was nothing of the sort, so it was just solid blackness beyond the net curtains.

A white face with black holes for eyes approached the window pane less than two feet from the women. They both screamed and ran to the hallway. Leslie unashamedly deserted her friend, and Heidi went to stay with her neighbour till Keith returned home. The couple had now truly had enough of the ghost, and they put the house on the market and went to stay with Keith's mother in Liverpool. Keith went to collect the mail at the house a week after this, and in broad daylight he saw the woman in black kneeling at the site of the buried doll in the back garden. The house was eventually sold, and no one knows if the new residents saw anything.

Just what that doll with the five daggers in its head represents, I do not know.

CAPTAIN STARLIGHT

The more I delve into the intricacies of time and quantum physics, the closer I get to insanity. In 2001, the *Liverpool Echo* and the *Merseymart* reported on a timeslip I looked into in which several people – including two policemen chasing a joyrider and a man racing home to get to a heavily pregnant wife going into labour – drove across an unknown bridge which spanned Runcorn and Widnes. After travelling across this unidentified bridge, the witnesses subsequently discovered it had vanished, and that bridge later became a reality in October 2017: it was the Mersey Gateway. In other words, the man rushing home to his pregnant wife and the police and the joyriders had all crossed a bridge that only came into existence, sixteen years into their future.

I have spent many years investigating these mind-boggling timeslips – where the past or future somehow becomes accessible in a most unexpected way, and I have also come across weird scenarios involving alternate futures and histories where people have glimpsed how thing might have been (if such a person had not died for example) – and the following is a case in point. Mike Osborne had been working abroad for many years, and he returned to his Liverpool hometown in December 1975 and met up with his old mates. They went on a pub crawl which started at 6.30pm in Kensington and ended at 11.30pm on Mount Pleasant, where a few of the pub-crawlers were ejected from the Beehive public house for being a bit too rowdy. Mike and his friends then got talking to two young women who said they were going to a nightclub. The girls led Mike and his mates up Mount Pleasant, and Mike imagined the club they were heading for would be something like the Blue Angel or the Jacaranda, but instead, the girls led the gang of intoxicated lads to a place called the Pink Banana, and it was situated on Benson Street, just off Mount Pleasant. The facade of the club was aglow with a huge neon pink banana, and the stylish frontage gave the impression of this being an above-average venue. The lads paid 50p admission and walked down a long sloping floor of red and white chequered tiles. The walls were matt black with neon music notes dotted upon them. Before the girls pushed open the huge silver swinging doors, Mike and his friends could already hear a thumping bass and someone who sounded like a cross between Elvis and Elton John singing an unknown song. The doors opened and Mike was dumbfounded by the chic interior of the Pink Banana. It was immense, and must have cost a fortune to put together. The walls were a mosaic of scarlet and purple mirrors, and lights of every colour in the spectrum shone down onto the crowds of club-goers gathered around the circular performance space. Mirror balls turned on a black ceiling dotted with blue-white constellations of stars. A rich, invigorating incense, mingled with the perfumes and aftershaves of the clientele hung in the air, and there, in the middle of the disc-shaped stage was some glam-rock singer with a sparkling knee-length coat, close-fitting silvery pants and glittery jackboots. He was blonde, with a huge quiff, and he wore a red star on his left cheek and a four-pointed Star of Bethlehem over his left eye. Mike thought the coat was of a military style from the four circumferential stripes round its sleeves – obviously signifying the singer was a Captain. The singer was almost doing the splits as he held the microphone stand as if it was a guitar. 'Who's this fellah?' Mike asked one of the girls who had led him to the amazing club, and she had to shout the answer down his ears because the band was so loud.

'Captain Starlight and the Men in the Moon!' she cried.

Mike's best friend Tony tapped him on the shoulder and handed him something that looked just like a baby's bottle. It contained a green liquid, and Tony had one of these strange bottles too, only the contents of his one was purple. Tony sucked at the teat and then gave an approving nod. Mike went to drink from his bottle, but one of the girls playfully snatched it from his hand and sucked at the teat. She then thrust the teat into Mike's mouth. It tasted sweet, and minty, but within a minute he felt as if he was not there and that what he was seeing was a mere projection on some screen. He felt detached and everything seemed unreal. He realised that the bottle had not contained some mere liquor – it had obviously contained a drug of some sort. He found his way to a bar, and got a round of the usual alcoholic beverages in for his friends and the girls, and the effects of that baby's bottle wore off.

Captain Starlight reminded Mike Osborne of someone under all of his theatrical make-up, and he kept asking his friend Tony if the singer reminded him of someone they had seen years ago, but Tony said Captain Starlight just looked like Bowie.

'No, Tony,' Mike yelled to his friend over the eardrum-battering music, 'there's something very familiar about that fellah! Who the hell does he remind me of?'

Captain Starlight jumped about the stage in his spangled costume beneath the twirling glitter-balls, sweeping beams of multicoloured light, and a stage that now lit up from a hundred bulbs beneath its translucent covering. Starlight started singing way-out songs about Martians, laser beams and dinosaurs – and then suddenly, Mike recognised him. Captain Starlight was none other than Rory Storm, a local pop singer from the 1960s who had a band called the Hurricanes – and Ringo Starr had played drums with that band before leaving to join the Beatles. Yes! That was it! It was Storm!

Mike asked a bouncer if Starlight was Rory Storm and the doorman nodded, and said, 'Yeah, he used to have the Hurricanes. He should go on *New Faces*, he's ace.'

One of the girls who had led Mike to the Pink Banana pushed him to a corner and told him they should go to a hotel when the club closed. Mike was single and the girl was extremely attractive, and he could not believe his luck. He nodded to her suggestion, and she offered him one of those odd baby's bottles, but he shook his head and continued to drink his pint of lager.

At the end of the seven-song set, Mike tried to talk to Captain Starlight but he couldn't get through the mob of fans charging the stage. 'Rory!' Mike yelled, and Captain Starlight's head jerked back, surprised, and he stopped signing autographs and looked at Mike, astonished, and then waved.

To Tony, Mike said, 'See him,' – pointing to Starlight – 'he used to just do rock and roll around the clubs, but look at him now; where did he get that image from?'

Tony nodded impatiently, and his eyelids drooped with all of the alcohol and whatever was in those strange bottles, and he grabbed Mike by the lapels of his coat in almost a threatening manner and said: 'Yeah, never mind all that, let's go and book a room at the Shaftesbury Hotel and take those birds with us, eh?'

'Sounds like a plan to me, Tony,' said Mike, and to Captain Starlight he shouted: 'Goodnight Rory!'

When Mike and Tony got outside, they could not find the girls, and the two men filled the air with profanities and Tony urinated in a doorway as Mike went to shout the names of the girls – but he could not remember them. He asked Tony if he could recall their names – and his mind was a blank on this matter too. Tony went to ask his friends, but they had all staggered away to the nearest chippy, so Mike and Tony hailed a taxi and went home.

Mike returned to the Pink Banana club on the following Saturday – and discovered it was the Unemployment Exchange. That club had vanished. He asked a passerby where the Pink Banana Club was and the man said he had never heard of such a place. Mike continued to ask around, and he even asked a policeman if he had heard of the Pink Banana; the constable said there was no such club.

'I drank in there, as true as God's in Heaven,' Mike told the policeman, who began to look at him in a condescending manner, as if he thought Mike was drunk or high. And when Mike told him about the narcotic drinks in the baby's bottles, the policeman simply turned away and walked off. Mike had spent so many years away from Liverpool working as a bricklayer, he had not known that Rory Storm had died – possibly from an accidental overdose of sleeping tablets – three years back, in 1972, and when a drinker told him this bit of information, Rory was naturally shocked. 'He can't be dead, mate,' he told the drinker, 'I saw him alive and well, and he was Captain Starlight.'

Eventually, Mike discovered from other people that Rory Storm really had died at his home in Broadgreen on 28 September 1972 – so how had he been leaping about on a stage a week ago? Mike was haunted by the memory of that night at the Pink Banana – a club which did not exist – for the rest of his life. The only explanation which made sense to Mike was the one I offered him – that he had somehow entered an alternative future that December night in 1975. Mike had entered a future where Rory Storm had not died from that overdose, and in this alternative world, the former leader of The Hurricanes had reinvented himself as a glam-rocker, and had become Captain Starlight. This had been the case with his musician friend Shane Fenton – who had married Rory's sister Iris. Fenton had enjoyed a moderate success as a singer in the early 1960s, but after becoming Alvin Stardust he had gone on to enjoy a second successful career in the 1970s era as a glam-rocker. In our 'timeline', Rory died in 1972, but through some strange occurrence, Mike and his friends had walked into another timeline – and entered the 'Earth next door' – where Rory did not die. This scenario is in total agreement with the latest findings in quantum physics – that there are multiple universes peopled with countless versions of ourselves in lives that have turned out differently from our life in this one – some by degrees, whilst in other lives we may be a different sex or look completely different. It really is a mind-boggling concept.

SHANGHAIED BY A GHOST

One sunny but blustery Sunday afternoon in March 2003, a 22-year-old Liverpool John Moores University student named Lisa was working part-time as a bartender at a certain pub situated in very close proximity to the Albert Dock, and there were only two drinkers in the place: two elderly regulars – Alf and John - seated next to one another on a long banquette type of bench, talking about times past, and Lisa could hear their conversation in a stillness spoiled only by the occasional blast of wind buffeting the plate glass windows. Around 1pm, a man wearing a hat that Lisa called a fisherman's cap, entered the bar. He also wore a long black coat, dark blue trousers, possibly jeans, pleated in an unusual way so the edges, rather than running down the front of the trousers, were at the sides of them, and the pants stopped just above the man's ankles, so Lisa could see he had on a pair of black leather ankle-length boots. He was about five feet and seven inches tall, but broad-shouldered, and he had big hands with weathered skin. The stranger had snowy curls sprouting from under the sides of the cap, and an equally white goatee beard which contrasted with his evenly tanned face, and Lisa thought his skin was tenné – the same shade of orange-brown as her friend Margot's lipstick. This man, who looked to be about 70, perhaps older, had a pair of amazing penetrating blue-green eyes. Lisa normally never found old men attractive, but this stranger really drew her attention, and he just had some aura of appeal about him. He asked for milk-stout, which Lisa had never heard of, and she blushed and apologised and eventually the man settled for Guinness. His accent was not a Liverpool one, but perhaps more of a Lancashire brogue. The young barmaid waited for him to pay, but he didn't, and Lisa thought it would be a bit discourteous to reach out and gesture with an open palm, and he began to talk about his ship, the [something] Rose – she didn't quite catch the first half of the vessel's name, and the man – who said he was nicknamed Red Silas, spun some amazing tales about the sea, and he took off his cap and bowed forward as he parted his thick white hair to show the girl a ghastly deep trench of a scar in his scalp. 'The blade of a Barbary pirate's axe did that,' said Red Silas, 'the brains were showing but I pulled through.'

Lisa shuddered when she saw the deep scar, but the old mariner continued to captivate her with the sensational salty stories, and Red Silas eventually said, 'Come and have a look at her – she's only berthed over there! Come on!'

'Have a look at what?' Lisa asked, puzzled.

'My ship,' said Silas, and he nodded to the plate glass window facing the dock. 'You can see her from here – come on! I'll show you around her before she sets sail.'

'I can't leave here, ' Lisa said, but Red Silas shouted

to the two old regulars and told them to look after the place while he and Lisa went to look at his ship.

The two old men at the other end of the bar looked at one another in astonishment. 'Why? Where are you two going?' asked the old regular drinker Alf.

'We're not going anywhere,' laughed Lisa, but Red Silas was very persuasive, and he gripped Lisa's bare forearm and pulled her from behind the bar. His grip hurt her, and she cried, 'Ow!'

'You okay there, Lisa?' asked the other old drinker, John, rising from the bench when he saw that the young barmaid was apparently being dragged from behind the bar.

Lisa nodded to John's question but she didn't seem to want to go with the old stranger.

'You'll be back in a minute, lass,' Silas assured the student. He let go of her arm as they walked along the cobbled quayside, and Lisa looked at the bruise on her forearm where he had grabbed her hard. The old sailor took her to the huge old-fashioned sailing ship moored in the Albert Dock, and she went up the gangplank with him, smiling, but inside she felt a bit anxious. She wondered if this man had anything to do with this ship – which looked like the type of historic ship that had been exhibited around the Albert Dock by the nearby Maritime Museum. He could be a lunatic for all she knew. As Lisa walked along the deck, the entire dock and its colonnades slowly faded to white, as if a fog had enveloped the ship. The sounds of hungry gulls that had been shrieking overhead could no longer be heard, as if the sudden fog had blanketed out the sounds of the waterfront. Lisa then saw the eyeballs of Red Silas turn scarlet. They changed colour before her very eyes, and then he pulled a large clasp-knife from his coat pocket, opened it and said, 'You stay put now, lass.'

Lisa screamed, ran from the man and lost her bearings for a moment, and then she bolted towards the gangplank, and by now, she could not see the quayside of the Albert Dock or anything at all beyond the deck of that ship. Everything was a silent white void with no traffic noise coming from the dock roads of Wapping and the Strand – and Lisa could not see even the faintest image of any building. She literally took a leap of faith, and ran down the gangplank and jumped into the white nothingness – and she felt her feet hit the cobbles, and she knew she'd sustain a sprained ankle at least. Immediately, she saw a blue sky above her, and the red pillars and the renovated brick warehouses of the dock. Everything around her had reappeared – but there was no sign of that sailing ship and its sinister captain. Two young men helped Lisa to her feet, and she experienced an almost electrical shock of pain in her ankle. She had indeed sprained it. She was so upset by the terrifying supernatural incident, she left her job that day, and she had terrible nightmares about that man in the fisherman's cap – a man who must have been a ghost. The two regulars in the dockside bar had seen him arrive and the ghost had even told these two men he was taking Lisa to see that ship, so no one could say that the barmaid had imagined the whole thing, and she even had a bruise on her forearm where Red Silas had held her when he forced her to leave the bar to see his ship. I have looked through countless old maritime records for a Red Silas, but have not found him to date, although he did say it was his nickname, and as such his real name might not even have 'Silas' in it. I mentioned the case on the radio during a programme on the paranormal, and no one seems to have any recollection of a sailing ship of the type described by Lisa being moored at the Albert Dock that March in 2003, and Lisa told me that she felt as if she was sleepwalking at one point as she went onboard the vessel. One therefore wonders how much of the ship's existence was a subjective experience regarding Lisa's mind. It really is a peculiar case, although there have been so many strange goings-on at the Albert Dock since it underwent a massive renovation project in the 1980s, and I have long noticed that any disturbance of old buildings seems to bring ghosts out the woodwork. Lisa believes that some ghostly captain of yore had tried to 'shanghai' her for some unthinkable purpose, and even today, she is reluctant to go anywhere near the Albert Dock complex.

THE MYSTERY OF ELVA

Love is a powerful emotion, and few can escape its influence. They say love makes the world go round, and that's largely true, but it can also destroy a person's world; it can join people together and it can also separate lovers, driving one into the arms of someone else. Love laughs at locks, and will always find a way to someone's heart – even the hardest heart – and that heart will be softened by love. You can't keep love out – it will stealthily creep in where it is forbidden. If friends fall in love, their friendship will be gone forever, such is love's transformative power. Love has a language all of its own and it can speak, even when the lips are closed. When love fully possesses a person, words are very few – and there have even been cases where people who didn't speak the same language have fallen in love and married. Love can strike in an instant, and in some cases, "love at first sight" really has occurred, like some mysterious instant chemical reaction between two strangers. Our first love, besides the affection we may feel for our mother, will never be forgotten, and unrequited love is probably the only love that never dies. According to the ancient Song of Solomon, love is as strong as death, and of course, lovers have committed suicide and murder in the name of love, as all is supposedly fair in love and war, and sometimes, love is played like a game in which the two players cheat. Love features so much in our short lives, it's bound to have some influence in the supernatural sphere – because where people have lived and loved, they will leave impressions of their emotions behind after death that will be picked up by sensitives for many years to come, and some ghosts are bound to this arena of the living by ties of love. The story that follows is concerned with this concept – romance and the supernatural, and it is a very sad and eerie tale.

Night after night, 42-year-old plasterer Jim Kennedy thought of hardly anything but Elva. Just a week ago, on the last day of November, 1970, he had met this beautiful lady by chance on Newington – that little thoroughfare which runs between Renshaw Street and Bold Street. She had been trying to drag a bulky padded Chesterfield armchair through the door of Number 23, to get it up to her flat, and Jim had offered a hand, and something had 'just clicked' between them as their eyes met. Corny but true. Three flights of stairs and a coffee later, he had asked her on a date, which surprised Jim because he'd never been successful with females and had only had two girlfriends in his life and he was forty-two. When Elva smiled coyly, raised her soft-arched eyebrows, then nodded to his question, Jim felt that butterflies-in-the-tum sensation he had last experienced when he was a child on a fairground ride. He had not expected her to say yes, but had felt he *had* to ask her out anyway.

The date was at a basement trattoria on Bold Street called La Bussola – a place Jim Kennedy had passed many times, but he had never set foot inside the premises. It had always looked a cut above the usual restaurants and Jim had always longed to take a girl there. He arrived at 7.50pm sharp in his new TJ Hughes suit, Ben Sherman shirt with a daft bow tie and a pair of black slip-ons from Clarks – and the heel collar felt like a razor pressing into his Achilles tendon. He smoked nervously outside La Bussola, and she turned up a minute before eight looking absolutely stunning and serene – the very epitome of sophistication. She wore a plain sleeveless black dress which reminded Jim of the dress worn by Audrey Hepburn in *Breakfast At Tiffanys*, and Elva's hair was consummately styled into an updo with a bejewelled comb atop of the bun. Jim quickly detected the very provocative perfume Elva wore, and it left him tongue-tied for a moment. They sat at a spot-lit table and Jim asked for Veal Marsala and Elva ordered some chicken parmigiana dish and they drank expensive wine as they waited for their orders.

'What do *you* do?' Elva asked, and she touched the knuckles of Jim's clenched fist as it rested on the table.

'I'm a plasterer,' he said, and felt an electric surge of pleasure upon her soft touch.

Elva smiled, muttered, 'A plasterer, eh?' and then she spoke fluent Italian to a nearby waiter, and he looked at his watch and told her the time.

'What do you do? If you don't mind me asking – ' Jim said, and found himself blushing. He felt so warm under his new suit and the starched collar of a shirt that felt as if it still had a holding pin in it.

'I'm an artist,' she said confidently, and she took out a pack of Pall Mall cigarettes and Jim plunged his hand into the inside pocket of his jacket to grab his lighter. With a slight tremor in his hand he lit her cigarette and said, 'A painter? Like in portraits and that? Or like a housepainter?'

'An artist,' she replied, and elegantly dragged on her menthol cigarette. She told Jim how she had studied at the Sorbonne and, now at 27, she was selling her oil paintings for a living.

'I forgot to ask last time, but what's your surname?' Jim asked, and he felt awkward and a bit too forward posing this question. '*My* surname's plain old Kennedy.'

'Zwack,' she answered, poker-faced.

'Unusual name,' remarked Jim, and he brought the wine glass to his mouth and its rim clinked against his front teeth. He ignored the faux pas and queried, 'Is it foreign?'

'Hungarian,' Elva told him, and then she patted the cigarette over the ashtray with the tip of her long slender finger, even though the ciggy had no overhanging ash, and she suddenly said: 'You have the most beautiful blue eyes I've ever seen, Jim.'

'Thankyou,' Jim replied, and the compliment threw him; no one had ever said anything like that about his eyes before. And then he felt the pointed toe of Elva's shoe in his crotch. She winked at him, and Jim felt his heart pound. She withdrew her foot as a waiter came over and apologised for a delay in getting Elva's dish, and once again she spoke to him in Italian. There were no further sexual overtures under the table, just small talk, and Elva didn't give much information about her background. What was she doing in Liverpool? Jim had wanted to ask her that, and he wondered if she was married; the absence of a wedding ring meant nothing nowadays. Every time he had tried to probe, Elva had made some flattering remark about his appearance or his nature. After the meal, Jim suggested going to a club, but Elva said she preferred a certain coffee bar close by on Bold Street, and this was the El Cabala. The couple went there and as they talked over a coffee, a foreign-looking gentleman in his early twenties on a neighbouring table called Elva by her name. She addressed this man in fluent French for a while, and then she told Jim that the man was a French poet named Albert, and she whispered to the plasterer about Albert's crush on her and how he often posted love letters to her. She dismissed him as a harmless, hopeless romantic. Jim felt welling jealousy towards the young man, and was glad when he finally left the El Cabala.

Jim walked Elva home to 23 Newington at midnight, and she kissed him. As she began to pull away he lunged forward and tried to kiss her back, but she giggled, tapped his nose with her index finger, and told him he could call on her on Saturday at noon.

Jim was about to say he loved Elva when she blew him a kiss, whispered, 'Night, Jim' and vanished into her flat. She closed the door, and he heard her heels going up the stairs.

The beautiful, sophisticated Elva could have anyone – so what did she see in a bald plasterer? Jim's friends wanted to know the answer to this and virtually accused him of inventing Elva, but he had a photograph of her. His friends said it looked like a photograph of the actress Tracy Reed.

'As if I'd do something as childish as make up a

girlfriend at my age,' Jim had told his sceptical old friend Ken Fisher as they had a lunchtime drink at the Belvedere pub on Sugnall Street on the day after the dream date.

'Could be a psychosis,' said Ken, gently sipping his pint of mild as he studied the topology of the barmaid.

'Could be what?' Jim asked, thinning his eyes – and he didn't like the sound of the term – whatever it meant.

'Psychosis,' Ken replied, turning to face Jim, 'is a psychiatric disorder. If you've got it, you lose touch with reality, like. A psychotic person retreats into a private world of fantasy because they can't take the harsh reality of life, you know?'

'I am *not* a bleedin' psychotic!' Jim protested, and his outburst startled the barmaid. 'I am going with a beautiful woman, Ken, and if anyone's got a screw loose it's you! You've turned into a real jealous sod.'

'Nothing to be jealous about, mate,' retorted Ken, taking out his Woodbines. He usually offered the pack to Jim first but he took a ciggy out for himself and lit it before putting the box back in his coat pocket.

'Look, Ken, put your money where your mouth is,' said Jim, bringing his face close to Ken's. 'We'll go down to her flat and you can see her yourself. If I'm lying I'll give you a hundred quid – and this girl here [and Jim pointed to the barmaid with his thumb] is a witness, okay?'

'You told me five minutes ago that she told you to see her again on Saturday,' said Ken with an agonised attempt at a smile, 'so show your sophisticated tart off then!'

'Alright, come on, shake on it mate!' Jim thrust out

his hand.

'Oh act your age Jim,' said Ken with a dismissive shake of his head, 'you don't have to shake on it.'

'I'm going to get a ring tomorrow,' Jim announced, and he placed both hands palms down on the bar counter and held his head back in a pose of sheer arrogance.

'Sounds serious,' said the barmaid, and she swung her large eyes from Jim to Ken and gave a feeble smirk.

'Oh, it is!' said Jim, annoyed by her washy smile. 'You want to see her figure – absolute stunner she is, love, and she's got the brains to go with it as well. Speaks all sorts of languages and she studied at that place over in France – the Sorbonne. One classy lady she is; there's none like her in this city.'

'And she's going with a plasterer,' said Ken, voicing his message in a hurtful stinging matter-of-fact putdown. And then he dragged on the Woodbine and thinned his eyes.

Jim turned and headed for the door without saying a word, and he heard the faint chuckle of the barmaid and Ken saying, 'It's true though, isn't it?'

Jim Kennedy went to H Samuel the jeweller and to a young assistant he pointed to an engagement ring with a large diamond that had caught his attention in the window. He wanted to know if it was 'a decent ring' and the young man said all the rings were decent, and Jim said he'd be back with the £300 to buy the ring. 'Ah, yes, but you'll have to know your fiancée's ring size first, sir,' said the smiling assistant.

'Ring size?' asked Jim, baffled by the term.

'Here, take this and find out what her ring size is,'

said the helpful assistant, and he handed Jim what looked like a bracelet with curtain loops strung upon it. It was a 32-piece ring sizer. Elva only had to slip her ring finger into a loop that fitted perfectly and Jim would know her size – but would she even agree to marry him? Was he getting ahead of himself? Jim asked these questions as he left the jewellers, and he convinced himself that Elva would agree to marry him – even though he'd only been on one date with her so far. Then every now and then the demon of doubt was conjured up in the plasterer's mind, and he would wonder if Ken was right about him being a psychotic who was hiding in a fantasy world – but then he recalled all of the compliments Elva had made about him; she seemed to actually love him. On Saturday at noon he planned to visit her, and then, when the time was right, he'd pop the question.

On that long-awaited Saturday at a quarter to noon, Jim Kennedy arrived at Newington, and he went to Number 23 – and found that the door to the house where Elva had her flat was not there. He was so excited by the prospect of the engagement he thought the exhilaration had hazed his mind and that he had gone to the wrong street, but no – this *was* Newington. He asked the tailor at No 24 and was told that 23 had never existed. He went to the shop at Number 26 and the woman behind the counter there told him there was no Number 23; 'There are only even numbers on this side of the street, love, ' she told him.

'It was a house with flats in,' Jim told the woman, his left hand unconsciously tracing out the square shape of the house in the air, 'and she had a flat there. Her name's Elva.' Jim dipped his hand into his inside jacket pocket, took out his wallet, and tried to find the photograph of Elva that she had given him. It wasn't there. He never did find that photograph. 'Zwack, her surname is, ' said Jim, putting his wallet back in his pocket, 'Elva Zwack.'

The woman shook her head and did a mock double take at the mention of the unusual surname. 'Zwack?' she asked, 'I don't know anyone of that name round here, and there aren't any houses with flats on in this row. I think there's a house like that on Slater Street, but that's about a hundred yards away from here – just turn left when you come out of here, it's like a continuation – ' the woman was saying, but Jim slowly shook his head.

'No, it was definitely in this street love,' Jim told her in a broken voice, and he fidgeted with the ring sizer in his jacket pocket. 'I'll try further down; thanks anyway.'

Noon came and went, and after asking several unhelpful passers-by if they knew were 23 Newington was, Jim Kennedy stopped a policeman on his beat on Renshaw Street and asked him if he could find the apparently non-existent address.

'Well,' said the towering policeman, 'if it was going to be anywhere it'd have to be on that side of the street, mate,' the policeman said, nodding to a store on Newington called Kelly's, but next to that store there was only a long sandstone wall.

'She told me to meet her here, you see,' a numb, deflated Jim told the policeman, 'and I was going to ask her to marry me.'

'Ah, as she stood you up, eh?' the copper asked, faintly smiling but with sympathy in his eyes.

'But I actually went to her flat, and the door was right there between that tailor's shop and that other shop there. It doesn't make sense, officer,' said Jim in an uneven, broken voice.

'Sorry I can't help, mate,' said the policeman, 'Hope you find her. Cheerio.' The officer of the law left Newington and headed back to Renshaw Street. Ken Fisher walked past that policemen as he arrived on Newington. 'Sorry I'm late – the bus broke down on Hardman Street,' explained Ken, 'just walked down from there now.'

'The door to her flat's gone,' Jim told his friend in a barely audible voice.

'What's gone?' asked Ken.

'You know the door to the house where Elva had her flat?' Jim pointed to the narrow length of brick wall between the tailor's and a shop. 'It's gone.'

'How can it be gone?' Ken asked, and immediately began to fear for Jim's state of mind. He knew Jim was not pulling his leg, but *had* evidently hallucinated the whole Elva thing.

Jim Kennedy was left heartbroken by the mysterious disappearance of Elva and almost had a nervous breakdown. Ken advised him to see his doctor, but Jim reacted angrily and said he had not been suffering from hallucinations. He begged Ken Fisher to go with him to that basement trattoria La Bussola on Bold Street, because the waiters in there would surely remember Elva. Ken eventually agreed to go with his friend, and sure enough, the waiter Elva had spoken to in his native Italian said he certainly recalled the 'beautiful lady' who had accompanied Jim that evening. Jim then took his friend to the El Cabala coffee bar and there was the French poet Albert, and he not only recalled Jim and Elva from that night, he told Jim that he had written many love letters to Elva at her address – 23 Newington – and Albert was apparently unaware that this address was no longer in existence.

'So, I'm not a psychotic, Ken,' said Jim. He stood with a dazed look in his tear-slicked eyes, and he looked at the ring sizer in his palm. 'People remember her, but she's vanished off the face of the earth.'

Ken gently took hold of his friend's upper arm. 'Let's go and have a few bevies Jimbo, and we can try and get to the bottom of this.'

They went for a drink at the Newington pub, and Ken told the barmaid what had happened, and this young lady, upon hearing the name of the vanished love of Jim Kennedy, stopped pulling the pump handle for a moment.

'Elva Zwack.' She said it in a flat monotone voice and nodded once. She had a knowing look in her eyes.

'Yeah,' said Ken, intrigued, 'you know her?'

The barmaid said she had, and that about three months ago, a regular drinker at the pub named Terry had come in and told his friends he had met the girl of his dreams. They had all laughed when he told them her name – Elva Zwack. Terry had seen Elva trying to light a cigarette one day in a doorway on Bold Street, and he had rushed to her aid and lit her cigarette – and then they had struck up a conversation and it had ended with Terry asking her on a date. Elva said she'd love to go out, as she hardly went anywhere because of work commitments. Terry took her to the theatre to see a musical and another date followed a few days later – a concert at the Philharmonic Hall, and then a meal at an upmarket restaurant. Terry was the envy of the men in the pub because a few of them had seen Elva and said she had movie star looks and an aristocratic way about her. And then Terry said Elva had disappeared off the face of the earth, and he could not find her flat on Cropper Street – just around the corner from the Newington thoroughfare. Instead, Terry found an old garage where Elva's ground floor flat had been, and this really puzzled him. Like Jim Kennedy, Terry had been planning to pop the question to Elva, and was left heartbroken by her vanishing act, even though he'd only been on two dates with her.

In 1972, Jim Kennedy had met a woman named Barbara and they now shared a flat together which was located over a shop on Richmond Street in the city centre. In March of that year, Jim went in search of some carpet for the flat and paid a visit to Taffy's Cut Price Carpets (which existed where the Petticoat Lane shopping arcade now stands) on Bold Street. As Jim was looking in the window at the selection of carpets, he caught a glimpse of Elva reflected in that window as she strode along towards the Berry Street end of Bold Street. Although Jim was happy with his partner Barbara, he was intrigued to see the mysterious and very elusive Elva, and so he shouted to her – twice – but she didn't react. Jim followed her, wondering where she was going. He could have easily caught up with her, but he wanted to tail her to see if she was going to her latest flat. She wore a tartan-patterned swing coat, black pencil skirt, dark brown tights and heels. Elva surprised Jim by taking a sharp left into Roscoe Place – a short cul-de-sac about 30 yards in length. Technically, Roscoe Place is not a blind alley because it leads to Back Bold Street and although this very narrow street is mostly used for shopkeepers to leave their premises via the back door (as well as being a place where the waste bins of the shops are kept) a person could use it to gain access to that narrow continuation of Heathfield Street which leads back onto Bold Street. Jim turned into Roscoe Place seconds after Elva had done the same, and he heard the click-clack of her heels stop. Elva was not on Roscoe Place. Jim went to the end of the dead end street and looked down Back Bold Street – and saw it was deserted. This was the only way Elva could have gone, but she was nowhere to be seen and there were no places – no doorways or niches where she could be hiding. As he stood there, contemplating the eerie way Elva had disappeared, Jim had an intense feeling he was being watched, and he quickly left Roscoe Place and rejoined the swarm of shoppers on Bold Street. Jim has not seen the enigmatic Elva since.

I mentioned this intriguing case on BBC Radio Merseyside's *Billy Butler Show* in 2007 and received some very interesting feedback in the form of letters and emails. A woman named Jayne who worked at a wallpaper store on Bold Street in the early 1970s told me how her brother, Denny, who was just eighteen, had visited her at the store one afternoon in July 1974 with his friend Geoff. Denny had been in town shopping for jeans and had called into the wallpaper shop just to see his sister, and Jayne told him off for coming into her workplace to mess about. A very attractive and shapely woman came into the wallpaper shop and told Jayne she needed someone to decorate her flat, and she made eyes at Denny, and made it clear that she fancied him. She looked as if she was in her mid-twenties and Jayne thought she was too old for her brother, who seem besotted by the woman, as did his friend Geoff. 'I can decorate,' Denny joked to the woman, and she said she'd be willing to pay him and that her flat was literally just around the corner on Berry Street.

'He's only eighteen,' Jayne told the woman, who bought five rolls of flock wallpaper, a packet of wallpaper paste, a paper-hanging brush and a plastic bucket. Denny volunteered to carry the wallpaper rolls and bucket to the woman's flat, and Jayne shouted after him, 'Be careful you!'

For the next fortnight, Denny talked about nothing but Elva, the woman who had come into the wallpaper store that day. He said she was a model and that he wanted to marry her. Denny even resorted to stealing money from his mother's purse so he could take Elva out. Then one day, a young woman named Nancy, who worked in a pharmacy in the Kensington area (where Denny lived), said Denny had been in to buy condoms. Jayne told her mother and Denny's father pulled him up and said: 'I hope you're not messing round with a married woman.'

Denny assured his father that Elva was single, and that she was a beautiful model, and that he planned to move in with her soon and, as soon as he could get a decent job, he'd marry her.

Two weeks after meeting Elva, Denny was at her flat one evening when she told him to strip. 'This is the night you lose your virginity,' she told him, and said she was going to have a shower.

Denny was stunned, and became plagued with first-time nerves, and as Elva went up to the bathroom to shower, he took off all his clothes and got into her double bed. He waited...and waited.

Eventually, after about half an hour, Denny tired of waiting and left the bedroom. He went up the stairs to the shower, and noticed something odd; the stairs were no longer carpeted. His bare feet were walking on bare wooden steps, and the wallpaper on the stairs was gone. In its place was flaking maroon paint. The shower upstairs was empty, and looked as if it had not been used for years. Denny got the shock of his life when he returned to the bedroom – it was empty, and not only was the bed missing, the carpet was gone too. The lights went out, and Denny could not get them to come back on. He tried the switches, and then with mounting panic he realised that he could not find his clothes and underwear – they had vanished in that bedroom along with the bed and carpet. He cautiously opened the front door, and he tried to tell a passing old man what had happened but the elderly man eyed him suspiciously and walked on. A woman in her fifties then passed and Denny called her, and had to talk with his head around the door because he was naked. He told the woman he had got out of the bath and discovered that his flat had been burgled and everything – including his clothes – had been taken, and he asked the woman if she could telephone his home and tell his mother or father what had happened. The woman did this, and almost an hour later, Denny's parents and sister Jayne turned up at the Berry Street house. Denny's mother handed him a tee shirt, jeans and a pair of old pumps, and the lad's father wanted to know what had really happened. He never believed his son's story but Jayne did, because she knew her younger brother simply did not possess the type of imagination needed to make up such a bizarre story.

This is just one story regarding Elva, and in the other accounts I received regarding this baffling and cruel woman, she exhibited the same pattern of heartless behaviour. So, Elva had been going out of her way to break the hearts of men young and old over the years. She beguiled them, captivated them, kissed - and even petted them – only to subsequently vanish like scotch mist. She has been doing this for God knows how long – possibly since the 1950s – perhaps even much earlier – who knows? What is she then? She never seems to age, for she always looks as if she's about 25 or 27, and when I asked a lot of the witnesses and 'victims' to describe her, their descriptions always matched. I showed them dozens of cards featuring the old Hollywood actresses she'd been compared to – and every person who laid eyes on Elva had matched her with a photograph of the late actress Tracy Reed. Is there something supernatural about her? I'd say so; I just feel as if there is something about her that doesn't quite add up, though – something we are missing when we analyse this strange case. Is she a men-hating witch? A ghost that is hell-bent on breaking men's hearts?

There is an eerie footnote to this case. Just after I'd drafted this chapter, I had to visit the city centre of Liverpool to meet an old friend, and afterwards, in the late afternoon, I was walking up Bold Street on my way home when I suddenly noticed a woman with a very strong resemblance to the actress Tracy Reed, standing on the steps of the Lyceum building. I had the unsettling feeling that I was looking at the mystifying Elva. She smiled, and I looked straight ahead and kept on walking...

YOU ARE EVERYTHING

On the Friday morning of 31 January 1975, 37-year-old Eric Johnson bought a Ben Sherman shirt from C&A, and then he visited the bookies and put his bus fare money on a horse running in the Barr Novices' Hurdle at Ayr, so he'd now have to walk four miles home to Knotty Ash. The orange shirt would complement his tangerine-coloured suit tomorrow, he imagined, when he was due to marry. His fiancée's dad had paid for the wedding and Eric's generous friends had paid for everything else, as they knew Eric was clinically incapable of saving up with his gambling problem. On this sunny but cold morning, Eric had just reached the corner of Roscoe Street on Mount Pleasant when he heard a familiar girl's voice calling him. He turned and saw it was Ruby Barnes, the 27-year-old he'd lived with for years before they split up six months ago. She lived in the basement flat round the corner on Rodney Street next to the YWCA (the Young Women's Christian Association).

'I should congratulate you but I can't,' she said, with a sorrowful look. 'All those years I wanted to marry you and you said you didn't believe in marriage – so why are you marrying this one you're with now?'

'Don't start, Ruby,' Eric sighed, glancing away and walking on, 'I'm marrying Jenny and that's that.'

Ruby walked by his side and asked: 'So the stag do is tonight then?'

'Yes it is – why?' Eric asked, full of suspicion, and he

nervously adjusted his spectacles as he watched the faint grin on Ruby's face. 'Ruby, you're not planning to turn up at my stag do and start a scene are you? I'd have to go to the police if you did!'

'No, don't worry Eric, I couldn't do that,' Ruby replied, looking at the pavement as she walked along. 'Seems like only yesterday when we walked up here holding hands,' she ruefully remarked; 'how did we come to lose our love?'

'Ruby, let it go,' said Eric, halting at the kerb. He looked left, right, then anticipated a Cortina swinging round the corner from Mount Pleasant as he waited to cross Rodney Street. 'We went our separate ways six months ago Ruby – we're just incompatible. Bye now.' Eric then started to cross Rodney Street, and looked back, annoyed, seeing his ex was still following.

'You were my everything, Eric,' said Ruby, tears in her eyes, 'no one will ever love you more than me. Do you remember our song? *You Are Everything*? I did the Diana Ross part and you were Marvin -'

'Ruby!' yelled an impatient Eric, 'What do you want me to do? Call the marriage off? We both have separate lives now. I wish you all the best for your future Ruby, and I really hope you find someone; someone decent. I was a liability with my gambling – you deserved someone better.'

'You *were* the one, Eric, from the moment I first saw you at the Everyman Theatre.' Ruby grabbed his arm and pleaded, 'Eric, come to my place – I have some money you can have, and we can talk like old time's sake. Please – I have some booze in too.'

The mention of money tipped Eric off balance. He stood there on the corner for a while, looking up the gentle slope of Mount Pleasant, thinking of his future with a new wife – and a pretty wealthy wife too – but his head swivelled right and he looked at the well-remembered basement flat of Ruby, where there was money to be blown on the horses. 'Look, Ruby, just half an hour, and I can get a bus home instead of walking all the way back to Knotty Ash – and maybe *one* drink – and that's all, just for old time's sake.'

'You can get a cab home if you want, love,' Ruby said, and to Eric it was strange being called "love"; his present girl never called him that.

'I'll have to get back by two at least – I have a lot to do, you know?' Eric told Ruby as she pulled him along by his hand to the gate in the railings.

'I know, I know,' said Ruby, going down the steps to her flat door. 'I have some of that whiskey you used to drink,' she said, smiling as she put the key in the door, 'in fact it *is* yours – it's a bottle you left behind.'

'Good, I could do with some of that,' said Eric, 'the cold is kicking my chest off.'

The flat had not changed at all since the split, and Eric noticed his old dartboard on the back of the kitchen door. He also noticed a pair of red leather knee-length boots with platform soles. 'They yours?' Eric asked with a seedy smirk.

'No, they're my sister Joanne's,' said Ruby, opening the cupboard to get Eric's old ruby red Luminarc whiskey glass. He smiled when he saw the glass, but then the smile evaporated when he recalled Joanne. 'Where *is* Joanne?' he asked.

'It's alright love,' said Ruby, rinsing the red glass under the tap, 'she's staying at my mum's today. Won't be back till tomorrow.'

He enjoyed the glass of neat Bell's whiskey – and then he had another, and then Ruby said: 'Can we lie together in one another's arms for one last time? The way we used to?'

'Ruby, don't ruin this. I'm not risking my marriage!' growled Eric, but Ruby put a single on the turntable of the old Dansette record player. It was *that* song - *You Are Everything*, and as Eric pretended to cringe at the song, Ruby found some bottles of wine, and although Eric said he wouldn't mix wine with whiskey, he eventually started gulping wine from the bottle as he started to do a silly dance to Ken Boothe's *Everything I Own* - a record Ruby put on, only to start crying.

'Ruby, stop it,' said a drunken Eric, hugging his former partner, 'no crying allowed. Come on, I want to see your lovely smile before – ' and he found he couldn't say it. He held her chin in his hand as she looked up to him with tears down her cheeks, and he simply could not mention tomorrow's wedding.

'I'm sorry,' she said, all choked up, forcing the words as her throat closed up with heartache. 'I should just let you go, but you'll always be my Eric.'

They went to the bedroom, and he stripped to his underpants, and he took Ruby's clothes off until she only had on her knickers. They laughed, and she clung on to him. 'You're not having your way with me,' Eric joked, and they lay there as a stack of singles automatically took turns to flop down onto the turntable. 'She's a strange one, Sarah,' Eric suddenly told Ruby.

'Is that her name?' Ruby asked, her face pressed to his chest. He could feel her eyelash flickering against his left nipple as she blinked.

'Yes, and as I say, she's a strange one,' said Eric, stroking Ruby's hair. 'She never really shows affection. We wouldn't do something like this. Lie in bed and cuddle like this. I don't even really know what she sees in me – it's odd.' Eric reached for the bottle at the side of the bed and offered its neck to Ruby's lips but she pushed it away and said she was too upset to drink.

One thing led to another. Barry White was singing *You're The First, The Last, My Everything* as they made love, and Eric was full of so much alcohol, he blacked out at one point.

He awoke with a hangover from hell at 9.30pm, and Ruby was nowhere to be found. He went to the tiny living room and she wasn't there. He tried the kitchen and the toilet, and saw she'd gone. 'Oh my God!' Eric shouted to himself, realising his friends would be at his place soon to take him out on a stag night. He really didn't feel up to going out with a rowdy bunch with his head pounding. He got dressed, and went outside to get some fresh air. He went up the steps, looked up and down Rodney Street, and seeing Ruby was nowhere to be seen, he wondered if she'd gone to his house to sabotage the stag do. He found £25 in a biscuit tin and took it, and then he flagged down a hackney cab on Mount Pleasant and within twenty minutes he was home, where his stag night mates were waiting for him on the doorstep. He later confided to Chas (his best man) that he'd slept with his ex, and his friend looked puzzled. 'Eric, that's not possible,' said Chas, all sombre-faced.

'What are you talking about?' Eric asked, puzzled by the comment.

'I've been keeping this from you, mate,' Chas replied,

'but Ruby died a fortnight ago from a brain haemorrhage. Your mum told me not to tell you.'

There was a pause, punctuated by laughter and shouts from his other mates at the other end of the pub. 'Ruby's not dead,' said Eric. 'My old mum must have got hold of the wrong end of the stick because we slept together.'

'You slept with your mum?' asked one of Eric's mates, overhearing his remark.

Eric swore at him and said, 'Do you want a smashed face, eh?'

'Alright Eric, simmer down, mate!' said Chas, with his outstretched palms towards his irate friend.

'Look Chas,' said Eric, nervously adjusting his specs, 'I slept with Ruby today and she was very much alive. My mum's always getting things wrong.'

Chas just said, 'Oh, well, someone's given her duff info mate,' and he got in a round of drinks.

That morning, Eric came home drunk at 2.30 am and his mother had to let him in because he'd lost his door key.

'Hey, mother,' said Eric in a slurred voice, 'why did you tell Chas Ruby had died?'

His mother seemed shocked. 'Oh, so big mouth Chas told you did he?' said Eric's mum.

'Ruby's alive and well mother dearest,' said Eric, and he hiccupped and added: 'once again you have got it all wrong me old mum!'

His mother walked away and went into the living room as Eric clung to the newel post at the bottom of the stairs. He heard a drawer scrape open in the sideboard in the living room, and then his mother came back – holding a strip of newspaper. It was the newspaper obituary she'd snipped out of the *Liverpool Echo*; the notice of Ruby's death. Eric read it and kept saying, 'It can't be,' over and over.

'She died, son,' said Eric's mum flatly. 'She wouldn't have felt a thing. Those haemorrhages are quick. She was a lovely girl, but you've got to look forward now; you have Sarah to look after.'

The news sobered Eric up. He hardly slept a wink that night, and he got up at 8am and rode a taxi to Ruby's flat. It transpired that Ruby's sister Joanne lived there now and she told Eric that burglars had gained access to the flat last night without breaking the lock and they had stolen £25 from the place as she was staying at her mum's home. For some strange reason, the robbers had also cheekily finished off bottles of wine and almost emptied a bottle of scotch before they left. They'd even played records during their stay. Joanne thought she would have been attacked or even raped by the intruders had she been in at the time of the trespass.

Eric burst into tears when he realised that Ruby had loved him so much, she had somehow returned from the grave just to tell him how much she had loved him in their life together. Perhaps knowing that he was about to marry, it had all been too much for the restless spirit of his former partner and she had crossed over from the world beyond; love is a very powerful emotion and bonds of love do not break when one half of a couple dies. After some in-depth soul-searching, Eric wondered if he was in the right place in his life, and at ten that morning he telephoned his fiancée and told her the marriage was off, and Sarah simply told him, 'Alright Eric, it's your loss.'

Eric eventual managed to turn his life around; he curbed his gambling drastically and eventually he stopped altogether. He never married, and in 2014 he passed away after a short illness. I have a feeling he's with Ruby in eternity now.

THE SINISTER MARRIAGE-WRECKER

The authors of poison pen letters - those anonymous outpourings of anger or unmitigated detestation designed to thoroughly upset the recipient – saw delightfully twisted possibilities when the telephone was widely introduced into society in the early 20th Century. Now the poison pen letter-writer was able to literally give a voice to his or her vitriol, and the sinister hater could actually get live feedback from the victims, listening to their gasps of shock at some telephonic insult, and of course, some menacing callers derived a sexual kick out their verbal tirades. On 30 November 1955, the front-page banner headlines of *The Daily Mirror* read: POISON PHONE CALLS with the subheading: 'Glamour-voice Girl tries to break up happy marriages'.

The story, which was the talk of the country, concerned a number of sinister telephone calls initially made in Birkenhead. It all started in October 1955 when Lorraine and David, a newly-married couple in their twenties living on Birkenhead's Arthur Street, heard the telephone in the hallway ring one evening. Lorraine answered it because her husband was washing his hair in the bathroom, in preparation for a night out at the cinema. The sultry-sounding female voice of the caller asked, 'Is David there?'

'Why? Who's calling?' Lorraine asked. She half turned and saw the bathroom door open, and David stood there in the doorframe, stripped to the waist as he dried his hair.

'Well who are *you*?' asked the caller.

'I'm his wife,' said Lorraine, and David came over asking, 'Who is it?' But his wife held her palm out, gesturing for him to stay there.

'David's married?' the woman asked, and then after a pause she hung up.

The seeds of suspicion had been firmly planted in Lorraine's mind, and even though David said he was not seeing anyone and had not given out his number to any female, Lorraine seemed very upset. She decided not to go to the cinema, and the whole evening was thoroughly ruined. Unknown to the couple, the malicious marriage wrecker was dialling two more victims, minutes after she'd frozen the air in the home of Lorraine and David. This time the telephone rang in the lounge of a semi on a leafy stretch of Upton Road, where a 45-year-old lady named Penny - who was partially blind - answered. Her 50-year-old husband Huw, a solicitor, was at that moment busily reading through a client's papers upstairs in his study. A female caller asked for Huw, and Penny said, 'Yes, I'll go and get him; he's just up in his study.'

When Huw came down and answered the phone he discovered the caller had hung up, but she called back at 9pm sharp, and this time Huw was having a bath. Penny asked the caller if she had telephoned earlier.

'Yes, I couldn't wait,' said that sultry voice of a woman who sounded as if she was in her early twenties perhaps. She paused, then added: 'Could you tell Huw I won't be able to see him at the cottage as arranged?'

Penny and Huw had recently bought a beautiful picture-postcard cottage near Heswall which they hoped to let, once it had been completely renovated, and Penny thought this message from the unknown woman was a bit suspicious. 'What do you mean, meet him? Who is this?' Penny asked, but the caller hung up. As soon as Huw got out of the bath, Penny told him about the 'cancelled meeting' at the cottage and with a look of puzzlement on his face Huw said he had not arranged to meet anyone there. 'You do believe me don't you?' Huw asked, and Penny said: 'She must know you – she knew your name and she knew about the cottage.'

'Penny, I give you my word I am not seeing anyone behind your back!' Huw assured her, and when he saw tears fall from his wife's eyes, he hugged her and said: 'Penny, someone is pulling your leg, and if I get my hands on them so help me God!'

Penny mentioned her blindness and asked if she was a burden to him. Huw said he loved her so much he was going to renew his wedding vows, and eventually, as more and more people received the "Poison Phone Calls" the Press investigated the weird case and Huw read the ongoing newspaper articles to a relieved Penny. She realised she had been a victim of the evil home-wrecker who was now the talk of Britain. Liverpool CID and a host of Birkenhead detectives worked in concert to apprehend the wicked woman who had singlehandedly waged a campaign against happily married couples. As the police worked with the GPO (General Post Office - who were then in control of the telephone network) to try and trace the spiteful woman with the sensual voice, theories abounded about her identity, and armchair detectives had a field day hypothesising on the whys and wherefores of the woman making the damaging phone calls. One theory had it that the caller was horrifically disfigured, and unable to find love, she was determined to destroy those who were enjoying a blissful married life. Others believed it was someone working in the telephone exchange, and some even thought the culprit was a female impersonator who knew his victims. Then there was a strange statement from the police in December that year. They hinted that they'd had several public phone boxes disconnected in Birkenhead, and that the cruel crusade against married couples had been brought to a definite end. The weird calls stopped, and a rumour circulated across Wirral about the heartless caller hanging herself.

Around this time, couples living on the other side of the River Mersey over in Liverpool found themselves targeted by the warped woman. A Mrs Jones on Childwall Valley Road received a call one morning from a woman asking for her husband. 'He's not in at the moment,' Mrs Jones told the caller, then asked: 'Who is that?'

'I suppose he told you he was playing golf,' said the caller, with a chuckle.

'Yes, he is, why?' said Mrs Jones. 'Look, who is this?'

The woman gave a worrying reply. 'Golf's a summer sport – you don't stand on golf courses in winter. Ask him where he's really been when he comes home, and also ask him when he's going to tell you about little old me!'

The caller then hung up. Mrs Jones began to think about the anonymous caller's words, and she wondered if her husband really was on the golf course in winter. Mrs Jones rang her friend Susan in West Derby and asked her what she made of the call. Susan said her husband Terry played golf, and she asked him if people played the game in winter. Terry came on the phone and said: 'Yes, I know people who play in winter; the courses are deserted then you see and you can just stroll onto the first tee. Good way of getting practice, and if you can play alright in a harsh icy wind, playing in the summer is a piece of cake.'

Mrs Jones still thought there was something suspicious going on. How did that woman who had called *know* her husband was out playing golf? When Mr Jones returned home, his wife told him about the call, and he said: 'I don't know who she was; I'm as in the dark as you are.'

'Who did you play with?' Mrs Jones enquired.

'Brian Lawless,' her husband told her with an annoyed look in his thinned eyes. 'Why? You can ask Brian if you don't believe me.'

Mrs Jones tried to smile, and she said, 'Oh, I *do* believe you love, but what's her game? And who the hell is she?'

Three days later, that woman called the house of the Jones family again, and this time, Mr and Mrs Jones were out at a cocktail party at the house of a friend in Wavertree. The babysitter, a 16-year-old named Cathy, took the telephone call at 8pm, thinking Mrs Jones was phoning to see how the kids were, but instead, the teen heard a well-spoken female voice ask: 'Is Mr Jones in?'

'No, he's at a party with his wife and they won't be back till around eleven,' said Cathy.

'Oh, he has a wife does he?' said the woman, and then she paused, and seemed to be sniffling. She then said: 'Well you tell him from me that I am going to have his baby!'

Cathy was shocked by the woman's claim, and was stuck for words.

'Yes, you tell that no-good two-timing bastard to meet me at the usual place this Wednesday at five! Got that?'

'Yes,' gasped Cathy, and then she heard a shriek and the caller hung up a split-second later.

Mrs Jones telephoned the babysitter at 9.45pm and asked if everything was okay, and Cathy said: 'Some woman called at eight Mrs Jones, and she asked for Mr Jones.'

'What!' Mrs Jones yelled.

In a nervous voice, the babysitter told her about the shocking claim of the caller. 'She said she was having a baby by Mr Jones, and she called him names and said he's to meet her at the usual place on Wednesday at five.'

Half an hour later, the Joneses barged out of a taxi that had pulled up in the drive of their home, and already Cathy could hear the couple having a blazing row. Mrs Jones asked Cathy to go over the exact wording of the call, and Mr Jones asked the girl if she had ever heard the caller's voice before; she hadn't.

Cathy was paid for her babysitting job, and was only too glad to get out of the house. The children were crying upstairs as Mr and Mrs Jones had a verbal barney with one another. That night, Mr Jones slept on the sofa and his wife even threatened to take herself and the children to her mother's home. The next day, Brian Lawless paid a visit, and when he heard about the call from the unknown woman, he said it had obviously been some prank.

'Someone's gone to an awful lot of trouble to play a prank,' Mrs Jones told Brian. 'The same person called three days before – it doesn't make sense.'

'I am not two-timing you!' cried Mr Jones, grabbing his wife by the wrist.

'No one would have him,' Brian said with a smirk, and that calmed Mrs Jones down a little. Brian told the couple to sit down and made them some coffee. Then he told them the caller might be the woman who had been in all the newspapers: 'She's driven some couples to divorce; don't you read the papers?'

'Yes, I've seen those stories,' said Mrs Jones, 'but that's over the water – not in Liverpool.'

'I think it's her,' said Brian, 'I think she's spreading her net a bit. Now, I don't know if she knows you two or whether she's just giving you the impression she does – I mean, she might just be going through phone books. The best thing to do is ignore her.'

Mr and Mrs Jones took Brian's advice, and they never heard from the disruptive caller again, but she seems to have wreaked marital havoc in other Liverpool homes around this time, in places ranging from Litherland, Fazakerley and West Derby to Halewood and Garston.

A year then passed – and then the calls started again – or was it a copycat? The police thought so, but one call was traced to a derelict gothic house on Devonshire Road, Prenton, and here a chilling discovery was allegedly made by the police: a woman, aged about thirty, was found sitting in a high-back chair, with a connected telephone in her lap and a purring handset in her fist. She'd been dead for at least three days, and her body was never identified. Rigor mortis had been and gone. The macabre find was said to have been hushed up by the authorities while forensic experts tried to identify the woman. Some thought medical students had taken the body from a morgue or possibly from a medical school where the body had been bequeathed for anatomy studies. If this was the case, it was quite a black humoured prank. Whether the body was that of the woman who had caused so much upset and turmoil in the lives of dozens of couples remains unknown.

A TALE OF TWO WITCHES

Across Knowsley in early 1994, strange rumours circulated about a woman who was said to be a real-life witch who had the ability to cure all sorts of ailments and conditions. Raymond Gallantree, a 57-year-old doctor who had a practice in the Huyton area, learned of the so-called witch when his patient - 40-year-old Mrs Janet Scott – arrived for her annual medical check-up – minus her fibromyalgia. She said a white witch named Jane Thorogood had cured her of the debilitating condition with a special soup she had to drink once a week. 'Quackery, Mrs Scott,' Dr Gallantree confidently told his patient with a lopsided smile. 'There is no known cure for fibromyalgia syndrome, so this white witch is a con woman.'

'She is not a con woman, Dr Gallantree,' protested an outraged Mrs Scott, tapping her index finger hard on the doctor's desk. 'She has cured me, I tell you. All the muscle spasms, pain and the irritable bowel thing have gone, and my mind's clear as crystal.'

'They call it the placebo effect Mrs Scott,' said the doctor, glancing at his patient's records, 'but let's come into the 20th Century; I think we could try a new drug on the market called – '

Mrs Scott got up, shaking her head. 'I don't need any of your drugs, doctor – I'm cured, thanks to Mrs Thorogood, and I shan't even bother with the medical either! You doctor's aren't happy unless you're finding something wrong with people, just so you can treat them with your drugs!'

'Now wait a minute Mrs Scott! You can't just – ' Dr Gallantree was saying when his patient turned her back on him and left the surgery.

The next patient – 35-year-old Peter Cheeseman – came in to see a ruffled Gallantree. Cheeseman had been suffering from chronic insomnia ever since he'd been made redundant, and he'd been given mild sleeping pills, but they had given him graphic nightmares. He was also a hypochondriac who was convinced he'd die of heart-failure from these nightmares. Cheeseman said he had gone to see a woman – a Mrs Thorogood – recommended by his aunt. This lady dealt in alternative medicine and she had given him some special pillow which contained lavender and various herbs – and although Mr Cheeseman was now sleeping for eight hours at a time, he wanted to know if the pillow's herbs could have any side effects, as he believed he was developing a rash on the nape of his neck.

'Sling that pillow in the bin for a start,' advised Gallantree, and he claimed the pillow's soporific effects were all down to autosuggestion. 'Tell me, Mr Cheeseman, do you know a Mrs Janet Scott by any chance?'

Cheeseman shook his head and asked who she was.

'Oh, just another superstitious fool,' the doctor murmured, and inspected the back of Cheeseman's neck to see a minor patch of reddened skin.

Dr Gallantree heard more and more of the white witch Jane Thorogood as the months wore on, and even a nurse at the practice told the doctor how she had visited the self-styled witch herself because of her arthritis, and Thorogood had given her gin-soaked golden raisins and some purple potion to sip, and now all the joint pain had ceased, and the nurse maintained that her little finger was no longer crooked.

'I must say, I'm surprised you of all people would fall for this mumbo-jumbo, nurse,' said Gallantree. 'You know very well that it's all jiggery-pokery, and all that stuff belongs in the Dark Ages.'

A week later, Dr Gallantree heard more of the white witch from an unexpected source - Mike Carson – a doctor who had a practice in Prescot. Gallantree had run into him at a medical conference in Manchester. Dr Carson joked, 'I'm rapidly losing half of my patients to a hag who's haggling for business!' he quipped, then went on, 'Her name's Jane something, and she's evidently attracting quite a following amongst the gullible.'

'Thorogood,' said Dr Gallantree, flatly and with a look of utter resignation in his heavy-lidded eyes, 'Jane Thorogood.'

'Yes, that's her,' said Dr Carson with a brisk nod.

'She should be investigated,' suggested Gallantree, 'heaven knows what her potions contain. A lot of my patients have fallen under the spell of this woman – no pun intended.'

Then a friend of the two men – Richard Randall – another doctor – who had a practice in the Melling area – met them on a golf course, and he also spoke of 'some woman who claims to be a witch convinced one of my patients that her sciatica had gone.'

'This witch isn't a Jane Thorogood by any chance, is she?' Dr Carson asked. Dr Randall seemed very surprised at the question and slowly nodded. 'You've come across her too, then?' Randall asked.

'She's treating my patients and quite a few patients of Dr Gallantree,' said Carson, 'and it's all down to her white magic, they say.'

Days later, an old patient being treated for warts came into Dr Gallantree's surgery and said a woman his sister knew had put some tape around his fingers which had warts on, and she had told him that the warts would suffocate and fall off. Gallantree tried to remove the tape from his patient's fingers, but the elderly man said he'd rather 'try the witch's old remedy first.'

Within days, the warts fell off the old man's fingers, and he rang the receptionist at his health clinic and told her to pass on the news to Dr Gallantree. Not long after this, Jim, a man in his fifties seeing Gallantree for sinusitis showed the doctor the clump of hair on the top of his head – in the centre of his bald spot. Jim said the hair had regrown after he had soaked it each night with the juice of crushed onions and some herb. Jim's sister had obtained the natural hair tonic from a witch.

'Your hair loss is hereditary,' Gallantree told Jim, 'and nothing can make it grow back. Is this witch a Jane Thorogood?'

'I don't know her name,' said Jim, 'but my sister and her friends said she's the real thing, and doctor, that hair was not there a fortnight ago. I've even grown my eyebrow hair back as well, because half of my eyebrows had fallen out, and you said it was to do with my thyroid.'

Gallantree gave a false laugh and declared: 'Ridiculous! Onions are for eating, not for putting on your head!'

'I thought that,' said Jim, 'but the witch says it's the sulphur in them see, it feeds the hair, like.'

'It's a wonder she hasn't given you some bubbling potion to treat your sinusitis,' said Gallantree.

'Well my sister's asked her about that – ' Jim started to tell the annoyed medical man.

'You must stop seeking these charlatans!' Gallantree thumped his fist on his desk. 'Their cures can make your condition worse. These potions and concoctions could have strychnine and lead in them for all you know, man. Leave medicine to the medical profession – got that?'

'Yeah, okay Dr Gallantree,' said Jim, shrinking back into his seat, looking dismayed and a little flabbergasted at the doctor's outburst.

Dr Gallantree contacted the other two doctor friends and they arranged a meet-up at the Philharmonic pub in Liverpool with a solicitor named David Humble Jones to discuss a way of confronting this so-called witch. A most unexpected thing happened at the Philharmonic pub meeting.

'Perhaps we're all just over-reacting to this witch nonsense,' Dr Richard Randall suggested, and he sipped from a half-pint glass of bitter, and added, 'I mean these New Age fads come and go, but people always see through them in the end.'

'This is not a fad, Richard,' said Gallantree, 'more

like a cult, and it's getting more members every hour. My next door neighbour even mentioned that bloody witch this morning; he told me his daughter's going to see her because she's had trouble conceiving.'

'Well, from a legal point of view,' said Mr Humble Jones, lighting a panatela, 'we have to actually prove she is obtaining money under false pretences, and then there's the Fraudulent Mediums Act 1951 whereby... '

And as Humble Jones droned on in his monotone voice, spouting all sorts of impenetrable legal jargon, Dr Gallantree's eyes wandered over to the shapely legs of a redhead standing near the table around which the four men were seated. This woman was, in the doctor's estimation, about five feet and six inches in height, of medium build, and she wore a sort of dark blue poncho, black stockings and black flat shoes. She was standing with her back to the doctors and the solicitor, and as Gallantree looked up at her head of curly Titian red hair, the lady turned to look at him and said: 'I have succeeded where your medicine has failed! Your people bled patients to death with leeches once!'

The other doctors and Humble Jones looked up at the woman, startled by her outburst.

'The so-called medical profession used to treat coughs with heroin and drill holes in the skulls of epileptics – and you call my spells dangerous!' said the beautiful stranger.

'Who the devil are you?' asked Dr Randall, and before the woman answered, Dr Gallantree said: 'Jane Thorogood – I presume?'

'You see me as a threat, doctors,' said Jane, 'but before this week is through, one of you will beg for my help.'

And then suddenly – she was no longer there. She vanished before their eyes.

A woman who had just entered the pub with her boyfriend yelped and said, 'That woman just vanished!'

'What *was* that?' asked the solicitor, gazing at the space where the woman had stood seconds ago.

'A witch, that's what,' said Gallantree, 'and that is why she must be stopped – destroyed even.'

'Well, to be honest, gentlemen,' said a very unnerved Humble Jones, 'the supernatural is really outside the sphere of my work. You can't take legal action against a ghost – '

'She is *not* a ghost!' Gallantree snapped at the solicitor. 'She's a witch – a genuine witch but nevertheless a charlatan.'

'I agree with Mr Humble Jones on this one I'm afraid,' Dr Randall told Gallantree, 'we're getting mixed up in the shady and very dangerous world of the supernatural and black magic.'

'White magic – according to her!' Dr Gallantree told his nervous colleague, then asked him: 'You're not afraid of her are you, Richard?'

Dr Randall's face twitched and he replied: 'I'm not a surgeon but put it this way – I'd rather have a go at a triple bypass rather than take on a ghost – no thanks!' Randall then put down his half pint glass on the table and inspected his watch.

'She's not a ghost!' growled Gallantree.

'That was incredible,' Dr Carson began to mutter, and he got up from the table and walked to the spot where Jane Thorogood had stood. 'Perhaps it was done by hypnosis – but how?' he mused.

On the following day, Dr Randall's wife broke down

and said she'd been diagnosed with a serious life-threatening illness a fortnight ago, but she had kept the diagnosis from him. She had less than a year to live – perhaps a little longer if she underwent a very risky operation. As predicted by the white witch, Dr Randall put out his feelers and asked his patients to contact Jane Thorogood on his behalf. When the witch turned up at his surgery, Randall begged her to cure his wife and said he'd give her a blank cheque. For a month, Jane gave Mrs Randall all sorts of potions, and the woman made a full recovery. Jane took no payment in return. Randall quizzed her about her white magic and pleaded with her to share her strange knowledge so that it could be practised by doctors, but Jane said her spells would be abused and that the forces of nature would not be contained in bottles and pills and be commercialised.

Dr Gallantree still believed the witch's cures were all down to someone unknown science, but also hypnotic suggestion, and he tried to find her so he could accuse her – in the presence of his solicitor – of being a charlatan. He also enlisted a number of priests and reverends from various churches to tackle the witch, but he never heard from her again, and gradually, all of Gallantree's patients came back to him with their incurable ailments.

We now move a year forward in time, and fly by broomstick across the River Mersey to the mysterious peninsula of Wirral, where another tale of witchery awaits us...

For legal reasons I've changed a few names and minor details in the following story, but the rest, to the best of my knowledge, actually took place. In March

1995, a Wirral banker in his forties named Alistair Telford returned from work, arriving at his detached 5-bedroom house on Village Road, Oxton at 6.30pm. His 39-year-old wife Angela had made Alistair Spaghetti con Salse di Vongole from a recipe in a book her mother had given her years ago: *The Galloping Gourmet Cookbook* by the television chef Graham Kerr. Angela placed the dish down on the dining room table as Alistair dialled his financier friend Dominic on the landline, then clicked his fingers at his wife and made a drinking gesture with an invisible glass between his fingers and thumb. Angela was conditioned to leap into action at such gestures from her selfish husband, and she instantly rushed to the wine rack in the kitchen and uncorked a bottle. She poured a glass, carefully handed it to Alistair and told him the spaghetti was going cold as he talked.

'Yes, Dominic, you heard right; Thorn EMI's buying Dillons, and what do you think about the latest on the Barings fiasco? Well, it appears that – ' Alistair was saying when Angela happened to mention that the food was going cold again. Alistair exploded into a rage and told Dominic he'd call him later. He sat at the table and tried the dish, then smirked.

'What do you think?' Angela asked, sitting opposite.

'So-so,' he said, then grimaced as he sipped the wine. 'You shouldn't have just poured it after uncorking; you're supposed to let it breathe first.'

Angela looked sad at his reaction, and he gave an insincere smile and said: 'Don't be so thin-skinned, dear; you've made *better* meals; I'm just being honest; I'd never lie to you.'

'Took me hours making that,' she said in a broken

voice, and she dabbed the corner of her eyes with a napkin and seemed unsure what to do next.

'Oh yes, Angela,' Alistair said, pointing his fork at the ceiling, 'I've got to go and see Rex North later, and I might stay over if business goes on a bit, is that alright?'

'Again?' she asked with a resigned look. 'Is he the fellah who lives in West Kirby?'

Alistair nodded. 'That's him yes – close friend of Eddie George – and a very influential real estate investor. Wants to run a huge business idea by me.'

'Who's Eddie George? A footballer?' asked Angela.

'The Governor of the Bank of England no less,' Alistair bragged and gave a smug grin. 'Rex has an Italian wife,' Alistair told Angela, and looked dreamily into space. 'She's beautiful, and her cooking is out of this world.'

At 7.45pm, Alistair left in his Range Rover, but unknown to Angela, he did not head for Rex North's West Kirby residence; instead he set off to a filling station, bought a box of Hamlet miniature cigars, three Cadbury Flakes and a packet of condoms, and then he drove to the Meols flat of an 18-year-old cashier named Tammy. He'd been seeing her now for just over a month, twice a week. Angela knew something was going on, and yet she so desperately wanted to trust her husband of ten years. As soon as Alistair arrived at Tammy's flat he gave the teen the three chocolate flakes and she giggled and hugged him. Alistair stripped to his boxer shorts and went straight to the bedroom carrying his lighter and the cigars.

Angela, meanwhile, sat on the sofa, drank a little wine, then dozed off as she watched *Gardener's World* on BBC2. Angela had a very strange dream. A woman with white hair, a long gaunt pallid face, dressed in a black robe that went to the floor, stood in front of the TV, which was muted in the dream. In a quivering voice the eerie woman said: 'Your husband is having an affair with a girl half his age! He's no good for you, and he is evil, so I will get rid of him!'

'He's not!' protested Angela, 'Don't do that!'

The creepy woman walked nearer to Angela and continued: 'You will be free from the bastard, and you will find someone who deserves you and treats you as you should be treated. These men need to be taken off the face of the earth!'

The telephone rang, awakening Angela. It was Alistair. Unknown to his wife he was lying in bed with Tammy as he spoke to her, and Tammy was giggling under the duvet as she kissed around his navel. 'Everything alright Angela? Just checking,' said the duplicitous banker.

'Are you staying over, or are you coming back? I can make you your favourite supper if you - 'Angela was saying when Alistair cut in.

'Ah, no, I'm afraid this looks like an all-nighter, dear,' Alistair told her, and he covered the mouthpiece with his pressed palm and stifled a laugh.

'That's a pity, Alistair, it's not the same without you here,' Angela told him, and he could not hear the loneliness in her voice. He wasn't listening out for it.

Alistair wiped the tears of laughter from his eyes with his free hand and told Angela: 'So, I'll leave Rex's home in the morning dear, and I'll go straight to the bank from here, so you don't have to mess about cooking breakfast for me.'

'I don't mind making breakfast Ali –' she said and she heard the phone click. Her husband had hung up. Angela went into the kitchen and sat at the table, thinking of that weird nightmare about the old woman in black. For some reason unknown to her, Angela had the impression that the woman in the bad dream had been a witch of some sort.

That night at 10pm, the boyfriend of Tammy, a security guard named Adam, was on duty at a building in New Brighton, when he received a telephone call from a woman who sounded quite old. She refused to give her name, but she told him that Tammy was in bed with the manager of the bank she worked at, and she supplied all sorts of personal details which convinced Adam she was telling the truth. 'Thanks, whoever you are,' seethed Adam, then he asked: 'Are you someone I know?'

The mysterious elderly-sounding voice replied: 'All you need to know is that a whoremaster is copulating with your lady, and they are laughing at you behind your back!'

The woman then hung up.

Adam left his post at the building and arrived at the flat in Meols at 11pm. Tammy refused to let him in the flat, so Adam kicked the door in. He threatened to smash a chair over Alistair's head, but Tammy talked him out of it, and the banker offered Adam money but the security guard spat in his face. Alistair gathered his clothes and a disgusted Adam picked up the packet of condoms and put them in the banker's jacket pocket, then threw him out the flat into the communal hallway. Alistair then heard screams as the guard slapped Tammy and there were sounds of things being smashed in the flat, but the banker fled to his Range Rover and drove off, heading for home. Throughout the night journey, Alistair had the strange feeling of being watched – almost as if there was someone in the back seat of the vehicle looking over his shoulder. Alistair thought that this was an unusual thing to experience given that he was in a dreadful state after the encounter with Tammy's enraged boyfriend. He then heard a raspy voice hissing the c-word close to his left ear, and this really frightened him, so he put the car radio on. About fifteen minutes later, as he travelled down Prenton's Wellington Road, a woman with long white stringy hair and a ghastly emaciated face appeared out of thin air in the path of the vehicle with her skeletal hands reaching out towards the banker. She wore a black gown of some sort from the neck downwards, and Alistair heard her let out a piercing scream before the Range Rover smashed into her. Alistair closed his eyes, thinking he had hit a real person. That would have been the perfect end to this accursed evening! He had instinctively tried to swerve the Range Rover at the last moment in a vain bid to avoid the crazy old eccentric, and the car spun out of control and crashed. Alistair sustained a whiplash injury and burst a blood vessel in his eye. When he got home he told Angela a cock and bull story about deciding to come home to her after a heated argument with Rex North, and then he mentioned the figure of the white-haired hag in the long black robe who had appeared in front of his vehicle, causing him to crash. Alistair stopped short of saying the weird jaywalker was a ghost, but he said he had not found a trace of her after the crash. Angela then told him that she had seen a woman matching the description of the one who had appeared in the road in a dream – but she did not say what that dream was about.

An ambulance was called for, and at the hospital when a nurse was taking Alistair's coat off, a packet of condoms fell out the outside pocket of the coat. This was naturally a shock to Angela, and she glared at her husband.

Alistair became afflicted by a mysterious illness, and kept telling his wife an old witch was stalking him. He said she was the very same woman who had caused him to crash, and she appeared in mirrors at the house and he even saw her in his dreams. This crone had told him that she had lived in Oxton years ago and that her life had been ruined by a 'bastard untrue'. And now she had returned from the grave to do away with all men who cheated and lied with whores behind the backs of their wives.

Alistair suffered from a strange rash that started in each armpit and travelled down his arms and joined up in the middle of his chest. Half of each eyebrow thinned, and copious hair grew out of his nostrils and ears. Almost every night, Alistair had a vivid nightmare about his penis becoming detached as he showered, and he went to his doctor about these dreams and was given sedatives and advised not to sleep on his back. Angela stood by him through these crises, and he tried to make love to her but found it impossible to get an erection. Then one evening Alistair burst into tears and admitted he'd had numerous affairs over the years – and he even admitted that he had almost got his 18-year-old niece pregnant a few years back. He made many more confessions, some of them so indecent,

Angela decided enough was enough and she divorced him. Angela believed that the 'witch' who seemed to be taking revenge on Alistair probably *had* been the ghost of a woman who had been wronged by a man once, and she thanked the unknown woman for unmasking her cheating husband.

TIME TWINS

It was the second time that they had met, but neither of them knew this at the time. She was 31-year-old Geraldine Stephenson and he was 31-year-old Gerald Peake, and they met on this occasion at Leece Street Job Centre in May 1980. They both spotted the same job listed on one of the cards in the wall racks. The vacancy was for an executive secretary to the Tree Foundation, a fund-raising charity based in London's Belgravia district, and the salary was very good. Both Gerald and Geraldine loved gardening and horticulture and both possessed good secretarial skills including book-keeping. They both reached for the card at the same time and an argument ensued. A member of staff intervened and said they could both apply, but when they did, neither of them was successful. Then just over a week later, a dream job appeared on the board at the job centre, and as Gerald read the card detailing the vacancy, he was surprised and annoyed to notice Geraldine standing next to him; she was also reading the card and muttering the job description as she perused in a way Gerald found quite irritating. The job was for a couple (aged 30+) to spend an initial six-month trial period at a luxury private villa in the south of France, with one half of the couple assigned to act as a driver and the other half to act as a glorified housekeeper to a couple and their two young children. This was 1980 of course, and gender equality and equal opportunities in the sphere of employment were still embryonic, so it was assumed that the man would be the driver and the woman would be the housekeeper. 'Excellent remuneration for the right couple,' the card read. Gerald rushed out of the job centre and crossed Leece Street to get to the telephone box on the corner of Roscoe Street, where he phoned his girlfriend Jane to tell her about the amazing vacancy, but she said she wasn't keen on France and would feel bad being so far away from her mum. Geraldine, meanwhile, knew a woman who worked in a nearby florist on Leece Street who let her use the telephone to call her boyfriend Martin. Geraldine asked him if he was willing to live in southern France but Martin yawned and said he'd miss his drinking friends and preferred to stay put in England. Geraldine asked Martin to reconsider as it had always been a dream of hers to work in the south of France, but Martin simply said, 'Don't be daft; we're not going to live in France.'

Gerald, meanwhile, left the telephone box on Roscoe Street calling his girlfriend of two months an unaspiring ambitionless layabout, and he went to the nearest boozer – the Post Office pub on School Lane - to drown his frustration. Seconds after he had arrived at the pub, Geraldine came in, and they were both surprised to see one another.

'Are you following me?' Gerald asked Geraldine, and she answered with an indignant scowl, and then she fumed: 'Certainly not! What on earth would I follow you for?'

'Look, I'm sorry, I'm sorry,' Gerald said, looking at the floor as he pinched the top of his nose with his finger and thumb. He closed his eyes, took a deep breath, and sighed. 'I'm just a bit peed off with my life at the moment – well, peed off with my other half actually,' he said, and then he pointed to the bar and said: 'Can I get you a drink?'

'No, I'll get my own – thanks anyway,' said Geraldine, and she opened her handbag to grab her purse but Gerald was already at the bar ordering his drink, and then he asked Geraldine: 'Come on, let me get you one.'

'Lager and lime – just a half,' Geraldine said with a crooked smile, 'thanks.'

They got chatting, and simultaneously discussed the dream job in France, and laughed when they realised each had been let down by their partner. Then came the first shock. Today was Gerald's birthday – and it was also Geraldine's. They were two Geminis, but they had not only both been born in Walton Hospital on the same day, but within seconds of one another, and it transpired that their mothers had chatted to one another before and after they had given birth. Gerald's mum recalled how Mrs Stephenson's baby had been in the cot next to Gerald on the maternity ward, and she thought it funny how the two newborns had similar names. Gerald and Geraldine had the same books on their shelves, same record collection, supported the same football team, and watched the same TV programmes. Even their tastes in food were identical. It was as if they were long-lost twins, and inevitably they were drawn romantically to one another. Within the week, Gerald and Geraldine broke off with their incompatible partners, and just a fortnight after meeting they started dating. That dream job was still up on the board at the job centre. They both applied for it and went for the interview pretending to be married – and they landed the job. Gerald and Geraldine then rushed to the register office and married, and then they started their job in France. It was hard, but so worth it, and after seven years they returned to Liverpool, had a 'proper' church wedding, and settled in Childwall. It is claimed that such "Time twins" – as astrologers term people born on the same day – can be even closer than soul mates, and this was certainly the case with Geminians Gerald and Geraldine.

VAMPIRES ON LOWER LANE?

The following uncanny incident took place in Fazakerley in 1964 on the Ides of March – the fifteenth of the month; an ominous and supposedly unlucky date because it was the day upon which Julius Caesar was assassinated in 44BC. In 1964 the Ides fell on a Sunday, and upon that Sunday evening at 7.15pm, a 16-year-old girl – Judy Barratt of Norris Green – was picked up by her date – 19-year-old John McLeckie. He had told Judy he'd be borrowing his brother's Ford Zephyr to take her to the party in Fazakerley, but instead, John turned up in a big grimy-looking Bedford truck with an open cargo area. His brother's car was at the garage, John sheepishly explained, so he'd borrowed his uncle's haulage truck instead. Judy threatened to go to the party with someone else, but John begged her to go with him in the truck and he promised he had thoroughly cleaned the inside of the vehicle. 'You won't get any muck on you, honest love,' John assured her. Judy said that she'd go with him but warned John that he'd have to park well away from the house where the party was being held because she'd be a laughing stock turning up in a truck. Judy brought a bath towel with her and draped it over the seat of the Bedford truck just in case, and she wouldn't even wear her white shoes in the vehicle because the floor was so grimy. Instead, she held her stilettos in her lap. The truck pulled away from Judy's home on Sedgemoor Road coughing clouds of black smoke from its exhaust and shaking her bones with its rickety suspension. John was a terrible driver; he took a wrong turn down Faversham Road, and he kept taking sly glances at Judy's legs. 'Keep your eye on the road John!' Judy told him, 'Never mind my legs! Turn right – here!'

He swung the truck onto the East Lancs Road, and a minute later Judy caught him looking at her legs again and screamed at him to turn left at the Lower House Lane junction.

'I'm sorry Jude, I'm knocked out by your beauty,' explained John with a dopy smile.

'I'll knock you out if you don't watch where you're going!' the Norris Green girl warned him. 'Concentrate John,' she told him as he admired his Beatle cut in the wing mirror, and then she looked through the windshield at the black lonely stretch of Lower Lane. It had farmland to the left and a sprawling bleak sewage works to the right. 'And another thing John: you better not try that trick where you'll pretend to break down so we'll end up stranded in some lonely place. You are not getting your oats in this thing. I'm not that type of girl.'

'As if I'd do something as despicable as that,' John intoned in a low moaning voice. 'What do you take me for? I'm not that type of fellah either. God, that's hurt me that, you saying that.'

'I'm just telling you, that's all,' Judy told him, and fidgeted with her shoes. 'I've had lads try that one on me before.'

'Well I was brung up with morals like,' said John, and his voice seemed a bit choked up. 'I'm from a middle class family in Walton, me.'

Just under twelve minutes later, John dropped Judy

off at Montrovia Crescent, and already they could hear the music playing at the party house a hundred yards away. 'I'll wait here,' Judy told her boyfriend of nine days. 'Park this in the next street, and somewhere dark if you can. I don't want that Sheena Wilson knowing I came here in a truck. Her fellah's got an Alvis Saloon.'

'Stick with me Jude, and you'll end up with a Roller,' said a stern-faced John.

'Yeah, roller skates more like,' retorted Judy with a resigned look. 'Go and park this monster, hurry up!' she told him and put on her stilettos as John drove off. She cussed when a blast of smoky exhaust hit her legs.

John tried to park up on Hawksmoor Road but a man came out of a house and said, 'Hey, you're not parking that thing there. Beat it, go on.'

John eventually parked the Bedford truck on the corner of Moss Pits Lane, at a spot where a lamp post was out of order. He then ran all the way to Montrovia Crescent, where he found Judy being chatted up by a man named Peter Postgate, who was also going to the party. John McLeckie grabbed Judy's hand and dragged her away from Peter as the latter was still talking. 'John! I was talking to him!' Judy protested at being yanked away, but she also smiled at the jealous streak her boyfriend had shown. In her mind it proved that he loved her.

The party went on till four in the morning, and Judy had to be carried to the truck because she'd had too many Babychams, Ponies and Golden Godwins. The party had ended in quite a funny way. At 2.30am an elderly man had come round to the house to complain about the music and the young partygoers had plied him with drink and encouraged him to sing. After consuming quite a few glasses of neat whiskey the old man had started to sing the *Three Blind Mice* nursery song, and this made everyone laugh. A guitarist even accompanied the old man as he bellowed out the old nursery rhyme until he fell unconscious onto the sofa. Judy started singing the rhyme as John propped her up in the seat in the truck.

He climbed in and started the engine, even though he had been drinking. The drink drive limit would not be introduced until next year and the breathalyser was three years away in the future. After a crunching of gears, the truck lurched off on its short two-mile journey through the night. Judy smiled, and without opening her eyes she leaned to her right and rested her head on John's shoulder. 'My dad will have forty fits when I get home. What time is it again, John?'

'Four,' said John, and he wound the window down to get some cold night air into the cab to stop him from dozing off at the wheel.

'Three blind mice, three blind mice, see how they run...' Judy started to sing again.

'What did you think of my dancing, eh?' John suddenly asked, smirking as he recalled his attempts at doing the Twist.

'Ha!' shrilled Judy, 'That was dead funny! Oh at least you tried. Some of the fellahs there were more concerned with drinking.'

'You're a great little mover, love,' John said, and he placed his hand on Judy's knee, but she laughed and pushed it away, then squeezed his hand.

'Concentrate on the road, John,' she told him, then groaned and said, 'I think I'm going to be sick.'

'Well be sick out the window, Jude,' said John with a

concerned sidelong glance. 'My uncle will kill me if you throw up in his truck.'

'Three blind mice...' Judy whispered the song to keep her mind off the dizziness and nausea.

The truck headed south down Lower Lane, and John had to take extra care now because he could only see the road ahead by the light of the truck's headlamps.

'John! Slow down! I'm going to be sick!' Judy cried, and made retching sounds as her stomach went into spasm.

'Wind the bleedin' window down!' he told her.

She clawed blindly at the window, looking for a handle in the darkness. 'I'll be alright I think,' she told him and hiccupped. She looked ahead at the road, and saw something there. She shrieked and pointed at it. 'John! Look out!'

John turned his face from his girlfriend to the windshield, and for a brief moment he thought he saw a boy kneeling in the road. He thought the face of the boy looked towards the dazzling headlamps, and then Judy screamed, and there was an awful thump. John closed his eyes. He'd hit him!

John braked and pulled over, and then Judy started to make that retching sound again and this time he opened the door on her side of the vehicle and she threw up with some force. He heard the sick hit the road. He got out the truck with her and as she bent down and threw up again, he looked back. The sky was moonless and there were no lamp posts to show him the aftermath of the terrible accident. He walked in a daze down the pitch black road and felt for his lighter in his trouser pocket.

'John! Wait! Oh God!' yelled Judy.

He could hear her being sick again and spitting some of the vomit out. He flicked open the lighter cap and thumbed the wheel twice, and it lit. He cupped his hand around the flame and manipulated the flame height adjuster with his thumbnail. By the light of the flame he could see the remains of a fox smeared along the road with the tyre tracks of the truck in blood. He could see mashed organs and fur, but he could not see any boy. Had he imagined it? He hoped to God the whole thing had been an optical illusion. He heard the clicking of Judy's stiletto heels faintly through the thick fog of trepidation that was obscuring his sense of reason.

'John! Did you kill him?' Judy appeared at his right side and grabbed his forearm.

'Kill who?' he asked, dreading the answer.

'It looked like a lad,' she said, gasping for breath now, 'a boy. He was kneeling in the middle of the road over a dog.'

'A fox,' John corrected her, and he hoped this was a nightmare and that he'd wake up soon.

'Oh! Look!' Judy saw the remains of the fox spread along the road surface, and she started to alternate between sobs and making that retching sound.

'Maybe he ran off just in time,' said John, and he had to let the flame go out because the lighter was unbearably hot.

'No, I think you hit him John,' said Judy, and she started to shake. 'I closed my eyes when you hit him and the fox.'

'My Nan said today was unlucky. I should have listened to her,' said John, and he felt as if he couldn't breathe so he took deep gulps of air.

'Will we go to prison for this? Have we killed him?' she asked, and stumbled in the inky engulfing darkness.

John lit the lighter again and looked about. Had the impact knocked the boy over the fence? Was the body lying in a farmer's field in the darkness? Was he still alive? What was he doing in the middle of the road at four in the morning? What kind of parents would allow their son out at such an hour? The questions unreeled in John's frightened mind, and he suddenly became gripped with the urge to get away. 'Let's go!' he said, and capped the lighter. He pulled Judy along to the truck and helped her get in. He slammed the door on her, catching her elbow, and then he walked around the front of the truck on his way to the other door, and he saw the blood on the bodywork of the vehicle. He shivered, and then he got into the truck and stalled it. Judy was sobbing loudly as he started the vehicle again and drove off.

'Will we go to jail?' she asked, and started to pant.

'No, there's no body,' he told her, but there was no certainty in the tone of his voice.

'You were the one who was driving anyway,' she said, and John swore at her and told her to shut up, but quickly regretted his outburst and said he was sorry.

'Don't tell a soul what happened,' John suddenly said with a quiver in his voice. 'Don't tell your mum or dad or anyone, please Judy, don't tell them,' he pleaded.

'I won't,' Judy replied, and then she said, 'Maybe it was just a trick of the light. Maybe there was no boy, because like, I mean, what would a boy be doing out at this time in the morning and why on earth would he be kneeling in the road with a fox? It's just been a shadow or something now I come to think of it. You see things at night that aren't there, especially when you've been drinking.'

'We'll have to wash the front of the truck first – get rid of that fox's blood,' said John. 'I'll go to our house first and get a bucket; no, hang on, my dad's a light sleeper and I don't want to wake *him* up. I'll go to my uncle's house, he could sleep through World War Three.'

'I'm not washing any blood – ' Judy objected, and hiccupped.

'I'll do it, and then I'll drop you off and drive the truck back to my uncle's house,' said John, 'and go straight to bed, and don't say a word in the morning.'

'I won't be able to sleep,' Judy told him, then after gazing through the side window for a tense moment with her mind racing, she reasoned, 'And John, listen – no one can blame you for what happened. The police would say that boy - if he exists - shouldn't have even been in the road – and a dark road at that.'

John thinned his eyes and shook his head as he stopped at the lights. 'Yes, but I'm full of drink, Judy, and I shouldn't even be driving; I haven't even passed my driving test; I don't have a licence, not even a provisional one.'

'It's Monday now,' Judy realised. 'Read the newspapers later and listen to the news on the telly and the wireless in case they mention it.' Her teeth chattered as nerves got the better of her.

John drove the truck to the road where his uncle lived – Braybrooke Road – and he told Judy to stay in the vehicle. He was just going to get a bucket of water and a rag to clean the front of the truck, and then he'd drop his girlfriend off at her home. He gently closed the door so as not to wake up the residents or his uncle, and he took out the door key to his uncle's home. Then he happened to glance at the back of the truck, to the flat open boards of the cargo area – and he noticed something grey. He peeped at this object through the gaps in the long slats of wood enclosing the cargo area – and he saw it was a body – the body of a boy in greyish ragged clothes, and his arms and legs were bent at unnatural angles. He looked like a broken doll. John slowly climbed onto the back of the truck and by the light of a nearby mercury vapour lamp post, he saw the body of the boy, who looked as if he might be about ten to twelve years of age. He had a head of long black hair to his collar, and he looked inert; there was no sign of any life present. His eyes were open and they were heavy lidded. The impact must have somehow thrown him onto the back of the truck, John reasoned, but then he thought that this would have been unlikely. The truck had smashed into him at around fifty miles per hour, and a basic knowledge of the laws of motion told him that the body should have been throw ahead of the truck, not up and over it. It didn't make sense.

John hopped down off the back of the truck, and then he opened the door of the cab and told Judy what he had found. She started to tremble and said she didn't want to see the body.

'We'll have to get rid of it,' said John, and he took out a pack of cigarettes and lit one. He puffed on the fag and muttered to himself.

'What are you going to do?' Judy asked, and tears

rolled from her reddened eyes.

'Hang on, yes,' John said, and he looked at the wing mirror. 'There's a cemetery down there behind us. West Derby Cemetery; I'll bury the body there. Have to get a move on though before it gets light. I won't be a minute.' He left the vehicle and went to the side of his uncle's house and climbed over the fence. A few minutes later a spade was thrown over the fence, and then John climbed back over the fence from the back garden. He went to Judy and she would not agree to the plan. 'I can't carry the bloody body and this spade Judy. All I am asking you to do is carry the spade. I'll drag the body through the cemetery.'

'No, I want to go home John, I've had enough,' said Judy, and she bit her lip then started to cry.

'Alright then!' John snarled, 'I'll have to carry him over there and then I'll have to come all the way back for the spade because of you!' He got out the vehicle and went to the back of the truck, when a skeletal hand reached out for him through one of the gaps between the slats. It was the boy! He was alive!

John backed away, and he was in shock and unable to speak for a moment. He got back into the vehicle and he grabbed the spade. He went back to the rear of the truck as Judy was asking him what he was doing, and he saw the boy leap off the back of the vehicle and land with a gentle thud on his bare feet about fifteen feet away. He could now see that the boy was not human – not by any stretch of the imagination. He was about five feet in height, and his clothes were ragged, stained with blood – probably his own blood and the blood of the fox – but his skin looked very pale with a tinge of blue to it. The eyeballs were huge and pink and had small pin-hole irises, and when the mouth of the boy opened, John saw the fangs; two rows of yellowish pointed teeth. He immediately thought of a vampire. John swung the spade at the boy but he leaped up into the air, well above his own height, and landed a little further away. John dashed towards the truck and he saw the vampiric entity close in on him. Judy opened the door behind her boyfriend and screamed when she saw the entity approaching. Its neck seemed to extend as it looked up at Judy and smiled.

'Get back in the truck, Judy!' John cried, and he heard the faint clunk. Judy had not closed the door properly. John thrust the cutting edge of the spade's blade at the evil-looking being, and it made a hissing sound like a cat. John lifted the spade and tried to smash its blade down on the fiend, but it suddenly darted to the right and the head of the spade hit the ground so hard, the shaft broke. The mouth of the vampire opened so wide it reminded John of a cobra. The mouth was open by what looked like 90 degrees, as if the jaws of the nightmarish boy had dislocated. John could hear the muffled screams of Judy up in the cab of the truck. He recalled that the only way to protect yourself from a vampire was with a cross. He'd seen this type of cruciform defence in horror films, and so he quickly crouched and picked up the broken-off shaft of the spade and placed it at a right angle to the remaining handle and shaft he had hold of. Out of desperation he shouted, 'Depart in the name of Jesus! In the name of God, go away!'

The jaw of the unknown creature snapped shut, the pink bulbous eyes shrank to two slits, and the thing turned and ran off at a phenomenal speed towards Lower House Lane, where it fled around a corner.

Judy was in a dreadful state, and although her home was less than 700 yards away from Braybrooke Road, she clung to John throughout the journey home, convinced that the vampire was going to attack again. John saw Judy to her door, and her father came downstairs and roared: 'Do you know what time it is?'

'Dad, you won't believe what happened to us – ' Judy sobbed, and tried to get the rest of her words out.

'What do you think you're playing at bringing her home at half-past four in the morning eh?' he asked John, who found himself speechless.

'I'd better be going,' John told Judy, and then he nodded to her irate father and full of bumbling awkwardness he said: 'I'm sorry Mr Barratt sir, good night.'

Judy screamed and begged John to stay, but her father pushed the young man through the doorway and then he slammed the front door on him. John McLeckie looked about nervously and climbed into the Bedford truck. He drove up Sedgemoor Road onto Utting Avenue East, and continually scanned the deserted early morning streets in case that thing was still about. He intended going the long way round to reach his uncle's home on Braybrooke Road, and as he reached the junction formed by Lower House Lane and Utting Avenue East, he slowed as he approached the traffic lights, which were on red. He was suddenly startled by a little silhouetted figure which ran across the road, from left to right! John was that afraid, he went through the red light and tore around the corner, heading north to Braybrooke Road. He said the Lord's

Prayer, and then he said a silent prayer in his mind over and over: *Please Lord, keep that thing away from me...*

He parked the truck outside his uncle's house and then, on foot, he embarked on the two-mile journey home to Walton Hall Avenue. He kept looking over his shoulder, and he never saw another soul about. Not even a taxi or a milk float passed him, and he felt as if that thing was watching him somewhere close, ready to attack at any moment, so he started to whisper that simple prayer for God to keep the abomination at bay. Every now and then he wondered about the nature of the thing – what on earth was it? Had it been a boy once? Had it been drinking the blood of a fox that had been run over when the truck had run into it? He quickly turned his enquiring thoughts back to the prayer. He reached the end of Abbdale Road, where his walking broke into a trot up Scargreen Avenue. Once he was on the East Lancs he felt a little safer as two cars passed him. About 500 yards down the thoroughfare, John passed a tree outside a house numbered 65, and he happened to glance up into the branches of this tree – and there was the silhouette of what looked like a boy, perched on a branch. John cried out in shock and he swore, then ran, and he did not look back as he flew down the road towards the corner of Stopgate Lane, where he tripped and landed on his palms, skinning them. He picked himself up and without looking back he ran as fast as his legs could carry him, but as he passed under a railway bridge, he was forced to slow down and then stop by a stabbing stitch in his side. He looked back, and there was the shadowy figure of that unearthly fanged creature coming his way, walking in a strange manner with its legs bent. It was about a hundred yards away and it started to pick up speed. John cried in agony clutching the side of his lower abdomen as he hurried through the shadows beneath the railway bridge. He looked back and swore to himself, and then he hit something hard which naturally startled him.

It was a policeman on his beat.

'What are you up to?' asked the giant of a copper; he was well over six feet, broad-shouldered, and wore a thick walrus moustache.

'Oh, officer - I am being followed by something horrible!' John told him, feeling a little relieved by the presence of the officer of the law.

'I don't see anyone,' said the policeman, looking down at John with one raised eyebrow. 'You're the only horrible thing I can see, lad.'

'No, down there, look!' John turned and pointed, and there was no one there. 'He's gone,' John whispered, then turned back to the policeman and tried to explain what had happened, but the policemen raised his gloved hand and placed his index finger to his lips.

'Ssh! Listen mush, you stink of ale, and you're in no fit state to be walking the streets, so get yourself home and go to that place where any man of sense is at this hour – bed! Got that?'

'Yes, officer, thanks, I will,' said John, and he walked on, and then turned to shout: 'Good night officer!'

The policeman didn't answer; he walked on down the road.

John eventually reached his home and when he got in the house he bolted the door behind him, then went to the window of the living room and peeped through the nets. He could see no one. He also looked through the kitchen window at the back garden, and saw no one prowling about.

On the following day at 7pm he walked to Sedgemoor Road to see Judy, but lost his nerve. He thought her father would have something to say after bringing his daughter back from the party so late and in such a state. John hesitated at the top of his girlfriend's road, unsure what to do, when he heard a boy call his name. He turned and saw it was Judy's 10-year-old brother Micky. He was going to the shops for his mother and held a note upon which Mrs Barratt had written: 'Dear Mr Jones [the shopkeeper], Could you please serve Micky with 20 Embassy cigarettes and a box of Swan? Thanks, Mrs Rosie Barratt.'

Micky ran to John and said: 'John, can you come with me to the shop because I'm scared the vampire might get me...'

'A what?' John interrupted, 'Who told you that?' he asked the boy, taken aback by the mention of a vampire.

'Our Judy, and I wasn't supposed to hear what she said because me Mam sent me out the house but I listened by the door,' Micky explained.

'There are no such things as vampires Micky,' said John, but the boy still seemed a bit afraid.

'Can you go to the shop with me anyway John?' Micky asked, eyes wide with expectation.

'Yeah, come on mate,' said John, and he walked with the boy. 'I'll get you an ice cream if you'll do me a favour.'

Micky smiled and his bright blue eyes looked up at John.

'When you get home after we've been the shop, will you tell your sister to meet me here on this corner?' John asked.

'Yeah,' said Micky, and then he gave a thoughtful look and asked, 'does it have to be an ice cream? Can it be a quarter of pear drops and a Fry's chocolate cream bar please?'

'Yeah, of course, Micky,' John answered with a chuckle.

Later that evening, after Micky had gone home after the trip to the shop, John waited on the corner of Sedgemoor Road and Shottesbrook Green for about fifteen minutes, and then Judy turned up. She informed John that her father had told her to stop seeing him. 'You're not going to stop seeing me are you?' John asked.

'Of course not,' replied Judy, 'my mum told him to stop talking daft and she said in their courting days my dad was always keeping my mum out late when they went out for a drink.'

John was just going to tell Judy that he had been chased by that thing on his way home this morning but decided to say nothing because he didn't want to frighten his girlfriend. He felt closer to Judy now that they had been through that traumatic incident together, so in a way, John believed some good had come out of the macabre encounter with God knows what. He went steady with Judy for six months and then he took her to Reece's Restaurant on Parker Street (where Superdrug is now) one lunchtime, and over coffee and cakes, John proposed – and Judy said yes. Of course, she had to get her father's permission in those days, but Mr Barratt acquiesced because he had, over the months, seen that John was a decent hardworking young man. John and Judy married a year later and bought a house in the Fazakerley area. One wintry evening at 8pm in December 1966, John drove his wife to see her parents in Norris Green, and they found themselves travelling down Lower Lane, when a fog rolled into the area, so John slowed his Austin 1100 to 30 mph. Judy was visiting her parents to drop off some presents for her cousins, and her thoughts – and John's – were concerned with mundane matters; neither of them were thinking of anything remotely supernatural. There was only one other car on the road – a Ford Cortina by the looks of it – and it was travelling ahead of John's car at a distance of about sixty feet, and it was slowly becoming a greyish blue silhouette in the fog. All of a sudden that Cortina swerved dramatically as the driver obviously took evasive action, and within seconds, John's car had reached the spot where the car had swung out the way of something. There was a line of five people, all silhouettes, standing almost shoulder to shoulder in the middle of the road, and the leftmost one was the size of a boy; all the others were about six feet in height, and what's more, they all had glowing white points of light for eyes. Judy let out a scream as John spun the steering wheel, and in an instant the Austin 1100 was screeching towards the left lane, where John just about managed to regain control of it, but not without the kerb scraping the wall of his left tyres. He came to a halt, and then he checked the wing mirror, and saw that the five figures were now running towards the vehicle. Judy had turned to look back at the five people too, and she screamed when she saw them bolt towards the car. She and John recalled that this was the same stretch of road they'd been on that morning in 1964 when the Bedford truck had run that 'boy' over. That small silhouette among the other shadowy beings looked awfully like that boy.

John tore off and he accelerated that much he almost hit the rear of that Cortina which had first alerted him to the figures in the road.

'John, they're catching up!' Judy shrieked, and it was true – the five figures were emerging from the fog and they were running at a phenomenal speed – much faster than a human being could run. John beeped the horn of his car and overtook the Cortina and peeled rubber. He did seventy and went through the lights, bombing across the East Lancs Road, and he was so afraid he hoped a policeman would see his reckless driving and come after him, because he was convinced that those five entities in pursuit were out to kill him and Judy. No police cars gave chase though, and John didn't slow down until he had reached Dwerryhouse Lane one-and-a-half miles away. By then, Judy was in a terrible state. The couple agreed not to say anything about the incident, and they never travelled down Lower Lane again, even during the hours of daylight. Judy said she had the unsettling feeling that those weird creatures standing in the road somehow knew she and John were coming, and were lying in wait. Over the years the couple heard some very strange stories about entities being seen on Lower Lane, including an ink-black amorphous shape mentioned in some of my books, and also the "Thing" on Higher Lane in Fazakerley (less than half a mile away on the other side of Altcourse Prison) which has even been encountered by many people over the years, including policemen, and the Thing is occasionally active even today. The figures seen on Lower Lane are thought by some researchers into the paranormal to be vampires, as those unlucky enough to encounter them at close quarters have mentioned seeing fanged mouths and some have even seen them eating road-kill. Why these entities – whatever they are – seem most active on that stretch of Lower Lane only deepens the mystery.

JACK IN THE BOX

On a cold foggy afternoon one New Year's Eve in the late 1970s, nine men from many walks of life shuffled into the elevator at Liverpool's Lime Street Station, most of them carrying attaché cases and suitcases. All of them were bound for Wirral. The lift descended, shuddered and came to a halt between levels.

'Ha! I of all people should have *foreseen* this,' said Clive Spencer, a bushy-haired man of about forty in glasses and a lime corduroy jacket. He spoke clearly in a fine accent that some had interpreted as effeminate in the past.

'Why's that?' asked a police detective in his fifties named Roy.

'I'm a psychic – but I don't foresee everything,' Clive replied, and looked down at the elevator floor self-consciously.

'Psychic eh?' remarked Roy with a supercilious smirk. 'What's the gimmick?' the detective asked him, 'Confederates in the audience? Codewords?'

'I'm genuine, but well, think what you like,' said

Clive, head bowed, 'I've been laughed at all my life and I'm used to it all now.'

'You know what makes me laugh about you mediums?' said Roy, his eyes scanning the psychic's huge head of bushy hair.

'No, I don't know,' said Clive, and he gave a painful smile and said, 'Oh but I should know, because you probably think I can read minds all the time.'

'Why don't you call clients instead of the other way round?' said Roy, and he looked at the other faces in the lift, expecting a smile or a laugh but everyone seemed tense because they were stuck in this metal box of an elevator.

Billy, a 25-year-old Liverpool lad, went pale, took a deep breath, and then he pressed the alarm bell button. Seeing how distressed Billy was, Roy gestured for him to stop pressing the button and endeavoured to calm him down, saying, 'They'll fix it soon, lad; probably just a worn sheave. We'll be out soon – they know we're stuck in here.'

'Can you read palms?' Harry, an estate agent in his late fifties suddenly asked, and he thrust his palm out to Clive the psychic, who shook his head and turned his gaze away from him. 'Oh come on, mate, I'd like to know what the New Year has in store you see,' a smirking Harry went on, and Clive's face flushed from subdued anger.

Clive gritted his teeth then told the estate agent: 'Well, unless you stop hitting the bottle – and your wife – you might just end up dead or in prison! How's that?'

Harry was speechless for a moment, and then he swore and lunged at Clive, but a smartly-dressed debonair man intercepted Harry, and held him back, and then he shouted at the estate agent: 'Stop this bickering! All this movement might rock the lift, and a cable might snap!'

'What!' Billy the young scouser started to panic, but Roy shook his head and shot his best reassuring smile at Billy. 'No cable's going to snap, lad!' said the detective confidently, 'and as for you – ' he said to the psychic, 'could you keep your psychic act for the stage?'

'It's not an *act*, sir,' Clive told the policeman, 'I'm picking up all sorts of impressions from the people in this elevator; one of the reasons I hate being in crowded places – and I can't just turn my ability off.'

'You're *not* psychic,' said Harry with wounded pride in his forced laughter, 'you're a charlatan. Prove it! Go on, tell us something about our lives! Let the great oracle speak!'

'Put a sock in it fatso!' said a massive, square-shouldered man with a broken nose; he was a retired boxer in his sixties. To Billy he bawled: 'Ring that bell again, you!'

A gasping Billy nodded and duly rang the alarm bell.

The lights in the elevator faded slightly for a few seconds then returned to normal intensity.

'You work for the police, don't you?' Clive asked Roy, and the detective seemed a bit taken aback, but didn't utter a word of reply. Clive looked at Billy, 'You – you were in prison last year – for burglary – isn't that true?'

'How – how did you know that eh? Are you a jack?' Billy asked, and started taking anxious breaths again.

'You lie through your teeth,' Clive told Harry, 'and I

see houses, so you must be some estate agent.'

Harry made a dismissive waving away gesture with his hand, 'All guesswork – all kidology!'

'Yes, I've heard it all before,' said Clive, craning his head back and looking at the white translucent plastic ceiling lights with a big smile. 'Kidology – that's a new one. You would have burnt me at the stake for witchcraft once. Stay in your little safe corner of the universe and don't stray beyond the edge of human understanding. Stick to selling hard-to-lets to poor mugs.'

'Shut that trap of yours you puff!' said the retired boxer. 'Your voice is beginning to get on my tits!'

'I'm a puff am I?' said Clive, with an exaggerated puzzled expression, 'Even though I'm married and have three children. It's odd that you've chosen to call me a puff when you are wearing frilly knickers and stockings and suspenders, and you've never been with a woman in your life.'

A tense silence permeated the lift, and Roy the detective smiled as he watched the amazing reaction to Clive's accusation in the form of a squirming assortment of tics in the ex-boxer's face. The former pugilist opened his mouth but no words came out, and then he gritted his dentures, lifted his hand, and formed a huge fist as he shook with anger. 'You lying bent bastard!' he bellowed, and Roy, Harry and the well-dressed upper crust passenger had to seize the enraged old fighter, but he still managed to throw a punch, which missed Clive and hit the lift wall, missing Billy's head by centimetres.

'Right! Stop this!' cried Roy, 'Stop it now! Any more of this shit and I'll take you in!' he told the faded boxer, and then he turned to Clive and said, 'And I'll take you in as well! Trust me to get stuck in a lift with gang of plantpots!'

'Plantpot am I?' said Clive, 'A puff *and* a plantpot! No Mr Policeman, you've got far worse than that in here! Ha ha!'

'What are you talking about?' Roy asked, and he and the estate agent forced the boxer to the corner diagonally opposite the one Clive was grinning away in.

'Well, sir,' Clive addressed Roy, arms folded, leaning on the steel wall of the lift, 'there just happens to be a killer in this elevator!'

'What have I told you about stirring things up?' an extremely exasperated Roy warned him with a pointed finger.

'Typical queer!' shouted the superannuated bruiser, 'Anything for attention!'

'Don't get your knickers in a twist you punch-drunk pervert!' Clive retorted.

The past-it prizefighter roared and lunged forward, and it took Roy, Harry and three men to keep him from rearranging Clive's face.

'That is it!' Roy yelled at the medium, 'When we get out of here, I am going to throw the book at you! Have you got a death wish or something? I should let this man make mincemeat of you!'

'I'm just sick and tired of being a target!' Clive shouted back, and he slapped his hand against the wall of the elevator. 'I'll shut up from now on and keep the truth to myself!'

'You said there was a murderer in here,' said a worried Billy, and his face was shiny with perspiration.

'Who is he?'

'Oh I'm saying nothing!' Clive replied, and turned away, so he faced the corner. He seemed near to tears, and he adjusted his spectacles and wiped his eyes with the backs of his fingers.

'Ring that bell again!' the boxer told Billy, and he did what he was told but there was no response. No voice came from the lift intercom.

'*I* believe you,' Billy told Clive. 'My Nan went to see a psychic once and he told her she was going to come into money and she had a win on the pools.'

Clive turned left and smiled at the young Liverpudlian. 'You have a girlfriend named Rita, don't you?' he asked.

Billy was flabbergasted. 'Yeah, I do. How did you – '

'You're going to be a father soon,' Clive told him. 'I can see you painting the walls blue in a nursery so it must be a boy.'

'He's filling *his* head with shit now,' said the old boxer. 'He's moved on from the murderer; talking about babies now.'

'Oh no, believe me,' said Clive, and he turned to look at the eight faces in the broken-down lift, 'there *is* a killer in here, and not just an ordinary killer either, but a mass murderer.'

'The suspense is killing me,' said Roy, and he sighed.

'I'm not even sure if I should reveal his identity,' Clive said, looking at one wall of the lift. It was as if he was afraid to gaze at the killer he had somehow unmasked by his powers. Then he coughed and said: 'He has a knife you see, and by golly he knows how to use it!'

Roy the detective thinned his eyes and said, 'Who?

Who is he?' The policeman sounded convinced. He wasn't grinning now. He looked deadly serious.

'This is ridiculous,' said the debonair man in the fine clothes, 'absolute nonsense. I'm returning from my friend's wedding; I was best man. This has ruined the whole day – cooped up with a bunch of argumentative louts and name-callers. What a sad society we live in today. I hate to say this but this is why we have a class system; the working class leave a lot to be desired, all coarse language and my nose tells me that some of you in here don't even wash.'

'Hey you, you snob,' protested Billy, 'I'm proud to be working class.'

'You're not going to believe this,' Clive told the passengers in the lift, 'but the killer in this elevator is none other than Jack the Ripper.'

'What? You mean the Yorkshire one?' Roy asked, and his eyes darted from face to face.

'No, no,' Clive shook his head of bushy hair, 'the *first* one – the one they never caught in London! He's in here! And he's got his knife on him.'

'Oh boy, this crank is something else!' said Harry the estate agent, and he turned to Roy, smiled and slowly shook his head.

'He'd be a bit old wouldn't he?' Roy asked Clive, 'Only he was around thirty when he was going in the East End nearly a century ago – '

'He's a freak!' cried Clive, 'There's something wrong with him! He doesn't age. I can't explain it but he doesn't get old. I know it sounds far-fetched.'

'Well it isn't me!' laughed Harry, and the confined passengers looked at one another's confused and suspicious faces.

'It's him!' Clive backed into Billy in the corner as he pointed at the debonair 'best man'.

'What?' Roy looked at the man. He was about fifty-five maybe, not the centenarian Jack the Ripper would have to be.

'He's Jack the Ripper!' said Clive, and he grabbed Harry and got behind him, as if he thought the man he was accusing might attack him.

'Well, I've been called some awful things in my time,' said the elegantly-dressed man, 'but Jack the Ripper? That's definitely a first.' He then turned to Roy and said, 'Sir, when we get out of here, will you please honour your promise and take this lunatic into custody? His type should not be walking the streets!'

'Search him! He's got a huge knife on him!' said Clive, hiding behind Harry, who was struggling to get away from the terrified psychic.

'Do you mind if I *do* search you, sir?' Roy asked the man.

'Yes, I certainly do!' laughed the chic 'suspect'. 'I promise you that when we get out of this accursed lift, I shall be reporting you to your superiors, sir!' he told Roy.

But Roy persisted. 'Sir, *are* you carrying a knife?' he asked the middle-aged dandy.

The insulted-looking fop shook his head and told Roy: 'Oh for Heaven's sake! On the say-so of this veritable charlatan you are accusing me - a well-connected man who has a brother in the House of Lords - of being some long-dead murderer who was at large a century ago?'

'Sir, it's very simple,' said Roy, approaching the posh passenger in a very gingerly manner, 'are you carrying a concealed knife? And may I have your name, sir?'

'I am not obliged to tell you anything, but I have damn well nothing to hide. My name is Sir Henry Moon! I am not carrying a knife!' declared Mr Moon, and then he added: 'We have six sane witnesses here, and they are going to be subpoenaed to court when I get out of here, believe me! This is harassment, and all because of a self-proclaimed soothsayer! Ha! The papers shall have a field day with this! You can say goodbye to your career in the police force!'

'That's not his name!' cried Clive, cowering behind an agitated Harry. 'I can't focus on getting his real name yet, but it's not Sir Henry Moon! Watch him! He's going to kill us all! I should have said nothing!'

The elevator rocked and began to ascend.

Roy wondered if Clive might have been mistaken, and he was naturally worried now that Sir Henry would sue him. He quickly rehearsed an apology in his mind.

The elevator halted, the doors parted, and two railway guards stood there – and also a middle-aged woman known to the police as a prostitute who operated in the Lime Street area. She screamed when she saw that 'best man'. 'You!' she yelled, and hid behind a guard, 'He tried to kill me!'

The dandy who had been accused of being Jack the Ripper by the medium did not even react, but instead he casually walked out the elevator, but the detective Roy said, 'Not so fast, sir,' and reached out for the suspect's arm, and in a flash the immaculately-attired stranger pulled out a knife, either from the inside pocket of his jacket or from some hidden sheath tied to his chest, and in the space of a second the blade of this weapon sliced through Roy's purlicue – that piece of skin between the thumb and forefinger. The blade flashed through the tissue so fast, Roy felt no pain, and then he saw the blood ooze out of the wound. The man, despite looking as if he was in his fifties ran off as fast as an Olympic sprinter, and within seconds he was out the station and vanishing into the fog, with one out-of-shape railway guard trying to catch him, but that mysterious "Sir Henry Moon" was never caught and he was never traced. Roy had to say that the assailant had been an eccentric, for the policeman's superiors would not have believed the Ripper story, and who could blame them? At first, Roy wondered if Clive the medium had set the whole thing up as some publicity stunt, but the medium swore he had never seen Mr Moon before and never wanted to see him ever again – but Clive later sensed that the Ripper was following him. He asked Roy if he could swing it for him to get police protection but the detective told him that was out of the question; no one would believe that history's most famous serial killer – a man who had last been heard of in 1888 – was still around. Clive said he sometimes saw the apparently immortal murderer following him all over the country, sometimes on foot and sometimes behind the wheel of an old Daimler Majestic. No one believed Clive, except his wife Erica, for she knew her husband had a genuine clairvoyant talent and he had never once lied to her in all their years of marriage. She too saw the Ripper herself on several occasions and convinced Clive to move to the south of France with her and their three children. Erica had an uncle there who would let her and her husband and children live at his farmhouse. Clive agreed to Erica's idea in the end when he found that someone had slashed the tyres of his car one morning. Even in the south-west of France, near the La Roque-Gageac commune, Clive claimed that the shadowy killer from the past was still following him, so Erica bought a pistol and Clive slept with it under his pillow. A fortnight after Clive and Erica's arrival at the farmhouse, something terrifying happened. While Erica was out with her uncle and children at the market, Clive received a visit from a man who claimed to be a Government inspector, but he the medium could see it was his stalker in disguise. Clive ran up to the bedroom, grabbed the pistol, and managed to empty four shots into the chest and arm of the creepy unrelenting pursuer. The disguised man ran out of the farmhouse clutching his chest, yet curiously, not a drop of blood fell from him. Erica's uncle informed a Catholic priest about the strange and extraordinary situation, and the holy man blessed the house and even stayed at the farmhouse for a while. The priest was of the opinion that the man stalking Clive had long ago made a pact with the Devil. Clive and Erica never saw the "Ripper" again, and the medium passed away around 2009.

THE MYSTERY OF MERSEY HAFEN

The watch you wear on your wrist is a shackle that handcuffs you to the present, and all of your other earthly concerns also anchor you to the here and now, but when the mind is allowed to roam at large, via sleep or certain drugs, it occasionally glimpses other realities, and the following strange story, reported to me many years ago, seems to vindicate this view of the freed mind. In June 1967, the so-called "Summer of Love" arrived. It was an incredible and unprecedented movement involving mostly young people who distrusted their governments, refused to be part of the brainwashed consumer society, and were willing to alter and expand their minds through the use of meditation and drugs. A vast majority of the young during this (sadly, ephemeral) time felt as if they were part of a New Renaissance of the Mind, and during this period music, art, poetry, fashion and literature seemed to undergo a very refreshing change of direction. The Beatles had contributed to the Summer of Love and they were swept along with it. The world's most famous band went psychedelic in 1967, and even the Queen noticed it. During a levée for the Council of Knights Bachelor held at Buckingham Palace in the autumn of 1967, the monarch remarked to Sir Joseph Lockwood, the chairman of EMI: 'The Beatles are turning awfully funny, aren't they?' Her Majesty didn't mean funny as in humour, but *strange*. The Fab Four had just released the lysergic vaudeville album *Sergeant*

Pepper's Lonely Hearts Club Band and its release was hailed by critic Kenneth Tynan as a 'decisive moment in the history of Western Civilization'.

Against this backdrop of the short-lived "Flower Power" revolution, a 17-year-old apprentice plumber named Philip was lying on his back in a field near Speke Airport with a bunch of self-styled hippie friends. Most were drunk or stoned – and some were high *and* intoxicated with alcohol. One of them was finger-picking a Dylan song on a Spanish guitar, and Philip felt a little sad, despite the joint he was sharing, because he had just split up with his girlfriend, Abigail. She had decided Philip was not ambitious enough. She wanted to live in Paris as a model but Philip just wanted to stay in Speke and become the best plumber in Liverpool.

A man with long grey hair in a shabby suit came on the scene and sat among the bohemians. He said his name was Fred and that he was an 'experimental pharmacist'.

'Oh aye,' said Philip's best friend Darren, when he overheard the stranger make this odd assertion, 'you mean you're a drug pusher?'

Fred did not answer; instead he showed Philip a bottle of pink pills and said: 'They send people to some very strange places. Care to try one?'

'I don't take acid, man,' said Philip, raising himself up from the warm sweet-smelling grass by his elbows to look at the tablets.

Fred smiled and in an optimistic and melodic voice he said to the plumber: 'I assure you that these are not LSD – they're vitriac; they free the mind.'

'And why do you want to give one to me?' asked

Philip, naturally suspicious.

'Because he's a dirty old man and he wants your body, Phil,' Darren told his friend, all tongue in cheek.

Again, Fred paid no attention to Darren, and fixed his cold blue eyes on Philip's face.

'So these aren't acid,' said Philip, and he passed the half-inch-long marijuana joint to Darren, 'so what are they then?'

'Vitriac – whatever that is,' said Darren, and he swore because the joint went out.

'Could be bleedin' arsenic for all I know,' reasoned Philip, yet he couldn't take his eyes off the pink pills for long. He wondered how they could take him to those strange places Fred enigmatically spoke of.

'Oh come on, now. What type of person poisons someone with so many witnesses about?' asked Fred with a poker face, and then a smile dawned on his lips and he added: 'Hey? Who's paranoid?'

'A crank,' said Darren, 'a crank would kill someone in front of witnesses. Piss off dad and leave us alone.'

'Very well,' Fred smiled and got to his feet, but curiosity burned in Philip's mind and he got up off the grass too.

'Wait a minute,' the plumber said, 'I'll take one, but you'll stay here and if anything bad happens to me, my mates will give you a good kicking and then they'll take you to the police. Got that?'

'Don't be a nitwit, Phil,' Darren warned, but already, Fred had unscrewed the top off the bottle of pink pills. The stranger emptied one of the pills out onto Philip's palm. Philip shouted to a drunken friend named David and asked him for a swig of cider from his bottle to wash the pill down.

'You poison him and I'll smash your gob in, Fred,' Darren warned, as he saw Philip sit cross-legged on the grass.

'When will I feel things happen?' Philip asked Fred.

'About ten minutes,' Fred replied, and pulled the sleeve of his coat back and looked at his watch. 'So just relax, and let the pill take you out of all this.'

Sure enough, after ten minutes, an explosion of noise made Philip jump. It sounded like a bomb going off.

'You alright Phil?' Darren asked, kneeling in front of him – but then Darren vanished.

Philip looked to his right and saw that the blast of noise was coming from a giant black delta plane taking off from the runway of Speke Airport. It was like that futuristic plane he had seen a few times in the papers – but he could not recall its name. Philip would later compare this sleek plane as looking like the Concorde supersonic airliner, only its fuselage was longer, but its nose was dipped and pointed just like Concorde's. This plane also differed from the white supersonic airliner because it had the Nazi Balkenkreuz emblem on both wings. Philip had seen those markings on Nazi warplanes in films about the war, and this really struck him as bizarre. The Concorde-shaped plane bearing the symbols of the Wehrmacht thundered into the blue heavens, and Philip looked down and saw that his friends were all gone, but Fred was still there.

'You made it across, splendid,' said the enigmatic pill-pusher, but now he was speaking in German, and somehow, Philip knew this and found that he now spoke and understood German too.

'What's happened to me? Where are my mates?'

Philip asked, and he got to his feet and felt dizzy. Fred chuckled and held him by his right upper arm and took him to a strange station about a quarter of a mile away from the airport. At this station there were no normal trains – just a black rail which was suspended about fifty feet from the ground. Philip heard a faint whistling sound and he saw a monorail train arrive from the south. 'Come on,' Fred helped the disoriented youth into an elevator and they boarded the monorail. The guard on the futuristic train seemed to know Fred, and he smiled at him and directed him and Philip to two very comfortable padded seats. The passing sign outside the window read: "Mersey Hafen".

'Where are we?' Philip asked, and he felt his heart palpitate.

'Yes, that's the name of Liverpool here,' said Fred with a broad grin, 'Mersey Hafen.'

The high-speed monorail took the same waterfront route as the old Overhead Railway, and in minutes, Fred and Philip were in the city centre. The place looked superficially like the downtown Liverpool Philip was familiar with, only there were cameras and loudspeakers on poles all over the place. The police here were armed with small machine guns, wore royal blue German WWII helmets and shades, and there were swastikas draped from most of the buildings. Every car that passed looked like a domed Volkswagen Beetle – even the taxi cabs.

'Is this all in my mind?' Philip asked, 'It's horrible.'

'No, you've come across to the good version of Liverpool, that's all,' said Fred – or Frederich, as he later called himself; Frederich Fischer.

'Take me back, I don't like this,' said Philip, but Frederich said he was taking him to the luxurious Hotel Nietzsche – a transformed Adelphi Hotel with a towering statue of Hitler outside the entrance. The statue depicted the Fuhrer with a giant eagle on his gauntlet, and upon the plinth of this 60-foot-tall statue there was a laurel wreath encircling the swastika, and beneath this were words which said Hitler Unser Retter: 'Hitler Our Saviour'.

'Why have they got a statue of that bastard here?' Philip asked, and as he craned back his head to look at the top of the gigantic sculpture he almost fell backwards from another dizzy spell. Herr Fischer led Philip towards the Hotel Nietzsche, and the teen noticed a group of tall athletic-looking males and females who seemed to be around his age, and Frederich explained that these were the "Super Youths" – genetically-perfected humans. Over the entrance of the hotel there stretched a long horizontal black marble slab featuring a gold German Eagle.

'I don't want to go in,' whimpered a shaking Philip, 'you're going to kill me aren't you?'

'Certainly not!' laughed Frederich, 'You are a guest of honour, young man! Now come on in and meet the Intellekts!'

In the Hotel Nietzsche, Philip received a warm welcome by these "Intellekts" – a group of about a dozen men and women who were attired in smart black uniforms, and they shook hands with the plumber and seemed to sincerely like him, yet in the reflective surfaces of the hotel's foyer walls, Philip noticed that a few of these people were smirking and sneering at him behind his back. Philip believed that if he went along with them for a while, he could gain their trust and then at an opportune moment he'd have to make a dash for freedom. A tall thin man with short coal-black hair and a beautiful blonde woman detached themselves from the Intellekts and ushered Philip to a lounge where the carpets were so deep, he felt as if he was walking through quicksand. He sat at a low round table and was given a drink which reminded him of the schnapps he had last Christmas.

'You must be rather confused by this state of affairs,' said the blonde woman who had escorted Philip into the lounge with the gangly raven-haired man.

'You can say that again,' said Philip, 'that pink pill has scrambled my mind.'

The blonde lady smiled and said: 'No, vitriac has brought you across from the old place you knew — what was it called now?'

'Liverpool!' someone laughed; it came from one of the other Intellekts who were sitting in an arc on the other side of the round table.

'In this world, Germany won the war, you see,' explained the dark-haired man sitting next to the blonde, 'And thank God we did.'

'No you never, you lost,' Philip replied in a timid voice. He felt as if they were trying to brainwash him into believing in the Nazis. 'Hitler died in that bunker.'

The blonde closed her sky-blue eyes and slowly shook her head, then opened those eyes and they were glistening and full of sorrow. 'Our Saviour died last year in January. January 1965 to you, the same day as Winston Churchill. The Fuhrer is resting in his sarcophagus in the Great Pyramid in Berlin.'

'He was a good man, Hitler,' said Philip, pretending

he liked the dictator, because he thought that if he went along with these people, he could escape somehow, even though he felt terrible praising Adolf.

'Ha! You don't mean that,' said the blonde, and her eyes were now full of hatred. 'Don't underestimate us, young man,' she seethed. 'We've only allowed you to live because you are part of an experiment!'

The tall and slender Intellekt seated next to the golden-haired woman tapped the knuckles of her fist, which was resting on her lap, as if to tell her not to impart too much information to the guest.

Philip saw the faces of the couple seated next to him split into two for a moment. He had double vision, and then the faces returned to normal, but a moment later they were tinged with pink and green. He felt as if the pink pill was wearing off. The voice of the woman also seemed incomprehensible, for a while, and he heard echoes as she spoke as if he was drifting off into sleep, but he squeezed his eyes shut, and when he opened them again, he could see the Intellekts clearly. The couple took him into what seemed to be a cinema with rows of red velvet seats facing a screen. Upon this screen, a film was shown, and it was accompanied by classical music – possibly Beethoven. It showed Spitfires being blown to bits by rockets fired from Nazi planes, and it showed German soldiers in London firing off flamethrowers at civilians and soldiers alike, and the Intellekts cheered and laughed as people ran about with flames issuing from them. There were scenes featuring firing squads, double-decker buses crammed with burning passengers, and a surreal clip which showed a group of men and women tied to the top of a V2 rocket that was launched from

Trafalgar Square. Philip found himself in tears at the graphic scenes of the film, and the Intellekts started to mock him. One of them said they were going to find a way to get to the other Liverpool – the one Philip was from – so they could invade and conquer it, and Philip called the hosts murderers and a riot of laughter broke out.

The double vision returned, and Philip got up and as he tried to leave his seat he felt hands grabbing at his arms, dragging him back, but eventually he was able to break free. He ran out of the Hotel Nietzsche, and when he got out onto Lime Street, he felt as if the entire axis of the world was tilting. His balance had completely gone. He screamed and believed that the colossal statue of Hitler was going to fall on him, and he fell on the pavement, but when he rolled over and looked up he saw only the weathered frontage of the Adelphi Hotel. The Hotel Nietzsche had gone. The effects of the pill were evidently wearing off, and by the time Philip had reached Lewis's (almost being run down by a bus in the process) everything had reverted to normal. The swastikas and the Nazi police and the black Volkswagen vehicles and that monorail had all gone. He spat in his palm and sniffed the spittle – it had an aroma of something like brandy, and he recalled the schnapps drink he'd been given by the Intellekts. 'So I didn't imagine it!' he cried to himself, and passersby looked at him as if he was drunk.

He boarded a bus home to Speke, and when he got off the vehicle, the first person he saw was Darren, who asked him where he had gone earlier on. Darren told Philip: "You and that Fred were there one moment, and then you just disappeared. We all looked everywhere, how did you do it?'

When Philip told Darren what had happened, his friend couldn't take it all in. 'Sounds like LSD to me that, mate,' said Darren.

'No, it really happened!' Philip insisted, 'It wasn't a trip!'

'But we won the war, so how could it have happened?' Darren retorted.

'Darren, you know me; I'm not the brightest of people – so how could I come up with all that? What the hell is the Hotel Nietzsche? And monorails and vitriac and all that? How could I come up with that?'

'Yeah, that's true,' said Darren, 'you *are* a thick bastard, like.'

'Exactly, so *did* I go somewhere real?' Philip asked him, as if his friend should know.

'Its drugs though, isn't it?' Darren struggled to express his take on the mystery, 'Drugs can make you think you're seeing all sorts. Pink elephants and that, y'know.'

Philip told his parents about his terrifying but intriguing experience, and his mother and father, knowing their son was a simple lad, were convinced he could not have made up something as outlandish as the tale he had told. They also told him to keep quiet about the incident or he'd earn a reputation as a drug-taker and no one would employ him. Philip wrote down what had happened in an old school exercise book, adding more details as he remembered them, and although he had a tough enough job speaking English properly, he kept recalling German words and sometimes entire sentences, but this ability deserted him weeks later.

Perhaps the whole experience the apprentice plumber had was down to some drug, possibly even LSD, but I have the unsettling feeling that Philip was taken to an alternative future, where our history turned out a little different, but who took him 'across' and why is anybody's guess.

VOICES ON A BUS

One foggy Saturday afternoon in December 1970, a Tuebrook librarian named Peter Cavendish sat and stared at the blank page loaded into his typewriter. This was supposed to be the first page of a bestseller he hoped to write, but the words just wouldn't come, and so the budding author got up and paced up and down in his bedroom until his mother entered with a tray. On that salver was Peter's favourite orange mug containing his usual sweet milky tea, and next to it was a plate bordered with red and yellow rose prints upon which three digestives and an Eccles cake had been placed.

'How's it going son?' asked Doris Cavendish, eyeing the blank cream page wound around the platen of the typewriter.

'I've got writer's block, Mum,' confessed Peter, 'all the great writers have had it.'

'Your big mug of tea and biccies will help you, son,' Doris suggested with a smile. 'Don't they say: "food for thought" or something?'

'Something like that,' Peter nodded with fake enthusiasm. 'Ah, thanks mum,' he said with a warm smile, taking off his reading spectacles. But then he put them back on. 'Hey, wait a mo,' Peter turned away from the refreshments and went to his floor-to-ceiling bookshelves. He scanned the spines of the paperbacks and hardbacks, and located the book about creative writing and pulled it out with his index finger and thumb. He thumbed through the slim tome and quickly found the chapter he'd recalled. 'Yeah, this writer here says if you get stuck for words, go and mingle with crowds in shops and pubs and eavesdrop on natural dialogue for ideas.'

'Drink your tea first, Peter,' said his mother. 'It's nice and hot. It's freezing out there and foggy. You don't want to go out in that, son.'

'I've got to, mum, for inspiration,' Peter sipped the tea with a slurping sound and then he dunked his digestive in the mug as he read the book in his left hand. 'This is the part that's relevant to my problem: "Eavesdropping can provide the budding writer with naturalistic dialogue and also ideas. Take a notebook and pen with you." I'll do just that.'

'Don't speak with your mouth full Peter,' said his mother, and she left the room.

Fifteen minutes later, Peter wrapped his brown woollen scarf round his neck, put on his jacket, and left the house, bound for the bus stop. Out of the foggy limbo a number 79 bus approached, heaving its way up Childwall Valley Road, bound for the city centre. Peter boarded the bus and the driver mumbled something about a slight detour because of roadworks somewhere along the route, and although Peter did not fully understand what the driver had said, he paid his fare, nodded to the busman, and went upstairs to the top deck. He found a copy of last night's *Liverpool Echo* on the third seat from the front of the bus and started to read through it. He was the only passenger upstairs, but when the bus reached a stop near the Paddington area he heard two young girls come up and they sat behind him. He smiled as he listened in on their conversation for inspiration as he pretended to read the newspaper. If he heard anything inspirational he'd write it down in his Silvine notebook.

'Judy, you had nothing in common with Alan; forget about him now,' said one girl in an Irish accent.

A distressed-sounding Judy replied, 'I'll never get over him Nancy, and I did a stupid thing before.'

'What do you mean, you did a stupid thing?' Nancy asked.

'I took those sleeping tablets – your mum's ones,' replied Judy, and she sniffled.

'I hope to Christ you're having me on Judy!' Nancy said, and there was a pause, followed by some sobbing from Judy, who told her friend: 'No, I took all of them! I can't live without Alan! I'd rather die!'

'Mary Mother of God!' exclaimed Nancy, 'You'll have to get to the nearest hospital and get pumped!'

Judy burst into tears, and groaned, 'No!'

Nancy started shouting at her. 'Judy, get off the bus now! There's a hospital down here! Come on!'

Through the front bus windows, Peter could see the faint outline of the Royal Infirmary in the fog further down Pembroke Place. He continued to listen to the drama behind him.

'Oh Judy, please get off the bus! Please!' cried Nancy, and her distraught friend howled with grief. Peter decided he'd have to try and get the would-be suicide off the bus and into the hospital, and he stood up and turned – and found the upper deck deserted.

He was the only one there. Many years later Peter heard that the ghosts of two girls were often heard on a certain bus; one had an Irish accent. They'd got off the bus on Pembroke Place in the 1950s and one of them had been knocked down and killed. The other girl died in hospital days later from an overdose.

APPROACHING SHADOWS

The wine and business banter flowed at that certain restaurant – the most popular one in Liverpool – the scene for the crème de la crème. The optimistic spring sunshine of the year 2000 glared through the plate glass and bathed this opulent stratum of the bourgeoisie as they spouted their idealistic philosophies over lunch. One young man declared to the wine bibbers: 'the nation state will be dead soon! Everyone will be a citizen of the Net! We will trade in cyberspace and pay no taxes! To the Netocracy!' he lifted his glass triumphantly and a hipster named Calvin yelled, 'I'll drink to that!'

This was the start of that decade we now know as the Noughties, and two Liverpool men at that fashionable restaurant – Paul and Richard – were on the crest of a wave with their cutting-edge software development firm. Richard had just bought a brand spanking new pink Rolls Royce for his wife and Paul was dating the daughter of a powerful buccaneering merchant banker and due to move into a luxurious Chelsea flat with her in a fortnight. Paul puffed on a Cuban cigar as a young man demonstrated a prototype invention made of Lego bricks, cellotape and circuit boards with flashing LEDs. It was a new type of high-speed modem. Richard agreed to back the young inventor and wrote him a cheque for £5000. Earlier that morning he had – against the wishes of his partner – invested £50,000 in the development of a mobile phone that used the earth's magnetic field to communicate – even from the bottom of a coal mine, the inventor claimed. Richard was the reckless one, prone to finance the most absurd inventions and harebrained schemes, and Paul often addressed him as "Your Randomness" because of his unpredictable and cavalier habit of throwing the company's money about.

'It's odd isn't it?' Paul mused, leaning back in his chair at the table, and puffing a cloud of blue sunlit smoke upwards into the novelty pendant lightshades fashioned as bowler hats. 'We have reached the start of the Millennium. A thousand years stretches before us. I wonder what's in store? Hopefully a new era of love and understanding.'

Some sarcastic eavesdropper seated further along the table started singing the Robbie Williams hit *Millennium* – but then something very strange took place. A shadow fell over Paul's face – the shadow of a girl. She was aged about twenty, perhaps younger, and she had just entered the restaurant. She had straight black hair to her shoulders, a pale beautiful face, and she wore a black knee-length tunic dress and black ballet pumps. Her legs were bare, and Richard, who had a fetish about female legs, scanned her ankles, calves and knees and muttered, 'De jambes sexy.'

The girl casually took Paul's Cuban cigar from his mouth and gently placed it in the ashtray on the table, then sat on his lap, legs on either side of his, as she faced him. Richard looked at Paul's face, assuming he knew this young lady, and Paul had an expression that lay somewhere between surprise and intrigue.

The audacious girl started to sing in a very haunting mezzo soprano voice, and people smiled and laughed, thinking it was some stunt, but then some listened to the soulful song, and became uneasy. The first words of her song were 'approaching shadows' and she mentioned Paul and Richard by name in her ballad, which now sounded like a mournful hymn, and then she ran her hand through Paul's raven black hair, and got off him, still singing. Some of the men present emitted wolf-whistles and a few laughed, but the laughter sounded forced and hollow, borne of discomfiture and unease. As the beguiling singer passed tables she looked at the diners and seemed to be singing about them, mentioning some by name, wiping the smiles off their faces. She burst into a loud operatic voice and the disquieting lyrics told of people 'going to the wall,' and Paul recalled a part of the song that ran: 'towers of money in flames, here today, gone tomorrow, fear is the name of the game.'

The song then turned to a description of money being swept away in a flood. The unidentified girl paused, smiled, then returned to Paul and Richard's table and ended the song with a description of the two entrepreneurs going down in the world after 'the bubble had burst'. To whistles and ear-splitting applause, the girl then left the restaurant by another door and everyone expected her to return for the curtain call – but she didn't, so everyone sat there puzzled for a while. She didn't return.

'What on earth was that all about?' Richard asked, his voice amplified in the unnatural hush around that table, and there was a ripple of nervous laughter. Calvin the hipster popped his head over Paul's left shoulder and asked: 'Who was that beautiful girl, Paul? Some record producer could make a million with her.'

'I haven't the foggiest idea who she was, Calvin,'

Paul told him.

'Some spaced-out student probably,' Richard decided, 'and heavens knows what she was high on.'

'But what a voice,' said Calvin, 'gave me goosebumps.'

Paul felt there was something supernatural about the singer; something prophetic in her strange song, and where on earth had he seen that girl before? He had definitely seen her face somewhere, and he told Richard this, hoping he'd place her, but all his business partner would say was that the singer had 'fit legs'.

After lunch, Richard made his way back to the office (via a betting shop) and Paul took his usual walk to clear his head before returning to work. As he was strolling along Mount Pleasant he heard a familiar voice behind him shout: 'Hey, moneybags, lend me a few quid!'

He turned to see Richard. He had a thick unkempt beard, wild uncombed hair, and he wore a stained parka, shabby brown corduroy trousers and a pair of scuffed black trainers. He had the unlit stub of a rolled cigarette in his mouth and his eyes looked red and very sorrowful.

'Richard? What the hell are you dressed like that for?' Paul asked, and his nose detected body odour coming from his friend on the soft spring breeze. Richard held his grubby palm out, gesturing for Paul to give him money. His fingernails were dirty and yellow from nicotine.

The dishevelled figure then vanished. Paul stood rooted to the spot with the malodorousness lingering in his nostrils, and he went cold. Paul just knew this was some bad omen, and he immediately thought of the mystifying singer at the restaurant. This was not looking good at all. Paul had never believed in the supernatural and had never given an iota of thought to consider anything connected to the paranormal; his chief concern in life so far had been the mundane secular world of mammon and economics, of programming codes and cash flows. He *had* been working rather hard of late, putting in the extra hours at the office to develop some complex mind-bending algorithms for his award-winning software, but he'd been wise enough to get enough sleep – so he could not explain the apparition he'd just seen of a down-at-heel version of Richard. Had that singing girl put some drug in his glass of wine when she cheekily sat on his lap? He dismissed this possibility as unfounded and paranoiac, but still unable to explain away the 'ghost' who'd just asked him for a handout, Paul continued on his way to the office racking his brains for a rational solution. When he arrived at his workplace, he poured himself a black sugarless coffee and looked at Richard, who was now puffing away on his pipe as he read the *Financial Times*.

Paul just had to ask a burning question. 'Richard, do you have a half brother by any chance?'

His partner coughed, removed the pipe from his lips and shot a puzzled look at him. 'And you call me Your Randomness! No, I haven't, but why do you ask?'

'Oh nothing, just wondered,' Paul replied, and blushed slightly, feeling so silly.

'Come on,' said Richard, 'you can't just ask a barmy question like that without some good cause.'

'Okay, look, you know me,' said Paul, trying to smile as he looked into the coffee cup, 'I'm not the type who believes in ghosts and all that claptrap.'

Richard returned a puzzled look, put the newspaper down and bit the stem of the pipe.

'Well, after we left the restaurant earlier, I went for my walk, and on the way back as I was walking along Mount Pleasant, I heard a voice shout out, "Hey, moneybags, lend me a few quid!" And I turned to look – and it was you.'

'Me?' Richard recoiled.

'Yes, you, but you looked like – well, the only way I can describe it is that you looked like a tramp – ' Paul told him, but his friend interrupted him.

'A tramp? Is this some idiotic joke? What's the punchline?' Richard glowered, his forehead corrugated with wrinkles of disapproval towards his friend's ridiculous claim.

'Yes, hear me out, please,' Paul stammered and nodded with his eyes closed. 'I find it as hard to believe as you, but I swear that it happened. You asked me for money, and then you vanished into thin air.'

'And did anyone else see this *ghost* of yours truly?' Richard asked, angling his head sideways and looking Paul up and down as if he was evaluating his sanity.

'I – I don't know,' Paul struggled to recall if any witnesses had been about, adding: 'it was that brief. You were there one minute and then you were gone, and the smell – '

'Smell?' Richard scowled.

'Well, never mind, but I give you my word, I saw your double today, and it knocked me for a six.'

'Paul, I think you had *some* experience, but I don't think it was a ghost you saw; I think you've seen some beggar, and there are enough of them in this city, and he's just had a look of me. You've been working round the clock, mate, and we all know what that leads to. Remember what happened to Jim Rylands when he decided to take two jobs with four hours' sleep each day?'

'Yes, I know but – ' Paul sighed.

'Died in the barber's chair, heart failure, and he was younger than you,' Richard recalled.

'You're probably right,' said Paul, 'I better start taking it easy.' He still held his belief that he had witnessed something paranormal but thought he'd better keep it to himself as he seemed to have scared Richard.

That night, Paul had a very strange dream. He was sitting around a table with his usual friends; Richard was there too and Calvin, but they were all dressed in clothes that belonged to the 18th century, and they all had on white wigs of the type seen in those old paintings of France in the days of the Revolution. In the dream, Paul knew that he was in a salon – not a beauty salon, but a salon in the old original French meaning of the word: a gathering of intellectuals, usually in the house of a prominent or aristocratic person. This salon was in the magnificent drawing room of some nobleman and the people present were having a philosophical discussion with an amazing spread of food and wine upon the table. Into this room came the love of Paul's life, and it was *that* sybilline girl who had come into the Liverpool restaurant singing her prophecies. He knew her name now, it was Everléigh, and she was greatly feared because she could foretell the future and knew people's secrets. She would sing strange songs in a manner that some ascribed to demonic possession, and as soon as she entered the room, many of the affluent guests left the table, and some even opened a window to escape into the night, rather than hear the prophecies of Everléigh. She wore a flowing diaphanous night gown as fine as cobwebs and padded in her bare feet to Paul. She sat on his lap again, legs on either side of his legs, and she gently drew the tip of her index finger across his throat, right to left, as she sang about him losing his head. The room had a high ceiling, and upon the tall walls of the salon the shadow of a guillotine appeared with its blade poised to fall. The shadow blade of the silhouetted guillotine plummeted from the crossbar onto its victim.

Paul awoke with a start, and then, in the darkness he softly murmured the name of the girl he somehow knew; 'Everléigh,' he whispered. Within months the so-called Dot-com Bubble had begun to burst. This event had been caused by ultra-optimistic people over-speculating and over-investing on the potential of various new internet companies, and over five trillion dollars was lost as a result. Thousands of internet and tech firms went bust, and Paul and Richard's company was badly dented by the bursting of the bubble. Through bad management of the software firm's money by Richard, the software company went bankrupt, and while Paul recovered - thanks to a nest egg he'd sensibly stashed away (along with financial help from his prospective father-in-law merchant banker) - Richard turned to drink, his wife divorced him and he ended his days begging on the streets of Liverpool. In September 2001, after the terrorist attack on the World Trade Centre, Paul went cold when he recalled that line "Everléigh" had sung: 'towers of money in flames, here today, gone tomorrow, fear is the name of the game.'

The Twin Towers of commerce *had* indeed been standing one day, and were completely gone the next after they'd both collapsed after being struck by jet airliners, and the fear of further attacks by terrorists gripped the West for many years to come, which made Paul reflect on the line: 'fear is the name of the game.'

Paul later married and settled in London, and so far, he has not seen that oracular singer, nor has he had any further dreams about her. It's a strange case; it could be some form of reincarnation at work, or is Everléigh some immortal who tracked down a reincarnated Paul because he had been her lover back in the 18th century? It really is hard to say. I feel that Everléigh belongs to the same enigmatic genus of females as that other woman of mystery mentioned in a previous chapter – Elva, but this opinion does nothing to throw any real light on the riddle of the prophetic singer.

STRANGE WARNING

On 30 March 1968, which happened to fall on a Saturday, PC Jack Marshall sat having his tea in his Garston home as he watched an episode of *The Monkees* TV series. His wife Samantha said she had just bought a gold lamé dress and hinted: 'It'd be nice to go out some night and wear it.'

The hint went right over Jack's head as he tucked into bangers, extra-buttery mash, onion gravy and marrowfat peas and listened to America's answer to The Beatles singing the psychedelic song *Daily Nightly* – the first rock song to feature a Moog synthesizer.

'Any more tea, love?' Samantha queried, looking at the china cup by Jack's elbow. He didn't answer. He continued to gaze at the TV screen as he ate but his mind seemed elsewhere. Sam tilted the brown glazed teapot and refilled his cup, then poured the usual 'sterry' milk into Jack's tea and added a teaspoon of Tate & Lyle sugar. She stirred the cup carefully because Jack became annoyed at the ringing sound of a silver spoon against china. She then topped up her own cup, sugared it and sat down. Jack noticed the refilled teacup and muttered, 'Ta love.'

Sam smiled and said: 'Barbara was telling me that she heard that the Corpy are going to buy the Grand National; her husband knows a man who works in the stables.'

Jack turned to her at last and after a sneering chuckle, he asked: 'How can you *buy* the Grand

National?'

'I'm only telling you what Barbara said,' Sam told him, feeling silly now.

'Well Barbara doesn't know what she's talking about,' Jack replied. 'There've been rumours that the Corpy were going to take over Aintree racecourse for one and a half million quid, but it said in the papers that it was just a rumour. You take everything Barbara says as gospel, Think for yourself.'

Sam got up and went into the kitchen and ran the tap as she cried. She felt as if she was single again. Over the past five months the gulf between her and Jack had been widening; he was becoming more distant and they seemed to be living separate lives under the same roof. She turned the tap off, dried her eyes on a kitchen towel, and Jack appeared in the doorway.

'You okay?' he asked, 'You've left half your tea there.'

'Yes I'm alright, just got a bit of a headache,' Sam fibbed, and looked out the kitchen window.

'There's a film on tonight called *An Alligator Named Daisy* with Diana Dors,' Jack told her. She felt as if he was pretending to show interest now because of the abrupt way he'd talked to her at the table. 'You like Diana Dors don't you?'

'Ha! Red Alligator won the National today, as I predicted,' said Sam, picking herself up a little with a smile. 'What a coincidence – *An Alligator Named Daisy* on the telly on the same day.'

'Anyway, I just thought I'd tell you,' said Jack, and left the doorway of the kitchen and went upstairs.

Jack went on duty at 9pm that night on the city

centre beat, and midnight found him walking past the Adelphi Hotel, and here he saw a couple embracing as they kissed. He thought the voice of the woman was familiar – it sounded like Samantha. He turned and saw that the woman had a gold lamé dress on – like the one his wife had mentioned, but she had her back to him, and that ape with his hands around her looked just like his best friend Ted Cobley. Jack watched from the shadows as the couple went towards the entrance of the Adelphi Hotel. It was now plain to see that it was definitely Samantha, and that was Ted alright. She was supposed to be having an early night tonight with that headache, recalled Jack, his blood boiling. How long had this been going on? He cursed Samantha under his breath, marched to the Adelphi and hesitated at the entrance, then leaped up the steps to reach the foyer doorway. An old vagrant stood in his way in that doorway, giggling at him. Jack callously pushed him aside, went into the hotel foyer, and pressed the bell button hard at the front desk. A weary man appeared with red eyes and he put on his spectacles and said, 'Can I help you, officer?

'Yes you can,' snarled Jack, 'let me have a look at that guest book!'

'Why?' asked the man, guardedly, looking over the top of his spectacles in a suspicious manner.

Jack grabbed the book on the desk and slid it towards himself saying, 'Never you mind!' He looked through the names in the register. There were no recognisable names – not even a Ted and Samantha Smith or Jones. 'What bleedin' names have they checked in under?' the infuriated policeman muttered.

'This is most irregular, officer,' complained the man

behind the counter.

'Shush!' said Jack, sliding the guest book back to the hotel receptionist as he wondered what to do next. He considered knocking on the doors of each room at the hotel, but realised this would get him the sack.

'I'm just using this telephone a minute,' he said, grabbing the handset on the desk. 'How do I get an outside line?'

The hotel clerk tutted and pressed a button on the telephone.

Jack dialled his home telephone number, and bit his lip nervously as it rang. It continued to ring, and after a long twenty seconds he slammed the handset down into the cradle and shook his head. 'I would never have believed she'd do this to me, not in a million years. And I thought Ted was a good 'un – bleedin' whoremaster! Should have known he'd do this; anything with a skirt on will do for him.'

Ted looked down at the counter, closed his eyes, and then he looked up at the receptionist and said. 'You must have seen her – my wife. She's five foot five, 8 stone, almost white blonde hair, pale blue eyes – and she's wearing a gold lamé dress!'

'I haven't seen anyone like that come in here sir,' said the receptionist, 'and I've been on since four yesterday afternoon.'

'She walked in here minutes ago you idiot!' cried Jack, 'You must be walking around with your eyes closed!'

'Please keep your voice down sir, we have guests sleeping here,' said the receptionist in a hushed voice.

'She was with a so-called friend of mine named Ted Cobley – six foot five, black hair, looks like what's his name – The Saint – Roger Moore! He was with her for God's sake!'

'Will you please keep your voice down sir? No, I haven't seen him either.' The receptionist closed the guest book in a huff and Jack lunged across the counter and grabbed him by his tie.

'Are you in on this? Did they slip you a few bob and tell you to say nothing?' the policeman seethed and gritted his teeth, and his face came so near to the hotel clerk, the rim of his helmet struck the man's forehead.

'I'll report you to your seniors! You're mad!' the reception clerk said in a choked voice.

Jack released his grip on the tie and turned to leave the hotel. He continued his beat, and his temper bubbled with each step he took up Lime Street. He passed the Adelphi again at 2am, and this time he saw Sam and Ted in a passionate embrace standing on the grassy traffic island on Lime Street, situated in front of the hotel. Jack could not believe the audacity of the adulterers, and for a moment he thought about bashing their heads in with the truncheon, but he tried his utmost to stay in control. 'The games up, Sam!' he shouted, and he crossed the road and stepped onto the island, but the cheaters seemed oblivious to him as they kissed one another hard as there hands snaked all over the other's body. 'Enough of that!' Jack hurtled himself at Ted Cobley, ready to wrench him from Samantha and throw him into the road, but as the policeman reached out, the couple vanished into thin air. There was a pause of intense silence for a moment as Jack Marshall stood there on that grassy traffic island, looking at the space where two people had stood a moment ago. He heard the distant drunken singing of revellers, and he heard himself swear. 'Where did they go?' he said.

Then Jack noticed a shadowy figure out the corner of his left eye, and he turned quickly to see who it was. It was that vagrant he'd moved on earlier; the grinning tramp who had obstructed him as he went into the Adelphi Hotel. Now he sat grinning nearby in the grass.

'Hey, fog-lamp [old rhyming slang for tramp],' said Jack, 'did you see them disappear then?'

'Better start taking your wife out, eh Jack?' he said. 'All work and no play makes Jack a dull boy,' he added - and then he too vanished, only he faded away slowly, and the policeman heard echoing laughter fade away with the vagrant.

Jack returned to the station and said he felt ill, and he was allowed to go home – where he found Samantha asleep in bed. He also discovered that the telephone had a fault and so his wife had not heard it ring. She'd not left the house that night, and furthermore, when Jack made enquiries about the whereabouts of Ted Cobley on Saturday night, he ascertained that his friend had been in Wales visiting a cousin.

That Sunday morning, Jack Marshall brought his wife breakfast in bed, and he resolved to treat her like a princess for the rest of his life.

'What's brought all this on,' Sam asked him, as he laid the tray of breakfast across her on the bed. 'You feeling okay love?'

Jack nodded and smiled. 'Never felt better. I'm off tonight, love,' he told his wife, 'you can put that new gold lamé dress on and we'll paint the town red.'

THE VAMPS

The following strange story was related to me many years ago. It was Valentine's Day, 1980, and Karl Creighton, a 20-year-old Huyton man, browsed the latest LPs at the Probe Records shop on Button Street, in an area that is now known as the Cavern Quarter, because of the proximity of the world-famous Cavern Club. Shortly after leaving Probe, Karl noticed two women – smartly dressed and both in their mid-twenties - walking behind him. One was a brunette and the other was a brownette with sandy-coloured hair. Karl walked on into Whitechapel, and he looked at the Dolby tape decks and hi-fi systems in the window of a store called Beaver Radio, and in the reflection of the shop window, he noticed the two young ladies he'd seen behind him on Button Street. They were standing about six feet behind him, and seemed to be looking at him, but when he turned to face them the young women quickly averted their gaze and walked a few yards away. Karl was not a bad-looking chap, and from time to time girls did give him a second glance, but he had never been followed by members of the opposite sex. He walked to Woolworths on Church Street, and at first he thought the girls had stopped trailing him, but then he noticed them among the many shoppers milling about in the big store, and now he was certain beyond a shadow of a doubt that he was being followed – it was not paranoia at all – but what did they want? Karl dashed out of Woollies and turned right. Church Street was as busy as ever, and in those days there were stalls dotted about the thoroughfare with crowds gathered around them, so Karl thought he'd easily shake off the stalkers in the sea of people. The young man made his way to Bold Street and kept looking over his shoulder until he reached the House of Holland (a large emporium that stood at 108-112 Bold Street), where he decided that he'd shaken off the tenacious twosome. Karl decided the women had mistaken him for someone, and he went into the House of Holland and looked at a Campari frame tent, as he was into camping. A few minutes later he saw those two women again out the corner of his eye as they passed the window outside. They walked into the store and scanned the shoppers until they saw him looking at them. This really unnerved Karl, and he threaded his way through the shoppers and ran out of the store.

Instead of heading home as dusk gathered late in the afternoon, Karl called at the flat of his mate John Hickey on Roscoe Street, about thirty yards from the Roscoe Head pub. Hickey, an old school friend, answered with a Spanish guitar strung from his shoulder. With his upturned bowl-shaped hairstyle of flaxen blonde and impish grin, he was a dead ringer for Rolling Stone Brian Jones, and he seemed surprised to see Karl standing there. He invited his friend in and Karl told him about the two women who seemed to be following him and how he sensed there was something weird about them.

'Bring them in, man,' said John, in a jokey manner, 'I could do with some birds in my life. I'm like a hermit nowadays.'

'No, seriously John, there's something creepy about them,' said Karl, and he turned the light out in John's living room, crept to the blinds, gently lifted one of the plastic slats an inch and peeped out. The couple who had been shadowing him were standing there in the gloom on the other side of the narrow street, blatantly looking at John Hickey's flat. 'They're out there now!' said Karl, and John came over and asked: 'You been doing drugs or something? Where's all this paranoia coming from?'

'Have a look, go on – ' Karl stepped aside and John took his place and pulled a cord to open the blinds. 'Don't do that!' said Karl. 'They'll know we're on to them.'

It was too late – the blinds opened and allowed anyone in the street to see into the flat. 'They look a bit classy,' opined John, and he popped a cigarette in his mouth and lit it. The girls outside turned away and walked southwards, towards Leece Street. 'You sure you're not doing drugs, Karl,' John said, and exhaled blue smoke, 'only no straight guy in his right mind would be scared of two birds – especially birds like that.'

'Why on earth would they follow me all over the place?' Karl wondered out loud and leaned towards the blinds, trying to see where the mysterious women were going. John went and switched the light on, then sat on a beanbag, strapped a capo to the neck of the guitar and picked a dreamy tune. 'It's called *Serendipity* – an instrumental,' he said, and Karl could see he had obviously taken something from the inane smile on his face; he was in some psychedelic reverie. Karl made a coffee for himself and John, and then, against the wishes of his friend (who wanted to drop acid) he left the flat, and instead of going to the nearest bus stop, Karl decided he'd walk to Lime Street Station and get the train to Huyton, for he felt that those two women would try and get him into a car. Karl never thought he'd be afraid of two females, but he just sensed there was something very uncanny and unearthly about them, and he felt sick in the pit of his stomach. The logical part of Karl's mind thought he was being daft, but his intuition told him not to hang round at a bus stop, and he went with his gut feeling. As he reached the dark and secluded end of Roscoe Street which leads onto Mount Pleasant, he took a sharp left turn – and there, standing between the pillars on the doorstep of Number 66, were those two women!

They dashed from the step and the brunette grabbed Karl's left arm and the brownette seized him by his right forearm. Their grips were like vices, and as Karl tried to escape from their clutches, the brunette's eyes bulged and she said, 'Look at me, Karl!' and she had a slight German accent. Karl noticed her eyes – they were not human, but more like the eyes of a cat – and he found that he could not avert his gaze from the woman. It must have been some form of hypnosis, and he experienced paralysis in his neck. He could not turn his head away from her.

'Walk with us, and realise that you cannot escape,' said the dark-haired beauty, and she smiled – to reveal fangs. Karl immediately realised now that these women were vampires.

'It won't hurt,' the brunette said over and over, as she and the other woman clung on to Karl and led him to a black Transit van. Then there were screams, and

Karl snapped out of the hypnotic spell. He saw an old white-haired man with a large black metal crucifix held by both of his hands, and he was thrusting the cross at the vampires, and they ran to the van and it screeched down Mount Pleasant. The old man said he was a vampire hunter, and Karl pressed him for more information but the man said, 'Get off the streets as soon as possible, and here, take this – do not throw this away!' He handed Karl the large heavy crucifix. 'Sleep with this in your room, young man, every night for the rest of your life!'

'Who are they? Who are you?' Karl asked, shaking and looking about, thinking the female vampires would return in that van.

'Whenever you go outdoors, do not go alone, and wear a crucifix,' said the old man, and he delved into the inside pocket of his jacket and muttered, 'I usually have a spare crucifix but I seem to have mislaid it,' and Karl noticed a holster near the man's left armpit with a pistol in it.

'Are they really vampires?' Karl asked, 'Why are they after me?'

'Your blood must be unusual – must be rare,' said the old man, and his voice sounded weak. 'Get home as fast as you can!'

The man then looked about, then went to a car parked on nearby May Street and drove off.

Karl hurried to Lime Street, and he attracted some strange looks from the other passengers as he sat there clutching that oversized metal crucifix. He lived in mortal fear of those two women, and although he never set eyes on them again, John Hickey said they returned to Roscoe Street that February evening in the black transit van. They remained in the vehicle for about twenty minutes, and when John went outside to ask them if they wanted to come in and have a drink, the van tore off into the night. When John heard about the details of the attempted kidnap of his friend, he shuddered and realised he could have easily been abducted for some fate that did not bare thinking about.

Karl asked his doctor what his blood group was and was told that it was AB negative – one of the rarest blood groups in the world, with only 6% of the UK population having the blood type. Perhaps that is the reason why Karl was targeted, if indeed those women were bona fide vampires. I have a feeling that they *were* vampires of some sort, and I do wonder if they are still prowling about...

THE CARBON COPY PEOPLE

One evening around 6pm in the early summer of 2017, Lucie and Scott, a couple in their late twenties, left their new home on Parkside Drive, West Derby, and walked four hundred yards to their local chippy – the Beijing Palace – on Muirhead Avenue East. As the couple waited to be served, a 19-year-old lady named Kayleigh came into the chippy and tapped Scott on the shoulder. The young man turned, and Kayleigh said, 'Boo!'

A startled Scott shot a puzzled look at the attractive teenager, and his partner of six years Lucie looked at him with mounting suspicion in her narrowing eyes as Scott said, 'Sorry?' to the girl.

Kayleigh patted his bottom, asked, 'How's my adorbs?' then pouted her lips and said: 'Hey, what do you think of my Pink Barbie lipstick?'

'What in god's name is *this?*' gasped a fuming flush-faced Lucie - the "this" being a word she used to refer to Kayleigh. She looked the teen up and down, then grabbed Scott's hand.

'I – I don't know!' Scott replied, his face turning a shade of watermelon pink.

'You *do* know you two-timing 'arl arse!' Kayleigh seethed, and clenched her left fist, and for a moment it looked as if she was going to thump Scott. He raised his arm defensively in a reflex action. Kayleigh was wearing platforms and looked even taller with a huge inside-out ponytail bun on her head.

'I think you're getting me mixed up with someone else, love!' Scott told the irate teen, stepping back from her, and Lucie simultaneously yanked him towards her and faced up to Kayleigh so their noses were only inches apart.

'Your fellah's obviously a cheat!' Kayleigh informed Lucie, and she added: 'He said he was single and he hadn't been with anyone for over a year!'

'What?' Scott asked with a badly-feigned gasp of a chortle. 'I have never seen you before in my life!'

'Never seen me before in your life, eh?' Kayleigh recoiled, and her pink lips smiled but her eyes looked as if they were about to flood, and she lifted her right hand – which held her smartphone. She navigated through the icons and brought up photographs which clearly showed her and Scott hugging in what looked like a club or a pub. 'Well what are these you lying bastard?' Kayleigh asked, and she thrust them into Scott's face for a few seconds, and he said, 'Let's have a look, come on!' but Kayleigh then withdrew the phone and presented it to Lucie. 'He-yar! He's never seen me before in his life!'

Lucie looked numb as she studied the picture of a man who was obviously Scott with the side of his face pressed against the side of Kayleigh's face. Lucie took the phone out of the teenager's hand and she placed her finger and thumb on the touch-screen and zoomed in to see it was, beyond a shadow of a doubt, Scott in that picture. She swiped through the other pictures – about seven in all - and in the last picture Kayleigh was doing something disgusting with Scott. Lucie swore and she said to Scott, 'That *is* you, isn't it?'

To Lucie, he said: 'Giz a look! It can't be me you soft get!' And he reached out to take the phone off her when she screeched: 'That *is* you, isn't it! That is you,

you cheating tw-'

Lucie was interrupted by a woman in her forties queuing to be served at the counter, 'Aye, aye! There's a child here, you foul-mouthed mare!'

'That's not me! It's Photoshopped or something!' claimed Scott, looking at the photo on Kayleigh's phone with wide eyes. 'It's fake!'

Lucie marched out of the shop, and as she got to the door, she turned and shouted to Kayleigh: 'You can have him! Oh, and try and get him a job – he's shit-scared of work!'

'I wouldn't piss on him!' Kayleigh yelled back. 'I've had enough of cheats in the past!'

'Oh my God! The language!' said the woman with the child in the queue.

Scott ran after his partner protesting: 'Lucie! I'm not having an affair you divvy! And who's scared of work, eh? You know I've got chronic sciatica!'

'Hey, give me my phone back!' Kayleigh shouted, and ran after him.

To make matters worse, Lucie fell over as she tried to run off down the street, and landed at the feet of a gang of youths loitering around an off-licence. The members of the gang laughed at her, and Scott helped Lucie to her feet as she burst into tears.

'Ah, you alright?' Kayleigh asked, and she curled her arm around Lucie and walked slowly along with her.

'I'm alright, just in shock,' Lucie told her rival.

Scott was livid at the way the teenaged liar had the sheer audacity to show sympathy to his beloved Lucie after causing this outrageous situation. 'No, she's not alright you lying cow,' Scott erupted. 'I'm going to a solicitor first thing in the morning! This is defamation.'

Kayleigh ignored his ireful outburst and she and Lucie were mumbling something to one another in low voices, and then Scott heard the teenager say something that really got up his nose. Kayleigh looked at Lucie's palm and said, 'Ah, you've skinned your hand. See what he's caused?'

For nearly 400 yards the two females walked on as Scott ranted about legal actions and compensation for psychological damage. Lucie blanked Scott at the house and invited Kayleigh in. Scott found the first aid box in a cupboard in the kitchen and took out a box of plasters and a tube or Germolene antiseptic cream.

'If I'd have known he was with someone – especially someone like you,' Kayleigh told Lucie, 'I wouldn't have gone with him. Joely my mate said he was too old; should have listened to her.'

'Oh my God! Are you still coming out with that shit?' Scott bellowed, and Lucie told him to keep his voice down. The fall had given her a banging headache.

'You don't deserve her,' Kayleigh told Scott, angling her head back and looking down her nose at him as she spoke. 'Men are beasts!' she added.

'Look, love,' Scott leaned on the table where Lucie was seated in the kitchen and said to his partner, 'Those photographs on her phone will be dated – er, what do they call it? Yeah – timestamped, yeah?'

Lucie didn't even look up at him as Kayleigh dabbed her graze with wet warm swabs of cotton wool.

'Now, you know I only go out for a couple of hours every week with me mates, and we'll see if the dates on those photos match. Get what I mean?' Scott asked, his face in Lucie's face now.

'You won't man up, will you?' Kayleigh cut in, 'You're saying I'm a liar, instead of just being a man and owning up. I'm glad you got found out! I'm just sorry for Lucie having someone like you.'

Kayleigh had placed her mobile phone on the table as she tended to Lucie and Scott grabbed it.

'Hey! Giz that here!' Kayleigh reached out for her beloved phone but Scott turned it on and saw that it needed a passcode. Kayleigh swiped it out his hand and swore at him. 'Trying to erase the evidence was ya?' she asked.

'God, you are really annoying!' bawled Scott, and he asked the girl: 'Look, how did I meet you, eh? Can you explain that? Don't say on Tinder, either, because I can predict what your bubblegum brain will say.'

'Yes, how did you meet him?' asked Lucie, putting Germolene on her own palm. Her head pounded from the fall and all the loud arguing.

'See? You're starting to realise this is all a tissue of lies aren't you?' Scott asked Lucie, who again asked Kayleigh how she had met Scott.

To Scott, Kayleigh said, 'I met you at the Heebie Jeebies in March; stop trying to keep this pretence up!' The girl then fidgeted with her false eyelash.

When Scott asked her to name the dates of 'the romantic rendezvous' (as he called them), Kayleigh said the last time she had seen Scott had been last Saturday, around a quarter past nine in the evening in the Dispensary pub on Renshaw Street.

'Ha! I've caught you out!' Scott said excitedly, and punched the air above him with his fist twice. 'I was at home with Lucie last Saturday! Lying cow, lying cow!'

'Yes, he was,' Lucie told Kayleigh, 'he was skint and

I had a bad headache. We stayed in.'

'Unless it was the Saturday before that – ' Kayleigh murmured to herself, and then she started tapping her phone's screen. 'I've got a witness, hang on.' She put the smartphone to her ear.

Lucie and Scott could hear a faint ringing tone emanating from it.

'What?' said a squeaky female voice on Kayleigh's phone.

'Joely, were we in the Dispensary pub last Saturday or was it the week before?' Kayleigh asked her friend, and then she said to Lucie, 'I'll just put it on speakerphone so you can hear her.'

'Where's that?' asked Joely.

'That pub on Renshaw Street,' Kayleigh reminded her.

There was a pause.

Kayleigh impatiently sighed and jogger her friend's memory. 'Joely, the pub where that 'arl fellah who was around forty asked you if you was pregnant; remember?'

'He asked if *you* were pregnant Kayleigh, not me – ' Joely started to recall the pub in question.

'Oh God, whatever – Joely – what night was that? Was that last Saturday? You remember that lad I'm going with – Scott – don't you?'

'Yeah, the one with the big nose,' said Joely, and Lucie smirked and Scott scowled. Joely continued her recollection: 'I remember it dead clear because I started coming on and – ' the girl was saying when Kayleigh cut her reminiscences short.

'Joely shut up there's people here. I'll call you later.' Kayleigh hung up as her friend was asking who the people were.

'So,' said Scott with a smug smile, 'case squashed! It *was* last Saturday, and you got it all wrong, and you have accused me of all sorts and really upset my fiancée. That fellah you've been seeing *does* look like me, I'll give you that, but it wasn't me, and I don't want to see you ever again, have you got that?'

'Scott, stop it!' Lucie reprimanded him and asked Kayleigh if she had the phone number of Scott's 'double'. The girl's eyebrows rose and she gave a succession of dynamic nods as she found the number, assigned to the nickname "Adorbs" (derived from adorable). She called it – and the Z Cars ringtone played on the iPhone in Scott's trouser pocket. He looked at his phone, and there upon the screen, it said the caller was "unknown".

'How do you explain *that?*' Kayleigh asked with a lopsided smile.

Scott dismissed the call on his iPhone and looked at Lucie. She saw fear and confusion in his eyes, and somehow she knew deep down that Scott was not some two-timer. He himself had been cheated on in the past by a girlfriend and he had always said he hated people who cheated on their partners. Lucie told Kayleigh to sit down. She asked the girl how long she had been going with the man who looked like Scott, and eventually, Lucie became convinced that Scott could not be that person in the photos. Kayleigh said she'd had sex with Scott after a night out on St Patrick's Day, and the teen even recalled it had been a Friday – but on that memorable day, Lucie had been with Scott at a pub in Walton with her father, who was Irish born. Scott kept looking at the alleged photographs depicting him with Kayleigh when he noticed something very telling – the Scott in the pictures was missing a tattoo on his forearm in one snap. Scott, who supported Everton, had a tattoo of the team's emblem – Prince Rupert's Tower (also known as the Everton Lock-Up) on the ventral side of his forearm. That tattoo was faded now because Scott had it done when he was 19, and now he was 28. Scott eventually realised that Kayleigh had been the victim of some bizarre deception, and as it became clear that something very strange was going on, Kayleigh was naturally spooked. Who would go to such lengths to pretend to be someone else, and to even know the number of that person's mobile phone? It went far beyond a normal joke, and Lucie and Scott racked their minds trying to think of any pranksters they knew who could even perpetrate such a joke, but they knew of no one who could go to such lengths. The person would have to have an uncanny likeness to Scott, and Scott and Lucie knew of no such person. Lucie thought the whole thing smacked of something supernatural, whereas her fiancé believed someone he knew had gone to an awful lot of trouble to cause a rift between him and Lucie. Scott, Lucie and Kayleigh went back to the Beijing Palace, and Lucie paid for the meals. They then returned to the house on Parkside Drive and Kayleigh asked Scott if he had a twin or some cousin who looked like him.

'No,' said Scott, 'I've got two sisters, no brothers, and none of my cousins could be mistaken for me.' He turned to Lucie and said, 'You've met my cousins – do any of them look like me?'

Lucie shook her head, and as she started to dig her

fork into the meal from the chippy, she voiced her nagging suspicion that there was something *eerie* about the whole affair. Kayleigh seemed very nervous, and she asked Lucie to elaborate on her remark.

'I don't know, but I've read about these things called doppelgangers,' she said, and her voice was very low and almost a whisper.

'What are they?' Kayleigh asked.

Scott was also intrigued by Lucie's mention of the strange word, and he leaned on his elbows towards her at the table.

Lucie gave a little cough and said: 'They're supposed to be like weird doubles of people that have been seen over the years, like twins, and they used to say that if you meet your own double it's bad luck, or even death, like within a year I think.'

'Death?' Scott asked with a look of intense concern on his face. 'It gets better and better this.'

'Well, it's not always death,' said Lucie, 'people have met their own doppelgänger and lived. There was a famous person – I can't remember his name now – and he actually met his own double – came face to face with him, but he lived.'

'What *are* they though?' Kayleigh asked, and her pink lips formed a perfect o-shape.

'I haven't a clue, Kayleigh, but so many people have seen them down the years, and they can't all be lying,' Lucie replied, 'but I've read that sometimes these twins are evil, and they try to take over the life of the person they're imitating or sort of try to put the boot in.'

'You saying these doppelgangers are ghosts or spirits?' Scott asked his partner.

Lucie lifted her shoulders and eyebrows, shrugging at

the question. 'As I say, I don't know what they are, but people have seen them for hundreds of years. I think even Joan of Arc had one. They might be evil spirits, who knows?'

'Oh God, I just got a weird chilly shudder thing then, like someone walked over my grave,' said Kayleigh.

'This isn't some evil spirit pretending to be me,' said Scott with a dismissive shake of his head, 'it's some arsehole playing a joke.'

'Scott, he's gone to an awful lot of trouble hasn't he?' said Lucie, duffing up her boyfriend's theory. 'He's led this girl on here for four months, had his - well – *had his way* with her.' Lucie grasped Kayleigh's hand as she said the latter. She continued: 'And Scott, you've seen him in her photos – he looks the spit of you. Unless this fellah knows a Hollywood plastic surgeon, there's no way anyone pulling off a prank could make themselves look like someone to such a degree. I'm telling you, I have a *bad* feeling about this.'

'You're really scaring me now,' Kayleigh confessed to Lucie, 'what if *he* gets back in touch again?'

'Kayleigh, there's nothing supernatural about this,' Scott reassured her. 'It's some joker, and he's probably got a look of me, but he wasn't clever enough to get the same type of tattoo I've got. He wasn't that good, was he?'

'If he calls you, don't answer,' Lucie advised Kayleigh, 'and call me if you want. I'd love to get to the bottom of this.'

'Could yous walk me back to ours later?' Kayleigh asked the couple, 'Only I'm really scared at the moment. I hate anything like that – ghosts and all that.'

'Yeah, we'll walk you home – where do you live?' said Lucie.

'Down Broad Lane,' replied Kayleigh, and with great appreciation in her voice, she said 'Ah thanks.'

After the three of them had eaten their chippy meals, Lucie and Scott walked the frightened girl to her home, and then they headed homewards, and a full moon had risen upon this warm evening. Lucie looked about, and she told Scott she had the feeling someone was watching them.

'Oh don't start all that,' Scott sighed and rolled his eyes but Lucie grabbed his hand and held it tightly and she started to walk a little faster.

'There's something weird hanging in the air tonight, Scott,' said Lucie, her eyes darting about as she looked into the shadows beneath every tree on Parkside Drive. 'Don't ask me how I know, I just do,' she went on, 'and I think that doppelgänger knows we're on to it.'

Scott deliberately slowed down and tugged on his girlfriend's arm to break her out of what he saw as paranoia. 'Lucie will you please put a sock in it?' It's only ten o'clock and it's only just gone dark. This thing has taken over your mind. It's someone arsing around – someone we're overlooking – and if he knew you were like this he'd be getting his rocks off. Now stop all this supernatural nonsense, please.'

'Don't tell me to try and change my mood,' said Lucie, and she shook her hand from his hand and marched on. And as she and Scott reached the junction where Glentrees Road meets Parkside Drive, they saw a man, almost in silhouette with his back against the moon on the horizon, approaching from the Meadow Lane end of the road. He was laughing, and he held both hands over his face. He was wearing a camouflage patterned Hollister tee shirt, a pair of dark skinny jeans, and a pair of Converse boots – and when this laughing man covering his face with his hands passed by, Lucie could see he had the same shaped head, same build and wore the same clothes as Scott. Lucie even detected a zingy whiff of Hugo Boss Tonic which wafted from that uncanny double – the very same Eau de Toilette Scott had a habit of wearing. Scott could also see the startling similarity the man bore to himself, and immediately he thought of that doppelgänger Lucie had been talking about. The passing figure really scared Scott, but Lucie clutched her fiancé's hand and whispered: 'Scott! That's him! Oh my God! It's him!'

The lookalike took his hands from his face now that he had passed the couple but he didn't look back. He walked on down the moonlit street.

'Let's follow him – see where he goes!' Lucie said, dragging Scott after her.

'No bleedin' way!' Scott dragged the soles of his trainers across the pavement and resisted her manic pursuit of the unearthly man. 'He might just be some fellah who just looks and dresses like me Lucie; get a grip and let it go will you?'

'You're terrified, aren't you?' she hissed at Scott. 'We've got a chance now to get to the bottom of this – come on!' She pulled him along as the figure strolled on fifty yards away, heading in the direction of Muirhead Avenue East.

'I admit it's a bottle job,' said Scott, offering resistance, 'yes, my bottle has actually gone, but I don't care what you think, Lucie; these kind of things should be left well alone. It goes against Our Lord all this.'

'Well stay there then, Scott,' she said, letting go of his hand again. 'These things can't hurt you, only the living can do that.'

'Lucie, you really need to go and have a word with yourself!' Scott yawped and hurried after her. He overtook her and tried to reason with her. 'Luce, you don't even know what this thing is - now come home with me, come on, let's go back.'

She ignored him and followed the eerily familiar figure in the distance. It turned right and went onto Muirhead Avenue East, heading north. By the time Lucie got to the corner at the end of her road she was out of breath and she couldn't see the alleged doppelgänger – but Scott, who had excellent eyesight – said he could see the figure passing the Beijing Palace chippy.

An annoyed and unnerved Scott said: 'Lucie I know you're touchy about your weight, girl, but you're already out of breath – leave it!' And the moment he had uttered these words, Scott regretted saying them and tried to back-pedal. 'I don't mean weight, I mean your health.'

The remark about her weight really hurt Lucie and she ignored his advice and trotted after the sinister twin, puffing and panting with Scott running beside her, and that gang of youths that had laughed when Lucie had fallen a few hours ago were still outside the off-licence and they cheered when they saw her trying to run and one of them flicked the stub of his lit cigarette at her and missed her head by inches.

'He's crossed over,' said Scott. 'He's going down

Stalisfield Avenue. We'll never catch up with him; he's moving as if he's on wheels.'

And Scott was right; by the time he and Lucie had reached the corner of Stalisfield Avenue, they'd lost sight of the unearthly replica. Lucie reluctantly gave up the chase, but still hurting from the remark Scott had made about her weight, she never said a word to him until they got home.

The encounter with the apparent doppelgänger really shook Scott, and he did what a lot of people do when they encounter something beyond the edge of human understanding – he tried to rationalise the thing and translate it into mundane terms. He brought up his weak theory about the whole thing being someone's joke and he even suggested Kayleigh was in on the hoax. Lucie, in the meantime, was reading up on the subject of doppelgangers from the internet, and she even emailed me for advice. I told her that the doppelgänger phenomenon was on the increase locally and internationally but the doubles – whatever they were – rarely attacked anyone or caused any physical harm and were usually short-lived. Lucie said she'd try and get a photo of the possible doppelgänger and that she'd also get back to me if things got any weirder.

On the following Saturday, around 1pm, Lucie and Scott were in Basnett Street in the City Centre, sitting outside Sayers eating doughnuts and drinking coffee, and Lucie was contemplating on whether she should go to Liverpool One when her mobile vibrated in her pocket. She took it out, saw Kayleigh was calling, and quickly answered the call.

'Lucie?' Kayleigh asked, and then she started talking but her voice was drowned out by what sounded like a lorry rumbling past.

'Can you say that again Kayleigh?' Lucie asked, and Scott looked at his partner with some trepidation upon the mention of the teenager's name.

'I've just seen him in like some café on Bold Street, and he's with some other girl,' Kayleigh said, but the rest was unintelligible because of traffic noise on Bold Street.

'We're in town, Kayleigh,' said Lucie, 'are you still on Bold Street?'

'Yeah, I'm with Joely,' said Kayleigh and then Lucie's phone emitted a 'lost call' succession of bleeps.

'God! I hate this phone!' Lucie said and pressed the call back button, but got an engaged tone, as Kayleigh was calling her at the same time. Lucie tried to call the teen again and this time she answered. 'Kayleigh, stay there, we'll be over in a few minutes!'

'Hang on a mo, Lucie, Scott's definitely with you now?' Kayleigh asked.

'Yes, it's definitely him I hope.' Lucie replied, trying to make a little light of the scary situation, and as Scott rolled his eyes and moaned about going to Bold Street, Lucie asked the girl: 'Where about are you Kay? By the top of Boldy or the bottom?'

'Er, it's hard to describe,' said Kayleigh, 'I'll ask Joely, she knows round here.'

Scott, who held his ear close to Lucie's mobile phone whispered, 'How can you not know if you're at the top of a street or the bottom?'

Joely came on the phone and said the place where "the other Scott" was sitting was in a Peruvian restaurant next door to Raggas and facing the tandoori restaurant A Passage to India.

Still clutching a doughnut, Scott set off for Bold Street with Lucie, and he complained throughout that whole 600 yards (the distance to the Peruvian restaurant) and kept saying that he and Lucie would get nicked for stalking on the say so of a teenaged "scatterbrained ditz". When the couple finally met up with Kayleigh and Joely, who were standing under the awning of Matta's food store, Kayleigh led them to the window of the Chicha Peruvian Street Kitchen. 'He's gone,' said Kayleigh, pointing to the empty seat at a window table where a girl with blonde curly hair was sitting. The latter was eyeing Lucie, Kayleigh, Joely and Scott with a curious look as the teenager pointed at her. 'He was sitting talking with her and holding her hand,' said Kayleigh.

'And kissing her hand as well,' added Joely.

'Did you see him come out of this place?' Scott asked Kayleigh and the girl shook her head.

'He might have gone to the toilet,' said Lucie, and she walked into the vestibule area and pulled the doors open and said, 'Come on, let's go in and wait for him to come back.'

'No, let's wait by the window and see if he comes back,' suggested a plainly scared Scott.

Kayleigh and Joely walked in with Lucie, who went to the blonde girl sitting at the table. 'Excuse me love, has your fellah gone to the loo?' Lucie asked the girl, who was naturally taken aback by the peculiar and probing question.

'Why, who are you?' the young lady asked, with her knife and fork poised over her dish of what looked like haddock and some risotto.

'Is his name Scott?' asked Kayleigh, and then, as the

seated female's eyes widened with surprise at the mention of the name, Joely chipped in and said: 'And does he look like him?' Joely pointed at Scott, who was standing in the doorway. He tried to smile at the girlfriend of his alter ego but produced a crooked grin. He glanced at the half-eaten meal on the table where a living reproduction of him had sat minutes ago. He just wanted to run out of the place, he was that scared.

After a pause, the lady sitting at the table asked Scott: 'Are you Scott's twin?'

'No, his doppelgänger,' said Joely in a haughty manner, almost as if the confused woman should know about the supernatural twin.

One of the staff at the restaurant came over and Lucie pre-emptively said, 'I'll book a table for four now; I'm just going to the toilet first,' and she set off for the toilets, but she rushed into the gents. Moments later she came running out of the toilet, and bolted out of the Peruvian restaurant with Scott and the teenaged girls chasing her.

'What happened?' asked Scott, catching up with Lucie and seizing her by the arm.

'He was just standing there, and he had no face,' Lucie gasped, out of breath from the short run from the restaurant, 'just nothing Scott, just skin where his face should have been.'

'Ew, let's go and have a look!' Joely said to Kayleigh, but Lucie shouted, 'No! Please don't go back! That thing's evil! Scott's right, I should have listened. Oh God I feel sick. That face...'

'Come on,' Joely whispered and smiled to Kayleigh as she slipped away and went back to the restaurant.

'Joely you divvy, no!' her friend yelled after her, but

the girl sprinted to the doorway of the Peruvian restaurant and went in.

'Don't go after her Kayleigh,' Lucie pleaded, and a few minutes later Joely returned and said, 'He's gone, and that woman as well.'

'Let's go home,' Lucie said to Scott, and they walked up Bold Street with Kayleigh and Joely and a taxi was hailed on Berry Street.

Since that sunny afternoon, Scott and Lucie have lived in fear of the doppelgänger, but so far, it has not been reported to the couple and Kayleigh has not seen it either. What scared the 19-year-old most was the fact that she had sex with the thing, and when she explained the situation to her mother, she was told that Scott had cooked up the whole 'cock and bull story' after Lucie had found him out, but of course, Kayleigh knew this certainly wasn't the case at all, and like Lucie and Scott, she feels her stomach turn over every time she sees anyone with more than a passing resemblance to Scott.

I've investigated quite a few doppelgänger cases over the years, and while some have probably been down to nothing more than people who happen to be the spitting image of one another, there have been cases, such as the previous one, which are very difficult to explain, but the doppelgänger is usually at an advantage because people simply cannot believe that these sinister impostors are real, and so they often remain at large because people assume they actually are the person they are impersonating. Are they extraterrestrial in origin or perhaps from some other dimension? It's impossible to say. Thousands of illegal immigrants enter the UK each year because we simply don't have the technology to detect them when they are smuggled into the country in lorries, so you can imagine how powerless we'd be if higher intelligences wanted to slip into our world from somewhere else – we simply wouldn't know about it until, perhaps, they tried to blend into our society by copying the identities and physical likenesses of everyday human beings. There are many more files about these carbon copy people in my archives, and here's another one of these creepy but intriguing cases. This strange story was told to me many years ago by a prominent theatre director. I have had to change a few names for legal reasons. In the 1960s, Jeremy Richards, a Huyton-born artistic director of a well-known theatre in Liverpool – was looking for a certain type of actor to play the rôles of three separate characters in a very expensive production, and so, auditions were held at the Hope Street offices of Mr Richards, and one particular actor really impressed the latter; his name was Jonathan Gladwin, and he seemed to become the three separate characters during the auditions. Gladwin's voice underwent incredible changes so that he spoke in a Glaswegian accent one moment, and effected the upper crust voice of an aristocratic lord the next, and then he narrated an amazing 'duologue' between a cockney barrow boy and a plummy-voiced duchess.

Gladwin, however, turned out to be very temperamental and he also had a drink problem. He was caught drinking neat whiskey which he had poured into a yellow-tinted bottle of Lucozade during rehearsals, and when Jeremy Richards warned the thespian that no alcohol was allowed in his company until after the shows, Gladwin ranted on about whiskey deriving its name from the word *usquebaugh* - the Gaelic for "water of life", and eventually his drunken behaviour became so unruly, Jeremy Richards had no alternative but to fire him. A less talented actor named Stephen Bangarth replaced Gladwin, and after the nerve-jangling opening night of the new play, Jeremy Richards and the theatre's company of actors did a curtain call, and as they stood in a line on the stage, they enjoyed thunderous applause from the audience, followed by a standing ovation. Jeremy and most of the actors later left the theatre on a high and celebrated at the Philharmonic pub – where a stranger walked up to Jeremy and yelled, 'Stay away from my wife!' before knocking him clean out. One of the actors of the company, a man named Gerald Fairspear, ran out of the pub, seized the assailant in a headlock and dragged him back into the bar, where Jeremy was regaining consciousness in the arms of two actresses. The restrained man who had KO'd the director growled: 'I'm not a violent man, but I saw him making love to my wife in a car in the drive of my house! He's lucky I didn't shoot him!'

'And when was this?' Jeremy asked, getting to his feet as he rubbed his jaw.

'The night before last!' said the enraged husband, whose name turned out to be Ted Wallis.

'Then you have the wrong man! I have been in rehearsals with these actors every evening for the past week,' replied Jeremy, 'And they will all vouch for me! How dare you accuse me of having an affair with your wife!'

Mr Wallis was released by Fairspear, who stood between him and Jeremy. The husband fumed: 'I saw you with my own eyes before you threw my missus out the car and drove off! When I finally got your name out of the wife, I recognised your photo in the newspaper!'

'Then someone is playing a joke on you, and perhaps they gave my name because the blackguard resembles me!' Jeremy retorted.

'Oh for Heaven's sake! Just be a man and admit to it!' Mr Wallis lunged forward but Fairspear and another stocky actor grappled with the irate man and slung him out the door.

'Any more carrying on with my wife and I swear to God I'll empty the barrels of a shotgun into your brains!' Mr Wallis promised.

'Go on! Beat it!' Gerald Fairspear shouted at Wallis and closed the pub door on him.

'How extraordinary,' Jeremy said with a faint smile, 'talk about mistaken identity,' he went on, and the barman gave him a large brandy on the house to treat his shock. On the following morning at eleven, Jeremy telephoned his friend – the famous actor Rex Harrison (a fellow Huytonian), enquiring whether he would be available for a musical he had in mind – when there was a heavy knocking at the door of his Cressington home. It was a detective and a constable. The detective was following up reports of a serious shoplifting incident at a well-known department store in Liverpool – and many witnesses – including a policeman and a certain professional gentleman – had identified the thief as none other than Jeremy Richards. 'But I haven't left the house once this morning,' Jeremy protested, 'and who is this professional gentleman who says he saw me shoplifting?'

'Your former doctor, sir, Mr Quarritch,' the detective replied, adding, 'and there were six other people who saw you in the store as well.'

Jeremy had talked to the newspaper delivery boy at 8am, and his milkman, and his star witness – the former judge who was his next-door neighbour – had seen Jeremy smoking his pipe on his doorstep around 10am – when his lookalike was shoplifting in town. No charges were brought, and Jeremy wondered who was setting him up – first as an adulterer, and now as a shoplifter; the person would have to be a good impersonator...or a gifted *actor*. It *had* to be the actor he had dismissed from the play – Jonathan Gladwin! He had a very uncanny knack for imitating people. He'd obviously donned a wig and used make up, and dressed just like Jeremy – and he could replicate anyone's voice. Yes, it all made sense now – the disgruntled actor was getting his own back for being sacked. The last Jeremy had heard of Gladwin, he was living in digs over a shop on Renshaw Street, but no one in the acting company could trace the spiteful performer. Days later, on Valentine's Day, the mysterious person mimicking Jeremy Richards proposed to two former girlfriends of Jeremy at different restaurants on the same evening, and these two women had said 'Yes' – and now each of them refused to believe Jeremy's far-fetched tale of the twisted imposter out for revenge. Each of the girls threw their rings at Jeremy and turned the air blue with insults. The infuriating impersonator even withdrew a large sum of money out of Jeremy's bank, and so now it was a matter for the police. But the police discovered that the suspect – Jonathan Gladwin – had moved to Edinburgh days after being sacked by Jeremy – where he had been arrested three times for being drunk and disorderly, and he had not travelled back to England since. A week later, Jeremy returned from an evening stroll, and was at the gate of his Cressington house, when a familiar voice asked: 'Excuse me sir, is it 8pm yet?'

Jeremy turned – and came face to face with his exact double – same face, same build, even the same clothes, only the skin seemed a shade darker, and rather off colour – but otherwise it was the mirror image of Jeremy. The director hurried down the garden path to his home and fumbled with the ring of keys, trying to find the one to the front door. He heard deep laughter approaching from behind as he looked for the key, but he did not turn around. He unlocked the door, barged into the house, then slammed the door behind him and bolted it. As he turned the key in the mortice lock he could see a distorted, mottled image of his own face as it looked through the pane of Aquatex glass set into the door.

'Leave me alone!' Jeremy shouted.

The misshapen face came close to the rippled-pattern glass and Jeremy could see the undulating eyes of his twin from beyond, gazing in at him. He backed away from the door and fell when the heel counter of his brogue hit the bottom step of his stairs. He got up and listened to the footsteps of his menacing double walking away, and after that evening, Jeremy Richards never saw or heard from that creepy imposter again.

If someone should tell you that they saw your double in town, the chances are that it was exactly that – just a person who looks like you – but also consider the possibility that *something* might just be using your likeness as a mask as it goes about its sinister agenda. Doppelgänger incidents are on the rise, and – heaven forbid – it might only be a matter of time before one of these conniving copycats copies *you*...

VANISHING DEBRA

I've changed a few names, but the rest of this weird story is exactly how it was reported to me from two separate sources, and it suggests to me that some higher intelligences occasionally alter the parameters of our reality, to teach us a moral lesson or simply to amuse themselves. In August 1974, a 31-year-old DJ, Doug Greenking, set eyes on a beautiful 22-year-old redhead named Debra McDonald as she danced her heart out at the Moonstone club in St John's Precinct. The song Debra was dancing to could have been written especially for her: *Queen of Clubs* by KC and the Sunshine Band, as like the character of the song, Debra was very popular on the club scene, known by everyone and admired by many, and she lapped it up; she really did thrive on attention, especially from hot-blooded males. Doug introduced himself to Debra as he took a brief break from spinning discs and she also took a short rest from her energetic dancing as she stood at the bar. All the men were gathered around her and offering to buy her drinks but Debra only let Doug the DJ buy her half a pint of lager and lime. Doug took her to a relatively quiet corner of the club to talk, and during the conversation he learned that Debra was still living with her parents and was not working, but was trying her utmost to get into modelling. She was also thinking about forming an all-female dancing troupe similar to Pan's People which she'd call Eve's Apple. Doug said he knew a few agents who represented models and that he'd have a word with some of them to see if they'd be willing to have Debra on their books. Well, this promise did it. Straight away, Doug was Debra's boyfriend and she moved into his flat in Hartsbourne Heights. The DJ soon discovered that Debra had a very vain side, and she often told him she was the most beautiful girl in Liverpool. Often, as she dozed off next to him in his bed at night, Doug would hear Debra mutter: 'I'm popular,' over and over. Every time Doug and Debra were at the movies or watching TV, Debra would point to any young girl who came on the screen, either in the film or programme or even in the advertisements and she would invariably ask him, 'Is she better-looking than me?'

More than often, Doug would say, 'No, you're the most beautiful girl in Liverpool,' but one evening in September of that year he got fed up of her vanity and when his girlfriend saw the actress Madeline Smith in an episode of *Steptoe and Son* on the telly, she asked Doug: 'Do you think she's better-looking than me?'

'Yes, I do, to be honest,' Doug replied.

'What?' Debra seemed to freeze for a moment, and then she grabbed Doug by his arm and said: 'You're just saying that because you've got a cob on over something. What's up with you?'

Doug shook his head gently and faced Debra to tell her what was 'up' with him. 'Debra, I'm sorry but you have a bleedin' superiority complex regarding other girls. Everyone's noticed it as well.'

'What *are* you talking about? What complex?' she asked, and Doug could see that she really didn't get it.

'Every time we see some woman – even Marilyn Monroe or – who was it last time?' He fought to recall the actress's name. 'Brigitte Bardot! Yes, Brigitte Bardot – and you said you were more beautiful than her. Debra, you're not plain or ugly and you *are* really pretty girl, but you have this self-inflated idea that you're some absolutely stunning siren of the silver screen – and I hate to break the news to you – but you're not!'

'Well I know I am, and if you can't see that I am, what are you with me for?' she asked, letting go of his arm, and Doug could see her eyes glistening, ready to cry.

'I am with you, Debra, because I happen to love you, and believe it or not, if Brigitte Bardot or Sylvia Kristel made a pass at me I'd tell them where to go.'

'But you said I was the loveliest girl in the world,' Debra told him in a faltering voice, 'and now you're saying I'm not.'

'No, Debra *you* said you were the loveliest girl in the world, and they say beauty is in the eye of the beholder.'

'Well I won't even ask for your opinion from now on,' Debra decreed, and she clenched her teeth, closed her eyes, and seemed to be holding back a flood of tears for a moment. Out of her choked-up throat she managed to say, 'As long as I know I'm the best, that's all that counts.'

She left the living room, slamming the door behind her, and about a minute after this, Doug went to see where she was. He found her in bed with her eyes closed, pretending to be asleep, but her eyelids flickered and her eyebrows twitched now and then as he went into a long lecture on how she should be more modest and less catty and bitchy about other girls who were also pretty. At the end of his diatribe he stripped down to his Y-fronts and tried to hold her but she elbowed him and said, 'Get off.'

In the end, Doug gave up, turned the air blue in the bedroom, and turned away from her so that there was a gap between them. There was a heavy downpour outside and the drumming of the rain on the roof had a calming effect on Debra, and she dozed off. She awoke at around 3.40am to the sound of jingling bells, and her immediate thought was that the sounds were coming from a radio, as Doug often slept with the radio on, but the young lady soon learned that this was not the case at all. Debra happened to look over towards her right, and she saw what looked like the head of a grinning man in a jester's cap, hovering in the air.

'Oh God!' she cried, and she slid towards Doug and shook his shoulder, but he didn't even react.

The disembodied head of the jester was glowing with a pale blue light, and the eyes were very sinister; they had pinhole- sized pupils, and the mouth of the apparition opened as it said something in what sounded like a very effeminate voice. The exact wording was: 'They'll all forget you soon Debra!'

Debra screamed and almost pushed Doug out of the bed as she shook him hard.

In an echoing voice, the creepy head said; 'Bye-bye-bye-bye-bye-bye..' and it kept repeating the word until faded away.

Doug let out a load groan and said, 'What is it? Talking to me now are you?'

'Oh Doug, I think I just saw the Devil! Doug!' Debra climbed over him and got out of the bed to turn on the ceiling light. She looked back at the space in mid air where the head with the jester's hat had hovered. She told Doug what she had seen and what the thing had said, and he simply yawned, punched his pillow, and said: 'Debra, you've just had a nightmare. Go back to bed.'

'I was not asleep, Doug,' Debra told him, with her eyes fixed on that point in the air where the chilling head had uttered those strange words about everyone forgetting her.

'Debra, your biggest fear is people not acknowledging you because you're so vain, and that is why you've had the nightmare. I'm not bleedin' Sigmund Freud but that's what it'll be; now get back in bed!'

'Can I sleep your side then?' Debra asked Doug, 'and you can sleep on my side.'

'Oh for God's sake Debra!' Doug lifted the blanket and rolled to the other side of the bed, and Debra switched the light out, then almost threw herself into the bed. She clung onto Doug throughout the night and until she managed to doze off, she kept daring herself to open one eye to take a look at the very spot above the bed where she had seen what could have only been some ghost.

The next day, Debra spent over an hour putting on her make-up, and wore a very revealing outfit, then went to the bank to make a withdrawal from the joint account Doug had set up, but no one gave her a second glance, and she stood in the bank queue for ages, and when it was her turn, the teller pulled the blind down. Debra complained, and the teller said he had not noticed her standing there. She then walked across Dale Street, and a bus almost ran over her. She ran to the bus in question and pounded her fist on the vehicle's door and called the driver a lunatic, but he simply said, 'Sorry love, I didn't even see you!'

She went into Lewis's, and waited to be served – but again, she wasn't noticed and had to wave her hands in front of the lady at the perfume counter to get her attention. 'Are you blind?' Debra asked the lady. 'Only I have been standing here for ages and you've been looking through me as if was invisible. Is it because of this outfit eh? Bit of jealousy eh?'

'I didn't see you!' the woman behind the counter retorted loudly, and added: 'I am certainly not envious of *you* dear!'

Debra went to the bus stop on Brownlow Hill, and when the bus approached she put her hand out – but the vehicle went straight past her. She decided to hail a taxi, but three hackney cabs with their 'for hire' lights on went straight past her, and in the end, Debra had to ask a woman to flag a cab down for her. When the cab was approaching the block of flats in Childwall where Debra was living, she shouted to the driver, 'This is it!'

The taxi driver seemed to be in a world of his own, and Debra repeatedly yelled, 'Hey, stop here!' until he finally heard her. 'Are you deaf?' she asked him, and the driver said: 'You were whispering love, speak up next time.'

That evening Debra was out with Doug and his friends in town at a pub called The Sefton on Cases

Street, just across the road from Central Station. At one point, as Doug was about to go to the toilet, he handed Debra some money and asked her to get a round in. Debra stood there at the bar in a bright red top, waving at the barman, but he didn't seem to notice Debra and served people who had just come into the pub. Debra shouted at the barman and even waved a fiver at him, but he did not look her way. When Doug came out of the toilet he was surprised to see that Debra was still trying to get served. Doug raised his hand and the barman immediately looked at him and said, 'What can I get you lad?'

Debra later pulled Doug aside and told him she thought that she had somehow been cursed by that thing that had appeared in their bedroom.

'Oh don't talk daft, Deb,' said Doug, lighting a Woodbine.

'Doug I'm telling you, it said "They'll all forget you soon Debra," that's what it said, and I feel as if I'm becoming invisible Doug. Am I being stupid?'

'Very stupid, Debra, now let's have no more talk about that nightmare,' said Doug, and he kissed her cheek, then said: 'so go and sit down with all our friends and let's just enjoy tonight. I don't get many nights off like this.'

Debra sat down at the big round table around which all of Doug's friends were seated, and she tried to get in on the conversation, but no one listened to her – even Doug. This scared Debra a little – it was as if she wasn't there. She was only too glad when she and Doug went home.

Doug's mum passed him and Debra on the following morning and she asked her son, 'How's

Debra?'

'Er, why don't you ask me?' Debra asked Doug's mother, 'I'm here!'

'She's alright mum,' said Doug, 'we're thinking of tying the knot around the beginning of next March.'

'Er, excuse me – ' Debra tried to butt in to the conversation.

'Ooh, don't marry in Lent, lad,' said Doug's mum, 'marry in Lent and you'll live to repent.'

The conversation went on for a few more minutes and then Doug walked on with Debra, who was furious at his mother for not even acknowledging that she was there. 'Are you listening to me Doug?' she fumed at her boyfriend, 'Or are you as pig ignorant as your mother?'

Doug whistled a tune and walked on.

More and more people started to ignore Debra, and one morning as she was walking up Renshaw Street, an old female vagrant grabbed her hand, and said: 'I was like you once – life and soul of the party, until *he* played a trick on me.'

'Who played a trick on you?' asked Debra, but the old woman walked away without a reply, and Debra could hear her sobbing. She told Doug about the old woman, but he didn't even reply. Debra almost had a nervous breakdown, and she walked out of the flat and wandered the streets, unsure what to do in this unearthly predicament. As she passed under the railway bridge on Childwall Valley Road, there was a terrific downpour, and lightning flashed and thunder rumbled in the grey low-lying clouds. Debra stood there, taking shelter from the pelting rain when she heard the voice of that ghost that had appeared over her bed. It said, 'Debra, Debra you're nobody now; nobody even knows that you're there; nobody cares a fig if you just shrivel up and die.'

'Go away!' Debra cried, looking around in the gloom beneath the bridge, but she could see no one.

The eerie voice somewhere close said: 'Debra, Debra you might as well die, and no one will cry as you're such a small fry.'

'Go away!' she squalled, 'Get away from me! I know you're the Devil!'

'Oh Debra, Debra they won't notice you, unless you do what I tell you to do!'

'Leave me alone!' she screamed and pressed her hands over her ears, but her words were drowned out by the mighty crash of thunder which shook the bridge and made its riveted metal plates ring like a deep-toned gong.

'Debra, Debra cut throats with a knife, and I promise you dear you'll be noticed alright!'

'No!' she screamed, palms still pressed against her ears.

A knife about fifteen inches in length appeared in mid air, and it had a long black handle and the blade was bluish grey.

Debra ran from under the bridge and she raced through the penetrating rain which felt as if it was drilling holes in her head, and she kept running through the sizzling lightning flashes and the thunder which made her body vibrate like a hundred lions roaring together. She felt something sharp in her back as she ran hell for leather, and she realised that it was the tip of that knife. Her mind burned as she tried to make sense of it all. People had died with stab wounds over the years and the killers were never caught. If this knife went through her and she died, no one would even think it was strange – it would just be another unsolved murder and she'd soon be forgotten.

Debra covered almost 200 yards until she found herself out of breath at the corner of Childwall Valley Road and Bentham Drive, and here the fire in her lungs was too much, and she fell to her knees, but she heard a voice cry out, and it was not the voice of that devil. Debra looked to her left and she saw a man in a black suit running towards her through the curtain of rain, and then she noticed his white collar and the thin strands of hair he'd combed over his balding pate were falling down into his eyes as he ran. The priest reached her, and straight away she knew she was saved.

'What happened to you?' he asked Debra as he helped her up, and then she saw him look at his left hand. There was blood, dripping from his palm in the rain. He told her she had wounds on her back and that the back of her blouse was soaked in blood. He took Debra to a nearby house and knocked on the door. An old man answered and the priest said, 'Are you on the phone?'

The old man nodded and the priest said: 'This girl has been stabbed by someone, call an ambulance!'

The priest took Debra into the house and she felt weak now, and she kept asking: 'Did you notice me easily enough father? Did you notice me?'

At the hospital, they discovered seven wounds in Debra's back made by some pointed instrument, but none of them had gone in more than five millimetres and none of the wounds required stitching, but she was kept in for a few days, and during that time, Doug, his mother and many of his friends came to visit Debra in hospital, and she burst into tears at all of the attention. The police asked Debra who had tried to stab her and of course, not wanting to be committed to a psychiatric hospital, she did not mention the ghostly head of the jester and the knife he had manifested, so she had to say a man with a scarf wrapped around his face had tried to mug her as she walked under the railway bridge on Childwall Valley Road.

Debra never again looked upon herself as the most beautiful girl in Liverpool, even though Doug often told her that she was. She married him in the following year and she gave up her dream of being a model and she also abandoned her idea of forming a dancing troupe. Debra found work in a florist's shop and in-between bringing up three children, she was also successful at painting pictures that were used by a greeting card manufacturer. That terrifying entity in the jester's cap was never seen nor heard from again after that traumatic afternoon under the bridge on Childwall Valley Road, but even today, Debra still has the occasional nightmare about the apparition. It's hard to speculate on just what that being was. These things often vanish for long periods of time, only to reappear decades later, but I sincerely hope that the bodiless head in the cap of bells stays well away from our level of reality.

MARJORIE

In 2008 a 60-year-old man named Rob Fairfax was walking down the aisle of a certain well-known supermarket in Woolton when a very attractive woman caught his eye. She looked as if she was in her late twenties, had sandy blonde hair, and wore what looked like a white tunic which suggested she was perhaps a dental nurse. She also wore a knee-length black skirt, and her legs were bare. Upon her feet she sported a pair of black flat shoes with buckles on. The woman's eyes were large, expressive and she had a very angelic face. She noticed Rob eyeing her and smiled at him, and Rob coyly averted his gaze. He knew she was young enough to be his daughter, and that he was already married, but he just felt drawn to the young lady. Rob was very loyal to his wife and did not usually have a 'wandering eye' when he visited the supermarket; he rarely looked at women and always remembered anniversaries regarding him and his beloved wife Jo. On this day, Rob felt what he could only describe as some strange – almost magnetic – pull which was attracting him to the blonde. She turned left at the end of the aisle and Rob wanted to follow her but decided to 'act his age'. When he got to the checkout after buying just a few items, Rob looked around for the young lady but she was nowhere to be seen. Rob couldn't stop thinking of this woman for some bizarre reason, and he made excuses to go to the supermarket the next day, but he never saw the lady. His wife Jo noticed the peculiar far-away look in Rob's eyes, and she asked him what he was thinking about. Rob snapped out of his daydream about the blonde in the supermarket and said he was just thinking of the work that needed to be done in the garden, but Jo just knew that something else had been on her husband's mind. She also noted how Rob was going to the supermarket almost every day to buy things they didn't even need, and Jo became that suspicious, she followed him one afternoon when he set out for the supermarket. She also asked a friend named Karen to follow him round to the superstore to see if he was perhaps meeting anyone there, but Karen later reported back and told Jo that her husband had just walked around the place, up and down the same aisles, and appeared to be looking for someone.

About a week after this, Rob was at the supermarket on one of his pointless shopping expeditions when he had a strong urge to turn around, and there she was, walking towards him with her basket. She smiled at Rob and suddenly said to him, 'You have the loveliest baby blue eyes I've ever seen.'

Rob blushed and chuckled, stuck for words. In all of his years no woman had ever paid him a single compliment about his eyes. He laughed, and as the blushing skin slowly turned to its normal colour, Rob told the girl he'd seen her before in the supermarket, and she said: 'I can't keep away from here – used to work here, see, years ago, when it was Bear Brand. My name's Marjorie by the way.'

'Mine's Rob – pleased to meet you Marjorie. I've only lived in Woolton for two years.' Rob felt so elated by the compliment this beautiful young woman had made about his eyes and when she asked him what he did, he chatted to her about his early retirement from a job in the City Council, and at some point he lost her in the wine aisle as a huge gang of rowdy teenagers swarmed between him and Marjorie. He looked all over the supermarket but she was nowhere to be seen, and he felt so down at not being able to find her. He realised he was falling for her, and he also felt so guilty – and a little scared; he was afraid he'd leave Jo for this girl, but he told himself he was just being a silly old romantic fool who was getting way ahead of himself. As Rob left the supermarket about ten minutes later, he caught sight of Marjorie on the far side of the car park, and he broke into a trot and tried to catch up with her, when he suddenly felt a stabbing pain in his chest. He tried to burp, and cough, thinking it was just trapped wind that needed to be shifted, but the pain became so intense, he gasped for air, and then his legs went from under him. Rob realised to his absolute horror that he was having a heart attack, and he collapsed on Vale Road. He lay there on his back at the foot of a beautiful towering horse chestnut tree. As his eyes looked into the upper reaches of the tree, everything went black, the agonizing pain in his chest ceased, and for a moment, Rob thought he had died – but then he felt himself being pulled - dragged out of his body – by Marjorie. She was dragging him into a dark swirling void where sinister faces were laughing at him. These faces were distorted as if Rob was viewing them through one of those door viewers with a fish-eye lens.

'Come on, you'll like it here!' she told Rob, but he cried, 'No, I want to stay in my life with my wife – leave me alone!'

Marjorie's face contorted and looked positively evil now as she tried to drag Rob into that all-enveloping darkness. She seemed to gloat from the tone of her voice as she said: 'You're dead now, and you're staying with us over here forever and ever!'

Rob thought of his wife Jo, and a recent memory of her was conjured up in his mind; it was of Jo lying next to him in bed with morning sunlight streaming through the blinds as she stroked his face and told him that she loved him.

'There's no going back now!' Marjorie informed Rob with a mocking voice, and he felt hands all over his body, grabbing at him and mauling him. Rob hadn't been to church in many years and he was not a particularly religious man, but he earnestly asked God to help him – and then he awoke in a bed in Broadgreen Hospital. He underwent a coronary angioplasty, was put on special tablets, and within days he was discharged. He was one of the lucky ones who had survived a heart attack.

Rob subsequently discovered that many years ago, there *had* been a factory named Bear Brand that had made tights, and it had been demolished in the 1990s to make way for the very supermarket where he had encountered Marjorie's solid-looking ghost. They say her ghost still occasionally roams the aisles of that supermarket, and she stands out because of the tunic-like uniform she once wore at that long-gone factory.

Is she really just visiting the supermarket for nostalgic reasons, or is Marjorie a mere agent of something evil that is constantly on the lookout for those who are near to death, so it can perhaps try and drag their souls off to some type of Hell?

SNIPPY

The following strange story took place at a beautiful redbrick 6-bedroom terraced house on Mossley Hill's Elm Hall Drive in 1971. The house had no supernatural history, and the mother of the family that resided there – 40-year-old Jean, had lived at the atmospheric Victorian house since she had been born. Her father had passed away ten years ago but her mother now lived with Jean and her family. Jean's husband, 45-year-old Eric, worked in a toyshop in the city centre, and the rest of the family incorporated 14-year-old Karen, 12-year-old Hannah and 8-year-old Bill. Since January, Eric's layabout Uncle Sid had also moved into the house after a messy divorce from his wife. The spare bedroom at the house was full of junk, and Karen was always pestering her dad to clear it out so she could move into it and have her own room instead of sharing a bedroom with Hannah. Jean had told Eric that if Sid could find it in himself to move out, Karen could have his room, but despite many hints being dropped to his uncle, Sid showed no signs of wanting to move out, and Bill loved Sid's tall stories.

One morning around 10.30am in the school holidays of 1971, Karen came downstairs to the breakfast table in the kitchen and yawned as she sat in her usual chair. Her mother was emptying cornflakes into her daughter's bowl when she noticed something odd about Karen's hair. 'Karen, have you been trying to cut your hair?'

'Eh?' Karen's sleepy eyes opened wide. She was obsessed with her hair and the idea of something being wrong with it really woke her to reality with a start. She lowered her head to the table so her chin was almost touching the tablecloth and she inspected her reflection in the side of the chrome toaster. Her hair was styled into what was then known as the long bob, and even in the imperfect mirror of the chromium-plated toaster, the teenager could see to her horror that there was a gap where some of her hair had apparently been cut away. Jean saw her daughter's face turn red and she watched her beautiful big blue eyes bulge as she looked at the reflection. 'Oh my God! I don't believe it!' Karen dashed from the table and she ran upstairs to go to the bathroom mirror and knocked Hannah – who was coming down for breakfast – into the wall.

'Hey!' Hannah cried to her sister's back as she flew up the stairs, 'Watch where you're going!'

Up in the bathroom, Karen turned her head to the right and she saw that a lock of hair, about seven inches in length and an inch in width had been cut from just above her left ear. The scissors must have been sharp because the cut was perfectly straight and the blades had gone through every hair neatly. The girl wanted to cry, and then she wanted to be sick, and then she felt a tremendous anger well up in her as she thought about the only person who could have done this: Hannah! They both shared the same bedroom, and Hannah seemed jealous of her sister's hair because Karen's was straight and easy to style whereas Hannah's was a mass of unruly curls which never seemed to grow.

'You did this, didn't you?' Karen yelled at Hannah as she appeared in the kitchen. She was pointing at the missing hair as she made the accusation.

'Did what?' Hannah asked with a baffled face.

Jean looked to her younger daughter and said, 'Someone cut Karen's hair while she was asleep.'

'Well don't look at me!' protested Hannah. 'Why would I do that?'

'Because you're a jealous cow, that's why!' Karen told her, and her face was pink with rage.

Hannah looked to her mum and said, 'I swear I didn't do it mum! I swear on Granddad's grave!'

'Don't say things like that, Hannah,' said her mother, plonking a plate of toast in front of her daughter. 'Disrespectful that.'

'But I didn't do it,' insisted Hannah, 'she must have done it!'

'What?' Karen drew the word out in a long questioning tone.

'You probably tried to cut your hair and made a mess of it,' said Hannah, 'but you're not blaming me!'

'You little lying toad – ' Karen was saying when her mother cried 'Enough! Pack this in!'

'But mum – ' Hannah stood up and was ready to argue her theory, but her mother said, 'Sit down!' And then she turned to Karen and said, 'Have you found the lock of hair?'

Karen realised her mother had a point and she turned and charged up the stairs to her room. She looked on the bed, in the bed, under it, and then did the same with Hannah's bed but the missing lock of hair was nowhere to be seen. Bill came into the bedroom and asked his oldest sister what all the shouting was about.

'Never mind, Bill,' Karen told him in a gruff voice, and wondered where Hannah had disposed of the 'evidence'.

'What have you done to your hair?' he asked, eyeing the gap in Karen's shiny bob.

'Look, mind your own business,' Karen snapped at him, 'and stay out of my room! Go on!'

The sisters did not talk to one another for hours, and when Karen went into the garden to listen to the DJ Mike Raven on Radio 1 on an old portable wireless as she sketched ideas for dresses, Hannah came out and said: 'Karen, I did not vandalise your hair.' Karen thought the choice of the verb 'vandalise' was ridiculous and smiled, and then she realised somehow that Hannah had not cut her hair as she slept – which obviously meant that someone else had. The sisters wondered if it was their young brother Bill, but Hannah said she was a light sleeper and would have heard him enter the bedroom, and what would be Bill's motive anyway?

On the following morning at 8am, Hannah got up to go to the toilet, and her father, who was already up, was also heading towards the toilet and he said, 'You're not going to be long are you?'

'No, I'm not,' yawned Hannah, her eyes half closed with tiredness. As she entered the toilet, her father said: 'Hannah? What have you done to your hair?'

Hannah quickly turned to face her dad and asked: 'Why? What do you mean?' And her hands felt through her curls.

'There's a big chunk of hair missing at the back of

your head,' her father told her, thinning his eyes as he looked at the gap in her curly poodle head of hair.

Hannah grabbed her father's shaving mirror from a shelf in the bathroom and angled it so that its magnifying side faced the back of her head as she looked into the big square mirror of the cabinet over the wash basin. She kept saying, 'Oh no,' over and over, and tears filled her eyes.

'Why don't you just go to the hairdressers like every other person?' her father asked, and he was in a mood because he wanted to relieve himself.

'I didn't do it!' she yelled at her father, startling him. 'But I know who did!' she cried and she placed the shaving mirror down hard in the wash basin, almost cracking it, before storming back to her bedroom.

Eric then heard a scuffle, a swear word uttered by Hannah, and then a scream. He rushed into the room and saw that Hannah was fighting with her sister and her hands were gripping Karen's hair. He separated the girls but his daughters screamed at one another. Jean came into the room and asked what was going on, and Hannah pointed to the back of her own head and shrieked: 'Look what she did!'

Bill's face peeped around the door, and he asked his father what all the shouting was for.

His father waved him away. 'Go back to bed, Bill, it's just a silly argument between your sisters!'

'You must think I'm stupid, Hannah!' Karen bawled at her sobbing sister. 'You cut my hair the night before, and then you decided to cut your own hair so you could blame me!'

'You're insane!' Hannah screamed, as tears flooded from her eyes. 'You ought to be locked up!'

Mr Reynolds, the old bachelor next door, thumped on the wall because of all the noise – on a Sunday morning too.

'Calm down Hannah!' Eric told his daughter, and then his Uncle Sid appeared on the landing outside the doorway in his dressing gown. He rubbed his eyes and made a suggestion which irritated Jean. He said, 'Let's all go downstairs and have breakfast, eh? A full English brekkie and a few cups of coffee will calm us all down.'

'Well you'll have to make it, Sid,' Jean told him, and she hugged Hannah, then looked at the back of the girl's head. It was quite a large chunk of hair missing.

'I don't mind, Jean,' said Sid with a toothy smile, 'I worked in the kitchens of the Savoy many years ago and I can rustle up a breakfast of champions before you can say Jack Robinson.' And then to Karen and Hannah he said, 'Come on you two – you're always fighting like the Kilkenny Cats! Come and help your Uncle Sid.'

The girls said nothing in reply and Sid whistled as he went alone downstairs to the kitchen, apparently unaware that he was unaccompanied.

'I'll go and see if your mum wants anything, love,' Eric told Jean, and he went off to his mother-in-law's bedroom, leaving his wife with the battling daughters.

When the news of the mysterious hair-snipper reached Nan via her daughter Jean, the old lady paused with a pensive look, and then she said a curious thing. 'When I was a little girl – I must have been about seven or eight, I was playing in the back garden of this house – when I heard the girl in next door's garden scream. I stood on an upturned plant pot and looked over the fence, and the girl – I can't remember her name now but her mother was a Mrs Bruce – had one pigtail on her head – the other had gone. Her mother was trying to console the girl, who said something had cut it off. I asked my mother what had happened and she said it was "the bad hair-cutting fairy" and that she'd cut my hair off if I misbehaved.'

'Trust you to have some supernatural story about something cutting people's hair, mum. What it is with – ' Jean was saying when her mother interrupted.

'I haven't finished Jean,' Nan said, sternly. 'Two other girls in this road also had pieces cut out of their hair, and some thought the whole thing was a joke but others said a ghost was behind it, and they called it Snippy.'

Jean gave a slow dismissive shake of her head as she smirked, and said: 'Well this isn't a ghost, mum, it's Karen and Hannah playing silly buggers.'

Later that day, Jean told her husband Eric about Snippy the ghost as they were in the kitchen preparing the Sunday dinner, and young Bill overheard them. He went upstairs and told his sisters about the hair-cutting ghost. They told him no ghost was at work and each blamed the other and an argument kicked off again.

On the following morning, Bill came downstairs for his breakfast at 10.30am, and his mother immediately noticed that his fringe was missing. It had been cut off in a perfectly straight line. The boy was upset and baffled, and when the sisters saw their brother minus his fringe, they blamed one another, and then Hannah said that Bill might have done it himself so they'd think it had been a ghost and stop all the accusations – but Bill threw a very uncharacteristic tantrum and said it hadn't been him. 'Nan's right! It's a ghost! It *is* Snippy!' he yelled, and his father told him to calm down. Later that day Bill's mum took him to the barber's to get a good old fashioned short back and sides haircut in an attempt to cover up the inexplicable loss of his fringe.

A few days later, Karen woke up at around nine in the morning and saw a lock of her hair on the duvet. She shot up in the bed and thought someone had been at her hair again, but it turned out that the lock was the one that had been cut from her head days back. Later that day, Bill found the hairs of his missing fringe on the window ledge of his room, and then the chunk of curly hair that had been cropped from the back of Hannah's head was found by her in the corner of her room. The reappearance of the hair that had been lopped off seemed eerie to Jean and Eric, and when Nan heard about it from Jean, she said, 'I told you — it's that ghost. After all those years it's come back. How strange.'

Eric was never one to give any credence to supernatural matters, and he said the hair-cutting incidents did seem weird, but he was convinced one of his kids was to blame. Around 4am on the following morning, Eric awoke in bed, and felt the urge to go to the toilet, but was so warm, comfortable and utterly relaxed, he found himself hesitating. The early daylight was already seeping through the drawn curtains and Eric looked at the pale bluish light filtering through the geometric patterns on the drapes when something floated across his field of vision, but he couldn't see what it was because he didn't have his glasses on and the thing was just a blur. He rose up to a sitting position, reached out for his large-framed spectacles on the bedside cabinet and quickly put them on before looking about. There it was again! This time he saw it with great clarity, and what he saw chilled him to the bone. It was a hand – a disembodied one with no wrist or arm attached – and it was floating in mid air at the end of the bed, bobbing up and down slightly, and it held a pair of unusually large scissors with its thumb and index finger, with the middle finger pressed close against the pointing finger. The scissors looked as if they were made of a very dark metal, and the hand was making them snip.

Eric slowly placed his hand on his wife's right shoulder and gently rocked her till she said, 'What? What?' in an annoyed voice. She'd been sleeping almost face down and heaved herself over to see what Eric wanted.

'Jean! Jean! Look at this!' said an excited Eric, and Jean levered herself up by her elbows, then rubbed her eye. She looked at Eric, then followed the line of his gaze, and let out a yelp when she saw the single hand hovering in mid air with those huge black scissors.

Eric turned away from the chilling apparition and turned on the bedside lamp, and the hand flew towards his face with those scissors inches from his eyes, and they snipped loudly as Jean took refuge under the covers as she screamed.

Eric saw the cricket bat standing up in the corner; he kept it there, ready to whack a burglar with it should the need arise. He fell out the bed trying to get to the bat, and he felt something sharp pierce his right buttock as he was falling. He seized the bat, turned around, and looked for the gruesome detached hand, but it was nowhere to be seen. 'It's gone!' he shouted, and Jean came up for air from under the covers. She looked about, then said, 'Let's get out of here!'

'Did you see it? Just a hand!' a shocked Eric said to his wife as she got out the bed and headed for the door, and then he let out an agonised scream as something stabbed his big toe. He looked down and saw that hand and its scissors resting on the carpet in front of his foot. Eric pulled his foot back and he smashed the bat down on that hand, more out of fear than anger. The hand and the pair of scissors it held then shot under the bed. Eric ran out of the room, and he saw Jean hesitating at the top step of the stairs. 'Did you get it?' she asked, then screamed. Eric saw that her eyes were looking at something on the floor behind him, and he glanced back and saw the hand and its sharp-bladed scissors following close behind, levitating just a few inches above the carpet. Eric continued to run and made downward thrusts with the cricket bat, but the hand dodged the tip of the bat, and when Eric reached the top of the stairs he tripped and fell, landing with his arms stretched out. The discorporate hand vanished at this point, and Jean helped her husband to his feet. Eric thought he'd cracked a rib but had sustained nothing but a few bruises to his torso. Karen, Hannah and Bill came out onto the landing and asked what was going on, and although Eric shook his head to his wife, gesturing for her to say nothing, she had to tell her children about the floating hand and the scissors it held. Bill smiled and asked, 'So it *is* a ghost then?'

Jean told the woman next door – a 29-year-old woman named Denise Holly – about the ghost, and

Denise said she'd have a word with her brother-in-law Robin, a newly-ordained priest from Cheshire who had a longstanding interest in the supernatural. There were no further manifestations of the severed scissors-wielding hand but Robin turned up at the house on Elm Hall Drive later that week and said he felt as if there was some mischievous spirit at large in the dwelling. Robin even stayed overnight in the spare room, and allegedly made contact with the spirit behind the hair-cutting. The spirit said its name was Arthur, and that it had lived in the late 19th century. Arthur had been obsessed with collecting the hair of young females (a possible hair fetish) and had gone around in disguise to stalk children. He would cut their hair and keep it in an album, but became insane, and had decided to destroy his hand by thrusting it under the wheels of a tram. The tram severed his hand at the wrist and Arthur almost died from a great loss of blood. He then went slowly insane when his disembodied hand returned to him one night. His brother told Arthur he was imagining things, but one night, Arthur's niece stayed over at his house and in the middle of the night she was attacked by the hand, which now held a pair of scissors. The niece ran out of the house in her night gown with most of her beautiful blonde hair cut off, and the blade of the scissors had also sliced through one of her ears. Arthur hanged himself, and after feeling as if he was asleep in a black void for weeks, he found himself floating about in his house, and sometimes the hand he had lost would reappear and do whatever he willed it to.

'You must stop this and turn to God, Arthur,' Robin told the troubled spirit, and then you must repent and you will be at peace with your creator.'

'No thanks,' said Arthur, 'I'd rather stay here and frighten people. I get such a thrill when children scream. One of these days I'll kill one of them.'

Robin pleaded with the spirit to turn to God, but he lost contact with "Arthur" and resorted to blessing the house. The family had no further visits from the alleged twisted entity, but in my files there were many other mysterious instances of hair cutting in that area of Liverpool, but whether they were by a Victorian hair fetishist or some other uncanny being is unknown. In December 1922, the newspapers were full of reports of a weird-looking man who was seen to appear out of thin air in broad daylight on the streets of London before he grabbed young ladies and hacked off their hair. Whenever this bizarre fiend was chased by police and chivalrous men, he would literally vanish into thin air. The hair-cutting bogeyman scare eventually died down in the capital, but many years later there was an incident in Liverpool in August 1969 where a woman on the back seat on the lower deck of a bus travelling up Renshaw Street experienced an ice-cold sensation at the back of her head, and when she placed her hand there, she discovered to her horror that her long hair had been cut from the nape of her neck. The girl's mother inspected the back of her upset daughter's head and saw that whoever – or whatever – had made the cut, it had singed the hair off in a perfectly straight line for six inches – but of course, the girl had her back to the wall in that end seat on the bus, so there was no room for the mysterious barber. In May 1876 something invisible was at large in Nanking, China, cutting off the pigtails of many citizens, and the hair-cutting panic later spread to Shanghai. Demons were blamed, but no one ever got to the bottom of the matter.

On the subject of the supernatural snipping of hair, I must relate one more story to you, for I feel there are parallels with the Mossley Hill case, and the following weird incident, which took place in Wirral, also happened in the 1970s.

The spinechilling event happened at a semidetached and rather gothic residence on Park Road South, which, as its name implies, lies just to the south of Birkenhead Park. The house in question was owned by an elderly man named Mr Bryant, and he had divided the four-storey dwelling into flats which were mostly occupied by students. The house lay in shade all the year round because of a grove of towering sycamores in front of it, and there was a noticeable gloomy atmosphere in some rooms of the building which many tenants had commented on over the years. In May 1977, a 21-year-old Claughton woman named Judy Teare left her husband Paul when she discovered he was having an affair. Paul was a violent man, and had once threatened to shoot Judy if she ever tried to leave him. She had finally had enough of his philandering and plucked up the courage to leave Paul at their home in Liverpool, and now she had returned to her old neck of the woods with a school friend from Tranmere named Claire Jones who had also recently split with her boyfriend. The two friends now lodged in a large room on the third floor of the house on Park Road South, and on the Wednesday night of 25 May, 1977, the two young ladies were watching *Dawson and Friends* – an hour-long comedy sketch show starring Les Dawson – on a little black and white portable telly Claire had bought using her Giro money. She was in-between jobs and forever writing letters to prospective employers.

At 9pm the comedy show ended, and the TV and single tungsten filament bulb in the room suddenly went off. The sun had only recently set and there was pale dying daylight filtering through the net curtains. Mr Bryant the landlord came up the stairs and shouted, 'The fuses have blown! I've sent for an electrician! Sorry about this!'

A man in the flat below the girls was moaning because he'd been watching Liverpool versus Borussia Moenchengladbach in the European Champions' Cup Final on BBC1. Claire found candles in the cupboard under the sink, left there by the previous tenant, and she lit them and placed them around the room. The subject turned to the supernatural, and Claire suggested having a go at the Ouija board. Judy wasn't keen on the idea, but Claire cut out little squares and wrote the letters of the alphabet and the numerals 0 to 9 on each of them. The letters were arranged in a circle and a little whiskey glass was upturned and placed in the middle of the circle. The girls asked any spirits if they'd find a lover soon. The glass slid about as Claire and Judy rested their index fingertips on the top of the inverted glass. The word "HAIR" was spelt out. Each girl accused the other of pushing the glass. Another question was posed to the spirit world by Judy: 'Who will Paul marry?' – and this referred to Judy's partner over in Liverpool. The glass darted about back and forth, and spelt out the word "CLAIRE" twice – and then once again the word "HAIR".

'Stop messing about, Claire,' said Judy, 'as if Paul would go with you. He said you're plain.'

There was a loud rap at the door and the girls screamed. It was Mr Bryant, and he came into the room with a torch, and when he saw the upturned glass and the circle of lettered and numbered squares, he said, 'Oh no, don't ever mess with that bloody thing! We had trouble in here with that once.'

The lights then went back on and the TV set boomed out at full volume. Claire turned the TV down. Mr Bryant rambled on about the dangers of the Ouija, and then left. Soon afterwards, Claire did a cruel impersonation of the old landlord, making herself cross-eyed (as Bryant had strabismus), and putting on his Lancashire accent as she said, 'Don't mess with the Ouija.'

Judy laughed and told Claire: 'That really sounded like him; you should be on the telly with all these impersonations!'

The girls eventually retired to their beds, positioned at opposing ends of the room, at around 1 am. The next morning, Judy awoke at 8am, and discovered that her fringe had been cut. She accused a grinning Claire of cutting her hair, but Claire swore on her mum's life that she had not clipped off her fringe, and was only laughing because she thought Judy looked funny with her exposed forehead. On the following morning, Claire awoke and found locks of hair missing from her head. She blamed Judy, and said: 'You did it to get back at me because you think I cut your fringe!'

Judy shook her head, and then she reminded Claire about the messages from the Ouija board – it had spelt out the word HAIR twice. On the following morning around 3.40am, Claire had a vivid dream she was being French-kissed by her former boyfriend, but when she awoke, she realised that something was on top of her. It was a black mass of what looked like billowing smoke, and in this gaseous body there were two bright lights – like eyes – and they were fixed upon her. From this shapeless black mass, thin spindly limbs protruded and they were pinning Claire down, and some type of tubular protuberance from this sinister entity was being thrust down her throat. This brought back awful memories of the time when Claire had to be pumped after she had taken tablets she'd mistaken for Smarties when she was three. This thing moving steadily down her throat pushed hard against her tonsils before it snaked its way down into her stomach. Claire realised she was paralysed, and she felt something snipping off her hair. She somehow managed to move, and she threw herself out the bed. The black vaporous thing flew across the room and went into the disused fireplace. When the light was switched on, Claire saw locks of her hair on her pillow. She and Judy left the house that morning in terror. A month after this, Claire discovered she was pregnant, and admitted that the father was Paul – Judy's partner...

The gaseous abomination of Park Road South is still occasionally seen at the house, but what it is, I do not know.

THE SHAPESHIFTERS

No rational system of explanation can currently throw any light on the werewolf phenomenon. How can a person change into an animal and afterwards revert to a human being again? Our DNA contains the DNA of many 'lower' animals, and believe it or not, when the human genome was finally sequenced in 2003, it was discovered that humans, dogs and wolves share 84% of the same DNA. In theory, a werewolf could be created by genetically modifying a human with lupine DNA, but this would take time, whereas the bona fide werewolf undergoes metamorphosis within the minute. The scientist in me says such a transfiguration is impossible, but the occultist side of me knows otherwise – that through some supernatural force, a person really can change into a hideous wolf-like being, and the reports of werewolves are not only mentioned by such ancient Roman writers as Ovid and Petronius, they are even referred to in the Bible. In the Old Testament's Book of Daniel, for example, we are told that the handsome black Mesopotamian King Nebuchadnezzar suffered a type of mental breakdown for turning against God, and after stripping naked and walking on all fours, he sprouted claws, a feathery type of hair upon all of his skin, ate grass, turned into a beast, and lived in a forest for seven years.

Reports of werewolves down the centuries have been very persistent, and even today, occasional accounts of the mysterious shapeshifters come my way. Between Eastham Rake and Hooton on the Wirral, close to the place where the M53 runs over the railway track, scores of people – myself included amongst them – have seen a large unidentified animal roaming a field. I saw it from a train in 2004 and it struck me as a classic prowling "Big Cat" – a cryptozoological felid of the same ilk as the Surrey Puma, the Beast of Bodmin and the Beast of Exmoor – but others who have seen this creature at closer quarters have claimed that it was not a cat – but more like an unusually large wolf. The animal always seems to go to ground within seconds when it is chased, and some have remarked on its phantom-like vanishing acts when it is confronted. There simply aren't enough rabbits, pigeons and other sources of food in the area to feed the mysterious 'wolf' – and this adds to the air of mystery surrounding the unidentified animal. Could it possibly be a werewolf?

In 2002 at BBC Radio Merseyside I interviewed a former security guard who worked at a certain hospital in Wirral, and he told a chilling story that was later backed up by a porter, a policeman, and several nurses. The guard, Craig (not his real name), said that a heavily-pregnant New Age traveller, aged about 25, was brought into the Wirral Hospital after going into labour. She seemed delirious, and wanted to have her baby in a tipi – but an older man, possibly the woman's partner, brought her to the hospital before quickly leaving. It was a warm summer night and a full moon was out, and the woman belonged to a community of hippies who had camped down in bender tents and yurts on a tract of land close to the hospital. As the woman went into the throes of labour, the midwife and nurses attending to her saw the patient undergo a startling and very frightening transformation. The grimacing face of the young woman turned slowly into the face of some animal. The tip of her nose darkened, the skin became hairy and turned a strange greyish-pink colour, and long pointed teeth protruded from the mouth. The midwife and nurses backed away from the bed in terror as the woman began to make snarling noises like an animal, and a security guard – the aforementioned Craig - was called. When Craig reached the ward he saw the frightened nurses run past him into the corridor, and then he saw a figure in hospital clothes which looked humanoid, only the face was that of an animal with a snout. This entity ran to the plate-glass second-floor window and smashed it with its fists, before jumping through the frame into the garden. Craig reached the smashed window within seconds and caught a fleeting glimpse of the woman running off into the moonlit nightscape. Fearing the adverse publicity from this unearthly occurrence, the hospital managers advised the staff to say nothing about the incident, but many of them told their families and partners, and the story got out, but most who heard it classed the account as some urban legend. I mentioned the incident on a local radio station and was besieged with calls from people, including the security guard Craig, three nurses, a porter, and even a policeman who told me about a sighting of the apparently metamorphosed woman at a park near to the hospital. Enquiries were made at the travellers' encampment, but the police met a wall of silence – no one would admit to even knowing who the pregnant woman was. Days later the travellers were moved on. The whole affair continues to tantalize me; was that pregnant lady a shapeshifting werewolf, and furthermore - what became of her and her child? I think it will be a long time before we know the answers.

We now cross the Mersey to look at a few more werewolf reports in Liverpool.

There is either an exceedingly dedicated prankster at work locally who is taking a joke too far – or there is a werewolf on the prowl who really gets around. I and a few other researchers into the paranormal have had many reports of strange nocturnal howlings (always around the time of a full moon) and sightings of what seems to be a large wolf-like figure, sometimes running on all fours, sometimes on two legs, in places as varied as Edenhurst Avenue, Huyton, Bowring Park Golf Course, the Mill Pits, Knowsley Park and Rimrose Valley Country Park. Regular readers of my books will know that a werewolf has been reported in the Speke and Halewood areas for centuries, and many years ago something described as 'half-man, half beast' was hastily interred at Flaybrick Hill Cemetery after causing havoc on Bidston Hill. People often mock the idea of people changing into werewolves, yet the historical evidence for them is substantial, and even King John – who announced the foundation of Liverpool – was accused of being a werewolf. However, let us turn to more recent times in our search for the lycanthrope. On the last day of April, 1999, Jane, an asthmatic woman in Hale Village sent her husband Ken out to the garden shed one evening because of his excessive pipe smoking. Half an hour later, Jane heard a bloodcurdling howl, loud growling, and the sound of something being demolished. A bald man's face appeared at her kitchen window, and Jane suddenly realised it was her husband – but where had his hair gone? Ken barged into the kitchen and locked the door. He said he had been smoking in the shed when he had heard a weird howl. The face of some animal which looked like a wolf, appeared at the window, and it had bright green eyes and a white stripe running from its nose across its head like a skunk. It began to growl and claw at the shed, and Ken had been so scared he closed the door and kept it closed by pulling at it. The thing started to smash through the door and its massive claw came through a hole and swiped at him. It clawed off his hairpiece (which Jane knew nothing about) and injured his shoulder. Ken grabbed a gardening fork and stabbed the beast's left arm and it reacted by howling and running off. Jane said it must have been a large dog, but Ken said the animal had run off on two legs. On the following day, Jane saw her neighbour Jess with a huge bandage on her left arm. She said she'd had a fall, but Ken noticed that Jess had a white streak in her hair, and he recalled the white stripe on the head of that strange animal. Jane said he was being ridiculous in his insinuations, but was later asked to join a coven Jess ran, which involved having a crescent moon tattooed on the middle finger. Jane had it done, and each month when there was a full moon, she would go missing. Ken was so convinced that Jess was a werewolf, he gave his wife an ultimatum: move with him to Prescot or stay put and live without him. Jane reluctantly went to live with Ken at a house in Prescot and had to leave the coven. We now move forward a few years and return to Wirral for our next werewolf story, and this bizarre and frightening incident, like most of the stories in this book, remains unexplained.

On the Wednesday evening of 16 April 2003, two students – Misha Egerton and Bryony Claremont, both aged 20, got on their bikes and cycled almost two miles from their flat on Beckwith Street, Birkenhead, to a house on Wexford Road, Prenton, where their boyfriends Elliott and Jake (who were also students) had their lodgings, along with three other students. Tonight the girls, their boyfriends and ten other students were having a party and the guests were expected to bring their own bottles of wine and six packs of lager and beer. Misha and Bryony each brought two four-packs of Kronenbourg in their backpacks and when they reached the house on Wexford Road at 7.30pm the party had already started. By midnight, everyone was too drunk to dance, and the partygoers all sat drinking what was left and munching on Pringles as they watched a faulty DVD of the teen sex comedy *American Pie* which kept skipping. Misha said it was the most boring party she'd ever attended. Most of the males present ended up watching the "Battersea Bomber" Howard Eastman defending his British, Commonwealth and European middleweight titles against Scott Dann on BBC1's *Boxing* programme. The programme bored the girls stiff, and so they left the males in the lounge and went into the kitchen to bake some pizzas for themselves. Someone loaded disc 1 of the *Ministry of Sound Trance Nation* into the Boombox Stereo CD player on the top of the fridge. The music seemed to renew everyone's batteries. Bryony found 24 bottles of Peroni that selfish Jake had stashed away in two crates in the cupboard under the sink, and she shared out the bottles with the few girls who were able to continue drinking. The girls danced in the kitchen and one of them found a disco lights ball in the cubby hole under the stairs, and she set it up in the kitchen and they all laughed and danced. Misha mooched about in the fridge and found a bottle of cuveé Bollinger. She shared it with Bryony, then danced to Scooter, Energy 52, Rezonance Q and Dee Dee but then some of the men came into the kitchen trying in vain to dance and ruined the atmosphere. Misha had a blazing row with her boyfriend Elliott because he had called her 'an alky' (slang for 'an alcoholic') and she stormed out of the house, hardly able to walk in a straight line, with Bryony hanging onto her arm. Misha managed to call a private hire cab on her mobile, and around 3am, the cab turned up and passed the house but Bryony placed her fingers in her mouth and emitted an ear-piercing whistle - and the cab halted, then reversed to her and Misha. The girls almost fell into the vehicle and Misha told the cab-driver to go to Beckwith Street but to 'go slow and avoid the speed bumps or I'll hurl.' The route to Beckwith Street necessitated travelling through Birkenhead Park via Ashville Road, and as the cab approached this road three minutes into the journey, the cab driver started to cough so much, he pulled over, and seemed to be wheezing.

'You alright mate?' Bryony asked, and the driver turned in his seat and told his two passengers: 'Get out of here, quick!'

'What?' Misha asked, her hand on her forehead. She

felt so dizzy.

'If you value your lives - get out of here now!' the cab driver said in a raspy voice, and his hands flew up to his throat.

'Haven't you got an inhaler?' Bryony asked him, and the man wheezed and shook his head to and fro as if he was at the hands of an invisible strangler.

'Oh my God, we don't half get them!' cried Misha. 'We're not getting out here this time in the morning; we'd be raped – ' she was saying when the driver turned to face her and Bryony. At first the girls thought he had on some mask. His face had a sickly bluish tinge, but his eyeballs were black with golden irises, and his nose was dark at the tip. He started to growl like an animal, and Misha let out a scream.

'I warned you!' he snarled, and now he had hair protruding from under his eyes, and that hair seemed to be coming out of his face as he sat there, staring at the girls with those unearthly eyes.

Bryony undid her seatbelt, and then she undid Misha's too, and she opened the door and dragged her friend out onto a secluded stretch of Ashville Road that was illuminated only by the full moon. The girls tried to run, but kept falling over, and then they heard a loud howling – like that of a wolf. The thing that squeezed out of the cab was not human; it had a hunched back, and the head of an animal, and it walked on all fours as it coughed and spat. Its arms now looked longer than its legs, and the thing began to rip off its jacket.

Bryony dragged Misha to her feet and they ran screaming down Ashville Road. 'Hail Mary, full of grace...' Bryony prayed, and Misha gasped, 'Oh God please don't let it get us!'

The headlights of an approaching car blinded the terrified girls, and they thought they'd be knocked over by the vehicle for a moment. It slowed down, and Misha and Bryony saw it was a private hire cab. A door in the cab flew open and Elliot got out and walked towards them saying something but Bryony was screaming so Misha couldn't hear what her boyfriend was saying. He escorted the girls into the cab and Misha tried to tell him about the cab driver who had turned into some animal but Elliot was too busy dragging Bryony into the cab. Inside the cab, Elliot said that he had seen the girls get into that rogue cab minutes before, and then the cab they had called had turned up. He had got into it and told the driver what had happened. As the genuine cab passed the unofficial cab, something hit the vehicle so hard, the rear window smashed and the driver and passengers saw that metamorphosed thing in the road behind them, waving its huge hairy fist. It ran off like an animal into the night as the girls screamed. The rogue cab was nowhere to be found when police investigated, and that man – whatever he was – had also gone.

We now travel 31 years back in time from 2003 Wirral to the Huyton of 1972, to another alleged shapeshifting incident. This weird occurrence took place in the winter of 1972 in Huyton, and over the years, quite a few witnesses to the incident have spoken to me to add more detail to the account of the weird goings-on. It was January 1972, and it was the 9th birthday of a boy named Martin who lived at a semidetached house on Dinas Lane. Martin and his parents hadn't lived in Huyton long; they'd only moved to the area the year before from Blackburn, but already Martin was a popular boy with the local kids. Martin's parents let their son invite as many friends as he wanted to the party, and had it been in the summer months, there would have been a marquee in the back garden for the partygoers. Martin's parents had money and the lad's father was planning to build a big swimming pool in the back garden, just to encourage his son to swim with a grand view to obtaining Olympic medals one day. A small fortune was spent on the birthday party, and Sayers and Cousins did a roaring trade that week as Martin's mum bought boxes of cakes, pasties, sausage rolls and a huge jelly. The birthday cake itself was made by a local woman who specialised in wedding cakes, and she was paid £30 for her elaborate creation in sponge, jam, cream and icing. The party was held in the afternoon at half-past four, and a subzero fog had descended on Huyton by then. Martin's father was stranded by the freezing fog and black ice at his workplace in Widnes, and didn't get home in time for the party, but Martin didn't even notice his father's absence because he had so many friends over at his house. The boy's mother made all of the little guests welcome, and each was given a slice of the birthday cake on a paper plate, along with as many glasses of "lemmo" as they could drink. Most of the savouries went untouched during the party, and at one point, a 7-year-old girl named Jill – a school-friend of Marty – was put on a large dining table that doubled as a stage, and the child started singing *I'd Like to Teach the World to Sing* – a song by the New Seekers that was currently at Number 1 in the pop charts. Around half way through Jill's performance on the table, a rowdy child entered Martin's house. He was described as about 4ft 5, and he looked around Martin's age – about 9, possibly a little younger. He had a shaven head with only a few millimetres of blonde bristly hairs showing through his scalp, and a small pair of dark blue eyes. Although it was a bitterly cold January afternoon, the unknown boy wore only a thin grey tee shirt, black shorts, white socks (that had dropped down to his ankles), and black slip-on 'pumps' – or plimsolls to give the footwear its proper name.

This lad started to shout some very rude names at Jill as she performed her song, and at one point he picked up a custard tart and pelted the girl with it. The cake splattered upon impacting Jill's face and she fell backwards off the table, landing on two children. There were screams as the mischievous boy *changed* before the very eyes of the little party guests. The child's features seemed to melt at one point, and his body simultaneously stretched upwards, and this spectacle of terrifying transfiguration sent the children running from the living room in a state of utter terror. When Martin's mother came into the room she thought she was looking at a man covered in pink paint from his bald head to his feet, but the head was oval shaped and elongated, and the feet looked more like claws. The eyes of the entity were swept back and thin, and its mouth opened wide to reveal fearsome rows of pointed teeth. The thing hissed at Martin's mum, and a long thin tongue uncoiled from his toothed mouth like the unfolding tube of a party horn. The nightmarish entity then tipped over the table the birthday spread had been laid out on. Cakes and plates of abandoned food and bottles of lemonade went crashing to the floor, and then the mother of the birthday boy saw something that would haunt her for the rest of her life. The pink figure of the demonic being quickly changed into an animal before her eyes. The pink shiny skin was replaced by a grey coat of hair, and the face of the weird gatecrasher now resembled that of a wolf, minus the ears. Martin's mother ran out of the house with the screaming children into the fog and told a startled neighbour returning home from work what had happened. The neighbour, a Mr Thompson, thought that someone in a costume of some sort had just been playing a joke on his neighbour, and he went into the house and saw the overturned table and the cakes, rolls and pies all over the floor. He had a look around, and saw nobody hiding, and even checked the rooms upstairs. He came out of the house and convinced Martin's mum she'd just been the victim of a silly prankster, and she went back into the house with Martin and a few of his braver friends. Minutes after this, Jill, the 7-year-old who had been pelted by the weird boy, came out of the kitchen and said to Martin's mother: 'He's behind the fridge.'

Mr Thompson, the neighbour, overheard the girl's claim as he helped Martin's mum to clean up the mess. He smiled and said, 'It must be flat as a pancake to fit behind there, my love,' and he asked Jill to show him this hiding 'monster' (as he called it) . When he also saw the thing hiding behind the fridge – compressed into a gap of about three inches) Mr Thompson swore and recoiled in horror, shouting, 'There's an animal wedged behind there!'

Martin, his mother, and a handful of guests all withdrew into the hallway, and Mr Thompson grabbed a mop, and then he took a carving knife out the cutlery drawer. He poked behind the fridge with the mop handle, and then everyone heard a high-pitched scream. That boy in the grey tee shirt came running out of the kitchen, and in the few seconds Martin's mum saw him pass by before he ran out of the house, she noticed he had furry arms. This 'boy' ran out the place, into the fog of Dinas Lane, shrieking with laughter, and was never seen by Martin or his mum ever again. The usual explanations were trotted out: the overactive imagination of children, and mass hysteria, but something happened that wintry day in 1972, and whatever it was, it drove nearly a dozen children away from the tasty delights of a birthday party, so it must have been something very frightening. Something very frightening which has scared children and adults alike for many years is another genus of shapeshifter that's as enigmatic as the last one in Huyton, but this being is seasonal, putting in its terrifying appearances at the onset of autumn – particularly Halloween.

"Bouncy" is the nickname the locals of Woolton have given to an extremely weird bogeyman that manifests itself as a man in a red suit who changes into a form that is half way between a Space Hopper and a massive red balloon, and having no legs, the figure bounces along after his petrified victims. He has two long extendable arms, and one hand is a type of lethal-looking fork and the other sometimes brandishes a sword. His chalk-white grinning head has stringy grey hair which flies about as he hops after his prey, and he has a ruffled collar – which gives the impression of the creepy figure of fear being some clown. This description sounds ridiculous, but almost all witnesses who have encountered Bouncy, from Edwardian times to the present day, have described him almost exactly as I have done. He either appears as a man of about six feet in height in a scarlet suit who then changes into a legless, long-armed egg-shaped creature, or he appears as the ovoid monster then morphs back into a humanoid shape. I am currently researching an encounter with the pneumatic bogeyman that allegedly took place at St Peter's Mission Hall (now a nursery) on Rose Street, Woolton, in 1904. In 2015, many residents off Woolton's Quarry Street heard distant thumping sounds one October evening, and a rumour later spread that a weird-looking man inside of some bizarre inflated egg-shaped balloon was scaring teenagers in Quarry Street Playground. I investigated these reports and interviewed a witness – a drinker named David from the Victoria public house which stands next to the playground, and he said he saw what looked like a huge red egg-shaped inflatable, about 5-6 feet in height, bouncing along in the dark in the playground. Screaming youths were running from it, and the thing then vanished. 'It was there one moment,' said David, 'and then it literally disappeared and the bouncing noise it was making at is moved along stopped.'

I also interviewed a man in his sixties named Trevor, who told me how, in October 1959, when he was just 7, he got his head stuck in railings on Quarry Street one evening, and his friends were trying to free him when they ran off screaming. Trevor heard a girl shout: 'It's the Bouncing Man!' and then he heard the sound of weird laughter and rhythmic thuds getting nearer and nearer. He had heard about the weird ghost from his grandmother, and Trevor was so scared of being caught by the Bouncing Man, he pulled his head out the railings and felt as if he'd ripped his ears off in the process. The boy saw something resembling a giant rugby ball coming down Quarry Street, but could not see the oft-reported long arms or even a head on the oval mass, and he ran home in a terrible state. The lad's parents said the "ghost" was named Bouncy and it was just a deranged man in an inflatable suit, but his grandmother said it was something from the Devil and that she had seen it near St Peter's Church when she was a girl. Trevor had nightmares about the unearthly Bouncy for years. Is the modern Bouncy just some hoaxer in Woolton – or is it a shapeshifting being from the uncharted realms of the supernatural?

A very suave and eccentric – not to mention scary – shapeshifting being made its debut at Liverpool's Sefton Park in 1970, and this one was fixated with kissing young females. The strange account has the flavour of an urban legend about it, but I have interviewed so many people who either encountered the strange being detailed in the following section or saw him with their own two eyes. One can rarely completely rule out a hoaxer, but in this case I am convinced that something we cannot explain by the logic of this world was at large in early 1970s Liverpool. So many unearthly incidents have happened at Sefton Park over the years, and many of them are detailed in my books, so I am beginning to think the park might be what is known as a 'window area' in the sphere of the paranormal – an area of high strangeness where timeslips often occur as well as UFO sightings and other weird goings-on.

At first he was just a rumour, and a seemingly far-fetched one at that; a tall young debonair man was said to be confronting ladies crossing Sefton Park, forcing kisses on them before leaping off in enormous bounds reminiscent of that Victorian bogeyman Spring-Heeled Jack. Even today there is a grey legal area where an unwanted kiss may or may not be considered as an assault, but back in 1970 there was little the police could do to legally pursue the Sefton Park Romeo (as he became to be nicknamed) – and the authorities even doubted if the athletic amorist existed anyway. He first struck one Saturday evening in spring 1970 when the full moon had just risen and two 18-year-old girls, Anna Morrison and Tina Potter, were crossing Sefton Park on their way to a pub on Smithdown Road to meet their boyfriends. The girls were dressed up for the night out and Tina had just had her hair done by her older sister, a trainee hair stylist. A tall man, aged about thirty to thirty-five, in a black suit with unfashionable short slicked-back raven-black hair came running towards them and first seized Anna, kissed her hard, then did the same to Tina. Without uttering a word, he took two roses from his coat pocket and gave one to each of the stunned girls, and then he ran off towards Mossley Hill Drive, before taking three enormous leaps that would have broken Olympic long jump records. The girls, meanwhile, felt dizzy and drugged, and believed that the weird kiss-and-run fanatic had had put some stupefying chemical on his lips before he had smooched them. That evening, Terry O'Hare, a long-distance driver, had been taking a short cut through the park in his lorry (and testing his brakes, which he thought were playing up) when he witnessed the escape of the Sefton Park Romeo. He saw him make his gravity-defying leaps and prance across Mossley Hill Drive – almost being run down by the lorry which missed him by a few seconds. The bizarre prancing figure then ran down Ibbotson's Lane where he was lost in the shadows of the trees. Terry reversed the lorry, got out and went to the teens and found them staggering about, reeking of a sweet chemical smell the lorry driver believed to be hospital ether or chloroform. He asked the girls if the man had seriously assaulted them, and the dazed teenagers said he hadn't – he'd just kissed them, but he seemed to have had some substance on his unusually red lips that had made them feel drowsy. Both girls said they had never seen the man before but they'd be able to identify him if they saw him again. Terry gallantly gave the girls a lift to their homes, and during the journey, he asked them if they'd rather go to a hospital to see if they had been drugged by the weird man, but the girls just wanted to see their respective parents.

The "Romeo" made more attacks, always on Wednesday and Saturday evenings, and he invariable left red roses with his victims and always escaped towards the south of the park. On one occasion he jumped on a 21-year-old student from the branches of a tree, grabbed her hand and kissed her knuckles and although she managed to flee to her flat off Lark Lane, she later saw the frightening philanderer at midnight, standing in the shadows of an alleyway facing her home, gazing up at her window. A beautiful blonde lady of 22 named Jayne Kingsbury made the innocent mistake of walking through Sefton Park to visit a friend's house one Wednesday night at 9.50pm, when a man, about six feet in height with short black oily hair stepped out from behind a tree with a rose in his hand. Jayne said he was wearing a black suit with a white shirt and black tie, and the attire looked dated because the trousers were not flared (as most trousers were in the early to mid 1970s). The young lady also noted that the man's face was very pale and he had long slender fingers. His eyes seemed dark, possibly brown, and he wore a slight smile on his face. In a heartbeat the stranger lunged at Jayne, and she went to swing her handbag at him to strike his face but he moved with lightning agility and he swung her round to his right as he gripped her upper arms and pushed her against the trunk of the tree. He then kissed Jayne and thrust his tongue into her mouth, and the tip of it touched her molars and the back of her throat, which triggered a retching reflex. As he carried out this aggressive form of French kissing, the audacious man's eyes widened so he looked positively unstable, and he stared madly into Jayne's eyes as he pressed her hard into the trunk. He then pulled himself from her, and Jayne felt light-headed, but it was not through the usual blissful feelings stirred up by a passionate caress – Jayne almost felt drunk. The menacing would-be womaniser picked up the rose he had dropped during the forced French kissing, placed it in Jayne's hand, and she felt the thorn on the stem of the rose prick her palm. The man turned and ran away into the gathering darkness and was soon lost to sight. Jayne continued to her friend's home and found she could hardly stand up and found it difficult to speak. Her friend telephoned John, Jayne's boyfriend, a student at the Liverpool University's Robert Robinson Laboratories, and John suspected the crazed attacker of using some sort of hypnotic drug. He took swabs from the lips and interior of his girlfriend's mouth and established that some liquid or fine-powdery form of what seemed to be Flunitrazepam had been administered to Jayne by the assailant during the deep kissing, but John had never known this drug – today called Rohypnol – to exist in those forms; it was usually manufactured – and dispensed - in tablet form. Flunitrazepam is ten times more potent than Valium and it can be used as an anaesthetic and even a heroin substitute (as well as a powerful back pain reliever), so where had the bizarre libertine acquired it? Was the attacker some pharmacist, or even a scientist? And how was he himself not affected by the drug if it was in his mouth or on his lips? John wondered about these questions, and from then on he always escorted Jayne if she went anywhere near Sefton Park.

In the meantime the mysterious kissing maniac continued to prowl the park on Wednesdays and Saturdays, and a group of locals at the Rose of Mossley public house on Rose Lane noted that a certain well-dressed drinker named Tim always left the premises of the pub at 7pm sharp on Wednesdays and Saturdays, so he was suspected of being the over-affectionate park prowler. A few of the drinkers subtly questioned him about his whereabouts on those Wednesdays and Saturdays and Tim, who lived in the Aigburth Vale area, just a few minutes from Sefton Park, replied in a very cagey manner: 'Oh, just visiting my girlfriend, why?'

'I never knew you had a girlfriend,' said one of the drinkers.

'Where does she live? Is she a local girl?' asked another.

'She lives quite near to Sefton Park – why?' replied Timothy, finding the questions a tad suspicious.

A man named Jack who knew Tim said he was a loner who never seemed to be with anyone, male or female, and had another side to him when he was drunk. In drink, Tim was a sex maniac, according to Jack, and on one occasion when he'd had too many lagers, he had seized a woman in the Hunt's Cross Hotel and started to kiss her, and her boyfriend – a rugby player - had battered him.

It was starting to look as if the armchair detectives in the Rose of Mossley had found their man. Days later, on a Wednesday evening, Tim came into the pub around 5pm, had a few drinks and chatted to a couple of friends, and then, like clockwork, he left the premises. Four of the drinkers followed him, keeping a safe distance of about fifty yards from their suspect, and he headed down Rose Lane, then turned right into Palmerston Road. Tim then turned right onto North Mossley Hill Road, and after a hundred yards he turned left into Park Avenue, which, as its name suggests, leads directly to Sefton Park.

Tim walked through Sefton Park, unaware he was being tailed by four vigilantes – one armed with a knuckleduster and one of them carrying a cosh down his trousers. Tim went straight through the park and came out on the other side.

'Probably knows he's being followed,' said one of the pub vigilantes, 'but let's see where he goes.'

Tim was followed to a grand-looking three-storey house on Ullet Road, and the sign outside read: 'Judo and Karate Self-Defence Classes'.

Tim went in, and one of the four following volunteered to knock at the door of the house, and a tall muscular man answered. He was asked about Tim and he said that his 'pupil' came here twice a week – each Saturday and Wednesday evening for a two-hour self-defence lesson. When the band of self-proclaimed vigilantes returned to the pub, they felt real fools, but decided not to give up the hunt for the Sefton Park Romeo. They made a pact that they would patrol Sefton Park after dark and catch the Romeo red-handed – and they almost did. One evening, around 10.40pm in the August of 1971, the self-appointed guardians of south Liverpool's womenfolk were 'on patrol' in Sefton Park when they heard a girl screaming. As they ran towards her, the four young men saw the nimble Lothario running in the moonlight south of the Palm House. He climbed a tree in the park to avoid capture and when two of the unofficial law enforcers climbed that tree minutes later, they were startled by the descent of a huge black cat with strange eyes which ran off. The debonair debauchee had vanished. One of the men was very superstitious and he believed that the uncanny Romeo was some sort of devil, whereas another one of the unauthorised policemen said the perpetrator – given his amazing leaping abilities – had simply jumped out of the tree onto the branches of another one. The four self-styled protectors of the fairer sex searched the park but the Romeo was nowhere to be seen. I mentioned this case on a BBC programme about local mysteries on 2010 and three people who lived near Sefton Park during the sybarite scare told me of some very strange goings-on at the time. A 75-year-old Mrs Munford told me how, as a 36-year-old mum, she had been pushing a pram carrying her son through Sefton Park on a pleasant Wednesday evening around 7.30pm in 1971 when she saw two men chasing a man in a black suit who was running like a professional sprinter across the park. The man being pursued ran behind a small grove of trees and he did not come out the other side – but a black Labrador did and ran off. The two men who had been giving chase stopped and looked very confused at the man's apparent vanishing act. Mrs Munford told the men she had seen the man they were pursuing run behind some trees and how it looked as if he had turned into a dog, but her claim was met with looks of incredulity. The men told Mrs Munford to be careful because the man they were chasing was a sex pest who had been 'bothering' the women in the park. Another caller to the radio station named Doug told me how he had been a teenager at the time of the "kissing man" scare and he and a friend had climbed a tree in Sefton Park after reading about Robin Hood when they noticed a very smart-looking man in a black suit dancing about in a clearing among the trees. Doug recalled the strange scene. 'He was dancing like ballroom dancers do, and he had his arm curled around the waist of his imaginary partner and he had his other hand up in the air as if he had hold of her hand.'

The next moment, the man had vanished into thin

air. The two boys got down from the tree and looked for the 'barmy man' but he was nowhere to be seen.

The third caller, a man in his sixties named Gareth Sterne related a terrifying incident which happened in Sefton Park during the period when the Romeo was on the loose. Gareth was 26 at the time and was seeing a student named Brigit who was into botany, and in broad daylight around 6.30pm on a hot July day in 1971, Gareth and Brigit were collecting leaves from the trees in the park, when Brigit said, 'What's that?'

About fifteen feet away, something black and shiny was coiled around the thick trunk of an ash tree. At first, Gareth thought it was a thick flexible pipe, but when he and Brigit walked to the other side of the tree they received a shock that literally left them shaking. The thing coiled around the ash tree was a thick black snake with a grinning face and two large brown human-looking eyes. As the couple looked on, a Y-shaped tongue slid down out of the grinning mouth of the giant reptilian, proving that it was not some inanimate model that had been attached to the tree as a joke. Gareth backed away and pulled Brigit with him, and then the couple ran off, putting as much distance as they could between themselves and that freakish-looking snake. Brigit scoured books at the library on snakes and never found a species of snake that looked like that one in Sefton Park, which Gareth estimated to be around twelve feet in length. Gareth and Brigit had not been drinking and did not take drugs. What then, was that black reptilian creature which reminded Gareth of the Biblical serpent in the Garden of Eden? It might be straining credibility a bit too far, but could the Sefton Park Romeo – a very superphysical and outlandish individual – be just the humanoid version of some shapeshifting creature that can metamorphose into the black dog Mrs Munford saw when the "kissing man" was being chased? And if that's the case, was he also able to transmogrify into that giant black snake with the *brown eyes* - the reported colour of the eyes of the Sefton Park Romeo? Morphogenesis is a fascinating biological process by which organisms can change their shape, and it can happen from the cellular level right up to creatures ranging from the butterfly to a penguin, which undergo metamorphosis after they leave their eggs. Even a human being, when it is developing in the womb of its mother will undergo some very strange transformations, including the development of gills at one point, and some people are even born with tails – almost as if some ancestor from millions of years ago (possibly a tailed monkey-like being) is trying to come through. Biologists say the gills, tails and other strange features that arise in the embryonic human are just the result of now-defunct DNA from millions of years ago in our genetic make-up, but it's possible that life forms millions of years ahead of us in the evolutionary game might be able to alter their cells by will, transforming themselves into all sorts of forms and creatures. I am probably light-aeons off the mark, but personally, I have a feeling that the being we label as the Sefton Park Romeo was some intelligent but psychologically-alien life form that was curious to know what human love was about and after an unsuccessful attempt at wooing the females of this world, it probably gave up and went back to whatever world – in space or time – it originated from. On the cosmic scale we are so small, we are almost non-existent, and so we see very little and know even less. We'll probably never know the truth about the Sefton Park Romeo, unless the ultra-loving oddball returns to our reality one day...

RIGHT INTO TOMORROW TODAY

The following strange and terrifying incident unfolded one scorching summer's day at the end of May 2003. A heatwave was sweeping Britain and the 100 degrees Fahrenheit mark was broken for the first time. The tabloid newspaper 28-year-old Daphne Towers was reading – found on the table outside Lydiate's Running Horses pub - declared that Britain was now hotter than the Northern Sahara and claimed 'Brits will bake for a week in tropical temperatures' – which was the usual kiss of death for any hopes of the soaring temperatures continuing, and predictably, within a couple of days the rain was flooding every part of the British Isles within its fractalized coastline. But for today, Daphne was determined to enjoy her day off from that soul-destroying job in retail, and she sat sipping a small glass of wine as she tossed the tabloid aside and let the good old sun in the blue sky work its solar therapy and top up her vitamin D. She was surrounded by about thirty people of all ages sitting at the tables outside the pub, when she saw a familiar face. It was the weathered walnut-coloured face of a man in his seventies that she only knew as Mr Crabtree. He'd been a neighbour at her home in Halewood since she was around ten, and he hadn't really changed – he'd always looked old. Daphne wanted to get him a drink but Mr Crabtree pointed to two smiling women around Daphne's age and said they were his nieces and that they were taking him home because he'd had 'a skin full'.

'Oh, well, it's allowed Mr Crabtree,' Daphne told him, almost getting up, but he was moving away from her now. 'Lovely seeing you!' Daphne waved and the old man walked to his nieces but then stumbled and landed on the table where a teenaged couple were drinking. Daphne went to go to his aid but Mr Crabtree laughed, got up, apologised to the couple he'd fallen on, and then he waved at Daphne. 'See you Daphne!' he shouted, and then he walked to the car with his nieces supporting him.

A very petite and thin woman with short blonde hair came over to Daphne and sat at the bench on the other side of the table. She said, 'Hope you don't mind me joining you?'

'No, no,' said Daphne, saying the opposite of how she felt, and smiling and shaking her head.

'Daphne isn't it?' the woman asked. Her blonde hair was greatly contrasted with her almost orange tanned skin, and she had a pair of very pale blue eyes. She looked as if she was in her late forties, or maybe older. When some fair-skinned people age, they don't look as if they've aged; they look as if they've just woken up with bags under their bleary eyes and young haircuts usually make them look worse, and this woman was of that facial type.

'Yes,' said Daphne, thrown by the way the stranger knew her name.

'I heard that old man say your name,' explained the woman.

'Oh, yes, he's an old neighbour of mine,' said Daphne, and noticing that the woman didn't have a drink, she asked her if she could get her one, even though she didn't really want to do that.

'No thanks,' the woman replied, and seemed to have difficulty trying to smile. The end of her lips went up but a smile simply failed to form, and her eyes seemed cold now.

Daphne felt embarrassed at the way the woman was gazing at her so intensely, and she fluffed her words, saying, 'I'm Daphne – sorry – you *know* I'm Daphne – er, what's your name?' The truth of the matter was that Daphne wasn't in the least interested in the woman's name; she was simply making small talk and she wished she could just leave now and enjoy the long drive back home before the rush hour kicked in. It was too hot and Daphne just wanted to get home, get out of her bra, and get in a cool shower.

'Natalie,' came the answer in a low flat-sounding voice.

'Been out for the day? It's lovely isn't it?' Daphne asked, and fidgeted with the wine glass, gently rocking it to and fro and squinting at the spangly sunlight reflecting off the Prosecco.

Natalie didn't answer. She asked: 'Where are you from?'

'Liverpool,' said Daphne, resenting the impertinence of the woman's tone, 'you from there too?'

'I mean the *area*,' Natalie said, her voice louder now, and she clenched her fists as they rested on the table. 'What area are you from?'

'Oh – Halewood,' Daphne told her, and beneath her graphene-thin veneer of civility, she thought, *I'm sorry I didn't leave earlier; I would've missed this arsehole.*

Daphne then looked at her watch and said, 'Oh God is it that time already?'

'Halewood?' Natalie asked, ignoring her staged reference to time, and her thin over-plucked eyebrows rose with surprise.

'Yes, why?' Daphne noted her animated reaction.

'So you're from Halewood and your name's Daphne?' asked Natalie, as if she was drawing some conclusion from the two facts, and she thinned those cold iceberg-blue eyes as she lasered Daphne's face with attention.

'Yes,' Daphne told her, and rose from the table saying, 'and I must return to Halewood now. No rest for the wicked.'

'I'm going to Halewood myself now,' Natalie revealed, and she stood up quickly.

'Oh,' was all Daphne could muster. She had a bad feeling about this woman; she seemed unbalanced.

Natalie sprung the question and Daphne somehow knew it was coming. 'Could you give me a lift, Daphne?' she asked. 'I'm supposed to get a cab home but I had a really bad experience with a cab driver a few weeks ago and I don't feel safe anymore with these private hire – '

'Yes, come on,' Daphne interrupted, and brushed her long hair out of her eyes and walked with Natalie to the pink Volkswagen Golf Mk4. As the two women got into the vehicle, the trapped hot air inside the car wafted against them, and Natalie suddenly asked: 'You married, Daphne?'

'No, I'm a lonesome pine at the moment – ' she was saying as she put on her seatbelt.

'A what?' Natalie's eyebrows dipped and crunched together over her small turned up nose.

'I'm single – not even seeing anyone at the moment.'

Daphne pulled down the sun visor and looked at her fed-up eyes.

'It's shit being single, isn't it?' Natalie asked, adding: 'Especially when you *were* with someone you were put on this earth to love.'

Daphne nodded and asked: 'Where about in Halewood do you want me to drop you off?'

'Er, do you know Yew Tree Farm?' Natalie asked.

'Yeah,' Daphne told her, 'do you work there? I love that place – with the café and that.'

'No,' Natalie replied, 'I don't work there, I just live by there.'

Daphne, knowing the journey home would take around half an hour, wondered what she could talk about to make the time in the car fly by. This woman was no conversationalist. She tried sport. 'Are you a red or a blue?'

'Here's the man I lived with, let me just show you him,' Natalie said, rummaging about in her handbag for her wallet. She thrust the faded Polaroid snap in front of Daphne's face.

'Er, I'm driving Natalie,' Daphne said, tilting her head so she could see the road, but Natalie moved the Polaroid so she kept it a few inches in front of Daphne's eyes.

'Do you recognise him now, eh?' she asked Daphne. 'Stanley.'

'I'm driving, sorry, Natalie, ' Daphne's voice went up in pitch out of irritation as she turned the car right at the junction of Bell's Lane and Southport Road.

'You know him?' Natalie withdrew the photograph away from Daphne's face at last.

'No,' said Daphne. 'Why did you split up? Hope you

don't mind me asking that.'

'He went off with a younger woman — a much younger woman,' Natalie said, and it sounded as if she was forcing each word of reply through clenched teeth as she stuffed the photograph of Stanley back into her wallet, and Daphne heard her whisper the F word.

'I'm sorry about that,' said Daphne, and she reached to her left and patted Natalie's hand — but her passenger batted it away.

'You've got a cheek!' Natalie roared, and she reached into her bag and took out a steak knife and in a flash she held the tip of it to a point on Daphne's neck a few inches under her left ear. Daphne froze as she felt the icy sharp steel tip press into her skin.

'What are you doing?' Daphne said in a gasping voice, unable to turn her head left in case the movement caused the knife to go in. She felt dizzy and everything seemed dreamlike now as she went into shock.

'I recognised you when that old man said "See you *Daphne!*" and I couldn't believe my eyes.'

'What are you talking about?' Daphne went down a gear as she curved the Golf into Liverpool Road North. With a feeling of intense disappointment she recalled putting on her seatbelt, because she was considering jumping out of the vehicle when it stopped at any lights.

'Talking about *you*, you devious bitch!' Natalie moved the knife a centimetre away from Daphne's throat. 'You didn't think I'd find you, but I followed you and Stanley when you used to go to that pub in Lydiate.'

'Natalie, you have got the wrong person here,'

Daphne told her in a voice that was whispering out of a dried-up throat. 'I don't know anyone called Stanley.'

'You horrible lying bastard,' Natalie seethed, and she placed the point of the steak knife against the tail of Daphne's left eye. 'You break up relationships without so much as a little thought about the hurt you cause. Well I am going to cut you up when we get to Halewood, and I am going to give Stanley some of the bits. Those for a start,' Natalie's left hand slapped Daphne's bosom.

'They'll put you away for a long time,' said Daphne, and she coughed and wanted to throw up because of the fear welling up in her stomach. 'It's not worth it, and you'll be killing an innocent person.'

Natalie almost sung the reply in a carefree voice. 'They'll put me away in a nice cushy mental hospital because it'll be diminished responsibility won't it?' Natalie moved the point of the knife down from the corner of Daphne's eye to the corner of her lips. 'Crime of passion at least.'

'Natalie, *please* put that knife away, I beg of you. If this car goes over a speedbump you might do some harm.'

'I'll do more than that to you when we get to Halewood,' Natalie threatened, 'I'll cut that perfect nose off and your private parts and leave them somewhere for all the people of Halewood to see!' And as she finished the shocking sentence the mobile phone in the front right pocket of Daphne's jeans emitted a melody.

Daphne assumed it'd be her mum, wanting to know if she was coming round to tea later. With a lump of intense sorrow in her throat she wondered if she'd ever see her mum again.

'Don't answer it! I'll put this through you if you do!' Natalie warned.

'If you did, we'd crash,' Daphne told her in a broken voice, and made an involuntary gulping sound.

'I don't give a shit,' said Natalie in a nonchalant voice, 'the airbag might save me but you'll be dead, I promise you. I'll stab you before we crash.'

Daphne saw the lights were changing to red at the end of the road, and despite being numb with shock, she had the mental composure to indicate and move over to the left lane so she could turn onto the Westway.

The mobile phone stopped ringing as the lights changed to green a minute later, and Natalie started to cry. The car travelled just over 300 yards and turned onto the Northway route, and Daphne tried to reason with the demented Natalie again. 'Natalie, someone has hurt you, and I sympathise with you and I can tell you're obviously a decent person, but you've got the wrong person here – I'd never have an affair.'

'Liar!' Natalie screamed and she plunged the knife into Daphne's headrest three times. 'Come out with any more shit like that and I will take your head off!' she bellowed, and drops of her spittle hit the side of Daphne's face. Throughout the two miles travelling down Northway to the M57 motorway, Daphne tried to think of ways out of this nightmare as Natalie rambled on about Stanley and how perfect he'd been until he was taken away from her. The Golf curved onto Dunnings Bridge Road and joined the M57, and Daphne slowly changed gear and sent the vehicle's speed up to 75 mph. As the car passed under a railway bridge, Daphne looked in her rear view mirror and saw a police car cruising behind her. She decided to attract the attention of the cops in it by speeding, but she'd have to increase the speed in sly slow increments so as not to alarm nutty Natalie. Whenever Daphne ever so gently pressed her Keds canvas shoe onto the accelerator, she would make some remark in an effort to distract Natalie from the rise in the car engine's pitch. And it worked. On the first increase of speed, which took the car to 80 mph, Daphne said: 'How long were you and Stanley married?'

'Why do you want to know?' Natalie asked, clenching the knife handle in her lap with the blade tip pointing at the roof of the car. 'Feeling shitty now are you, after all the damage you did to the marriage?'

The orange-red needle of the car's speedometer indicated 95 mph, but Natalie was that wrapped up in the heated duologue between her and Daphne, she didn't notice it, and then she heard the police siren behind the vehicle.

'Shit, what do they want?' Daphne asked, looking in her rear-view and wing mirrors.

'Keep going!' Natalie warned, looking at the wing mirror on her side of the car. 'You stop and I'll put this right through your face!' she shouted, and held the tip of the steak knife under her captive's chin. A droplet of perspiration from Daphne's chin was transported by capillary action onto the tip of that blade.

'They'll cut in front of me if I don't stop!' Daphne told the disturbed Natalie, who started to swear as she realised that the police would indeed cut in front of the Golf, and even if they didn't they'd radio ahead to their colleagues and there'd be a roadblock waiting.

The police car drew alongside Daphne's car with its roof-lights flashing and its siren wailing and the cop in the front passenger seat gave the 'pull over' gesture with his hand. Daphne decelerated and as the car engine played a deep glissando tone, Natalie told her over and over that she would stick the knife through her if she tried to tell the police about the situation. She held the knife between Daphne's back and the car seat.

The car pulled over onto the hard shoulder at a point on the motorway just before a bridge. There was the gentle grassy slope of an embankment to the left and a pylon towering over the field there. The police car pulled over about twenty feet in front of the Volkswagen and a thickset policeman wearing shades got out and walked to the driver's window, which was already wound down. 'You the owner of this car?' he asked Daphne.

'Yes officer,' Daphne told him, and she could feel the blade touching the exposed part of her lower back where her tee shirt had ridden up from her jeans.

'You were nearly doing a ton then,' the policeman casually said, and Daphne noticed he was chewing gum. He looked back at his car as she spoke.

Daphne winked at him, trying to engage his attention and said: 'I'm sorry, officer, I didn't realise I was going that fast. I've just come from the Running Horses – it's a pub.'

'I *know* what the Running Horses is, love,' said the cop, 'and I must ask you: have you been drinking?'

'She hasn't touched a drop,' said Natalie, pressing the blade into Daphne's back.

'She went to a pub and didn't drink?' the policeman said, and he bent down to look through the window at Natalie.

'Help me,' Daphne whispered as the policeman's head came close to hers.

'What was that?' the policeman asked Daphne.

In a heartbeat, Daphne threw a punch with her right fist that caught Natalie off guard, and it made contact against the woman's nose. The punch stunned her, and as the policeman looked on in amazement, Daphne undid her seatbelt, and tried to open the car door, but the policeman was in the way, so she could only open it a few inches. She put all of her might into forcing that door, and she managed to squeeze out of the vehicle. She ran towards the back of the vehicle and she saw the policeman standing there, looking at her with a bemused expression. 'Where are you going?' he asked, and then he turned and looked at his colleague, and saw that he was already getting out of the police car. Daphne ran up the grassy embankment and shouted at the policeman: 'The woman in that car's got a knife! She was trying to kill me!'

Natalie got out of the car, and the policeman who had been questioning Daphne walked around the bonnet of the Golf and Natalie lunged at him and began to stab him in the neck and face. Daphne screamed as she saw the spray of arterial blood in the harsh sunshine issuing like a geyser from the neck wound. As the policeman staggered backwards and fell on the floor of the hard shoulder, his colleague reached for something on his belt and ran towards Natalie, and the unhinged woman ran in Daphne's direction. Daphne fell over as she reached the top of the embankment, and then she got up and ran across a well-kept stretch of grass where she could see the legs of the humming electricity pylon. She ran to the road at the edge of the grassy area – Brewery Lane - and looked back, expecting to see Natalie appear with the knife, but she saw no one. Daphne tried to flag down passing cars, and most of them slowed down but not one of them stopped for her. After about ten minutes – and subjective time is hard to gauge, especially when you're in a very emotional state – Daphne gingerly ventured back to the scene of the stabbing – and she looked down the embankment to see only her car. Had the police arrested Natalie and left Daphne's car behind for the forensic investigation? Something just didn't seem right. Daphne slowly ascended the embankment, and she kept looking around in case the mad knife woman was lying in wait for her. Daphne walked back to her car, checked the back seats and saw the vehicle was empty. She looked at the floor and saw no traces of that awful stabbing of the policeman on the hard shoulder of the motorway. Daphne quickly got into the car and locked the doors. The key was still in the ignition. She looked at the headrest of her seat and saw that there were no stab marks from Natalie's knife. Doubting her sanity, Daphne drove off and throughout the journey home she ached to call her mother on her mobile but she didn't want to distract herself from driving and her hands were shaking. As soon as the car reached the district of Halewood, Daphne drove to her mother's house. She told her the whole story, and Daphne's mum – Jill – said she must have had her drink spiked at that pub, but Daphne said the ordeal she had been through had been real – it had not been some hallucination. Mother and daughter watched the news and listened to the radio but there were no reports of any policeman being stabbed on the M57. Daphne was so upset at the weird and inexplicable experience, she slept over at her mum's house and she just couldn't get to the bottom of the mystery. A month later, Daphne went to a party at a house in Halewood, and a man who looked familiar to Daphne approached her and said he was an uncle of the girl who had thrown the party – a girl named Cheri who Daphne had only known for a few weeks. The man looked as if he was about 45 years of age, and gave his name as Stan. He soon made it quite clear that he fancied Daphne, and with a sense of mounting panic in the pit of Daphne's stomach, she recognised Stan; he was Stanley – the man in that Polaroid snap that Natalie had shown her during that ride of terror. Daphne was so shocked, she backed away from Stanley and toppled over a lad who had been crouching as he looked at a collection of vinyl records. She landed on a sofa on her back, and Stanley smiled and said, 'I love a young lady in that position.'

'Have you got a wife named Natalie?' Daphne asked, and she quickly got up off the sofa before he could even answer.

The way Stan reacted to Daphne's question convinced her that he was indeed the wife of the crazed woman she had met at the pub in Lydiate a month back.

'I was joking my dear – just breaking the ice, okay?' Stan said, obviously backpedalling now. He went to talk to another girl at the party who looked even younger than Daphne.

Daphne decided it was time to leave, but there was a knot of rowdy young men blocking the hallway, so she asked Cheri, the niece of the lascivious Stanley, if she could go out the back way as she didn't feel well. Cheri tried to convince her to stay but Daphne insisted and said she needed to go home. Cheri led Daphne out of the house via the kitchen, and she walked with her across the back garden to the door set into a tall wooden fence. A barbecue was in progress and a woman with short blonde hair shouted to Cheri: 'Fancy a nice cheeseburger with onions, love?'

It was *her* - Natalie. And she was standing there at a combination gas and charcoal barbecue grill – and she had a steak knife in her hand. 'No thanks Auntie Nat,' Cheri shouted, and then she turned to Daphne, smiled, grabbed her by the arm and looked back at her aunt to say, 'This is Daphne by the way, my new mate!'

'Oh, hi Daphne!' Natalie said, raising the hand with the knife in to acknowledge her. 'Do *you* want a cheeseburger?' she asked.

'No thanks,' Daphne replied and she quickly left the garden.

Daphne went straight to her mother's house and told her what had happened, and mother and daughter talked about the weird incident over drinks into the wee small hours of the morning, till Daphne went home at around 3am, and she called her mother as soon as she arrived safely at her place. Daphne's mum believed the whole thing had been some supernatural warning about getting involved with a married man. Daphne said she would never have gone with Stanley as he looked like a sleazeball. 'Yes, but when you've had a few drinks you let your guard down sometimes and slimeballs like that take advantage of you,' said Daphne's mum. About a month after this, Stanley ran off with a 19-year-old friend of his niece, and his wife later confronted the teen and gave her a black eye, so Daphne feels her mother was right – that something did warn her off, but to this day she still wonders just *what* that thing was which issued the terrifying warning.

THE WARNING EMOJIS

One sunny but razor-cold December morning in 2016, two young ladies in their twenties – Kristine and Elsa – were due to meet at the Starbucks situated off New Chester Road, less than a mile north of Childer Thornton. Kristine and Elsa, who both hailed from Hooton, had been friends since their childhood days but after Elsa had married a Liverpool man and moved to Mossley Hill two years back, the girls had seen less of one another – only meeting up now and then of a weekend for a day out. The young ladies did keep in touch via their mobiles though, and on this wintry day they were supposed to meet up at 11am to have coffee and cake as they discussed Kristine's idea about opening a vintage clothing boutique in Birkenhead. Eleven o'clock came and went, and at a quarter past the hour, Kristine decided she'd text Elsa to see why she was late. Before she could even key in the passcode to the mobile, it played a brief xylophonic ringtone, and a very strange text message appeared. It was a rather alarming emoji Kristine had never seen before: a little cartoonlike icon of a red-headed man in a coffin, with the uppercase letters RIP next to it. That little man in the coffin had a red beard and to Kristine's eyes it looked like a caricature of Rory – Elsa's husband. Who had sent this morbid text message? It was from someone called Heela – and there was no number listed. Kristine knew no one named Heela, but whoever he or she was, they had a sense of gallows humour.

'I thought that was my phone ringing then,' said a man who looked about Kristine's age. He'd just parked himself at the table to her left, and he almost elbowed over his drink. 'Shit!' he exclaimed, and seized the Starbucks cup with his two hands before it toppled. 'Don't want to spill my Caffè Misto,' he said, and smiled at Kristine.

'I've just had a weird anonymous text; bit creepy too,' Kristine told the stranger without taking her eyes off her phone. 'Look,' she thrust her iPhone out and the young man squinted at the morbid icon, then turned his eyes to Kristine. 'Just someone messing about,' he said, 'is a bit morbid though.'

Then Kristine's phone began to ring, and it displayed Elsa's name upon its screen. Kristine answered it and Elsa could hardly get her words out as she fought back tears.

'Krissy – it – it's Else – Rory's dead, he – he died – I –' began Elsa.

'What!' Kristine blurted out, numbed by the tragic and totally unexpected news.

'They – they think it was a heart attack,' sobbed Elsa, 'and me mum's only just called me to tell me. They only found him a while ago. Oh Krissy...' Elsa trailed off and burst into tears.

Elsa had reached Lime Street Station when her mother had called her to break the news so she was returning home now in a taxi. After Elsa had hung up, Kristine recalled that emoji of the coffin with the man in it who looked like Rory, and she turned to the man on the next table, who asked, 'You okay?'

Kristine told him what had just happened, and the

man – who later introduced himself as Stephen Sheridan, said that whoever had sent that distasteful emoji had to have known that Rory had died, and must have had software to make the little man in the icon look like him. 'And he obviously knows you and your mobile number,' Stephen added.

'I don't know anyone who works with phones,' Kristine replied, racking her brains to recall any acquaintance who could be such a cold-hearted joker, but it was so hard to collect her thoughts when she had received such a terrible shock. She had got on well with Rory and Elsa had always told her how she had found a soulmate in Rory.

'Can you think of anyone – maybe someone who works with computers, an IT savvy type?' Stephen said, but still Kristine knew no one in that line of work. Stephen asked Kristine if she'd like to go for a drink, as she'd received a bit of a shock, and he assured her he was not trying to hook up with her, but she said, 'I think I'll just go home, but thanks anyway.'

'Of course, I totally understand that – I was insensitive asking you,' Stephen said, his face looking full of awkward shame.

'No, don't be daft, maybe if we meet again under better circumstances,' said Kristine, with tears trickling from her eyes. 'I better go.'

Kristine got up from the table and Stephen handed her a paper napkin to dab her eyes. She called Elsa but her best friend's mum answered and said Elsa just needed some time to grieve and advised Kristine not to come over to Liverpool yet. Kristine left Starbucks in a daze, and she phoned for a private cab, and when the operator asked her who the cab was for, she could hardly reply because she was so choked up.

When Kristine got home, she looked over at the electric piano in the niche next to the fireplace. She had been trying to teach Rory a piece of music he was fond of: *Bella's Lullaby* from the soundtrack of the film *Twilight*. She wanted to sit down and play the piece, even though it would probably have her in tears. She sat by the fire for a bit, then decided to play the piece of music she associated with Rory when two strange emojis were sent to Kristine's mobile. The first was of an electric plug in a socket, and there was a plus sign (+) next to this image, followed by an emoji that looked exactly like Kristine – same profile and dark blue hair – bending over. Next to this image was an equals sign and the word OUCH!

Kristine was spooked and baffled by this latest text from "Heela" – what on earth did it mean? She found out when she bent down to plug in her electric piano; her back went. The pain was so intense, she almost passed out. She staggered to the sofa and fell on it. As she writhed in agony, she thought of the text message that had apparently predicted the painful mishap. These weird text messages with their eerie emojis continued to bombard Kristine, and they seemingly predicted two deaths, a fire, a miscarriage, a car crash, and even a life-threatening medical diagnosis concerning Kristine's mother, and then, on New Year's Day, the last text message from Heela was sent, and it simply read, "Have a Wonderful New Year". If some warped hacker was behind the weird text messages, how did he or she know in advance what was going to happen to the people they referred to? It's almost as if someone with a talent for clairvoyance was sending them, and Kristine herself believes that Heela was some mischievous spirit – and if this is so, why was Kristine on the receiving end of the frightening texts? The mystery remains unsolved.

THE READER

On the Sunday morning of 18 February 1996, a 22-year-old named Damon kissed the wife and then he left the flat on the top floor of the hi-rise tower block in south Liverpool. It wasn't *his* wife; he'd been having an affair with the 30-year-old married lady for three months and Karen had assured Damon her husband Frankie did not suspect a thing. Frankie, a security guard, was due home at 8am and the time was almost seven. Damon had cut it fine on this occasion because he'd got a bit carried away with his sexual shenanigans and on top of that the battery in the bedside clock had run down and he and Karen eventually noticed that it had been 6.20am for an awfully long time. Damon rode the lift down, left the tower block, and was about to get into his mini when he realised he'd left his lighter at Karen's flat. He'd flushed the roaches of the joints down the toilet and opened the window to let the cold February breeze blow the cannabis smoke out of the bedroom in case Frankie wanted to know where his wife had obtained resin, but he had been stupid enough to leave his blingy silver lighter – engraved with his initials – behind in the flat. He went back into the block of flats and he stepped into the lift after the doors parted even slower than normal – as if something was trying to delay him, he thought. He heard a heavy plodding of boots in the communal area, and then a towering muscular man, at least six feet and six inches in height, with a shaven head and a tough-looking sandblasted face came into the lift with him. The lift rocked on its cables as this man entered. Was this Frankie, home early? Damon wondered – he had never seen Karen's hubby, but she had called him 'baldy hole' and mentioned his height many times, and how he had thrashed the living daylight out of men who had merely smiled at her.

The man stabbed the top button inside the elevator with a thick square-tipped finger and folded arms that were each thicker than Damon's torso. Sixty feet up, the lift became stuck between floors.

The bald Goliath swore at the lift controls, slammed the ball of his hand into the buttons, then ranted: 'One of those bastard days! And you know on top of this, a mate of mine told me the missus has been having it away with some spotty little student while I'm at work.'

Damon's throat dried up and he couldn't even reply. Is he onto me? Damon wondered, and he could feel a nerve in his cheek fluttering.

'If there's one thing I despise in life, it's the home wrecker,' boomed the man, and then he turned to Damon, and said, 'I'm Frankie by the way. And you are?'

'Damon,' came the choked answer. Frankie smirked at the name, as if he thought it was a bit lad-di-dah and middle class – that was the impression Damon got from his sneer. Frankie then started raving on about infidelity, and what he was going to do if he caught his wife with the 'cockroach. 'When I catch the little shit, he's going right over the balcony – twelve stories. ' Frankie traced an arc in the air, showing the trajectory Damon would take when he was hurled to his death from the top floor of the tower block.

'You'd get done, though, is he worth it?' said Damon, sweating profusely.

'Nah, it was suicide wasn't it? The little shit jumped, and I even tried to stop him from taking his life; I struggled with him before I gave him a big shove,' said Frankie, smiling at this explanation, but then the smile died and he continued to seethe about adulterers. Then Frankie went quiet, and he turned to Damon and suddenly asked: 'Who you visiting, lad?'

'My Auntie, he said, trembling, 'Auntie Joan. She's been bad with her chest. Bronchitis. Been going on messages for her.'

'Joan Joan Joan;' muttered Frankie. 'I don't know any Joan up there. What floor did you say you were going to?'

'The top; the top floor.' Damon's face was glistening with sweat as he forced the words out of his dried-up mouth.

'I live on the top floor,' said Frankie, with a puzzled look, 'and I don't know anyone named Joan up there.'

'She's like a recluse – never goes out,' said Damon, coughing now because his throat was so arid. 'That's why you haven't seen her.'

'Don't take me for a fool you little spotty no-mark!' Frankie suddenly exploded, and he pinned Damon against the wall of the lift, then smashed his giant fist into the wall, denting the steel plating a few inches from Damon's head.

'Don't kill me please! I've got heart trouble!' lied Damon, his legs collapsing under him in a corner of the lift. He shielded his eyes, unsure whether he'd be kicked to death or be beaten to pulp by the sledgehammer fists of this herculean psychopath, but instead, the violent colossus stood bent over him with a faint smile. 'It's alright son, get up,' he said, then backed away exhaling as he thumped his right fist into the palm of his hand, as if he was bringing his volcanic temper back under control.

Damon slowly got to his feet and was so unsteady on them he had to lean against the wall to support himself. He looked confused.

'I'm not Frankie. So *this time* you're alright,' said the well-built hard-knock. He folded his muscle-bound arms and added: 'And, you're wondering how I knew you were screwing Frankie's missus; well, I read minds you see; it's a problem I've had since I was clobbered on the head a few years ago. I'm a bouncer by trade, and I switch my curse off most of the time. I'm always taking on other people's problems.'

Damon just looked on, speechless, leaning against the wall of the lift.

The bouncer looked Damon in the eyes and said: 'Your 'arl lady's name is Susan, and you have two sister's – Kate and Brenda, and a cat named Trixy. Your dad pissed off years ago to go and live with a woman over on Wirral.'

Damon still found the bouncer's claim about mind-reading hard to accept, and yet everything he had told Damon was true.

'So, sonny,' said the bouncer, 'go and get that lighter, and then stop seeing other men's wives because it's not nice; it happened to me you see, and I nearly killed the bastard who screwed my girl. Do you know what an orchiectomy is?'

Damon shook his head, still unable to get a word

out.

'Well you need something like this – ' the bouncer swung his hand around to his back jean pocket and took out a penknife with a 5-inch blade. 'You lift up the offender's prick and you cut his balls off. It doesn't half hurt. *He* nearly bled to death. Now, I know Frankie won't even be that light-hearted; he'll probably just make you suck on the barrels of a sawn-off shotgun and pull the trigger. So, well – you get the picture don't you lad?'

'Yeah – yes – thanks,' stammered Damon.

The bouncer leaned forward, palms on either side of the lift door so he faced the floor. He gave a little cough – and there was a faint humming sound above, somewhere up the shaft. The lift started moving. The bouncer got out on the fifth floor, and Damon remained in the lift until it reached the top floor. He called at Karen's flat, and said he'd forgotten the lighter. She asked him if he was alright because he looked very pale. He nodded and Karen searched the bedroom for the lighter. It was under her pillow. Karen held his hands and tried to kiss him as he stood in the hallway, ready to leave but he broke away from her hold, and when she asked him what was wrong, he opened the door and left without a word of reply. He went down by the stairs on this occasion, just in case the lift became stuck again, and he never returned to Karen and he never bothered with married women again.

VAMPIRE CULT

In the pages of the Bible's New Testament (John 11:25) it is written: 'Jesus said unto her [Martha, sister of Lazarus], "I am the resurrection, and the life: he that believeth in me, though he were dead, yet shall he live." '

The gospels make it clear; the only way to everlasting life is through Jesus Christ, but in the years 1967 and 1984, vampiric beings made a similar claim, and for years I have studied the accounts of these two strange beings to see if perhaps they were part of some vampire cult in which victims of the bloodsuckers would be turned into undying blood-craving creatures. I'll start with the first case.

On the Tuesday morning of 6 May 1952 at around 3.20am, a group of silhouettes was seen skulking about among the gravestones of St James's Cemetery, a vast sunken graveyard next to the sandstone splendour of the Anglican Cathedral on Hope Street. A resident named Phyllis was suffering from acute insomnia at her third-floor flat on Canning Street, and so she got up and went to look out the window with the light off. She had a good view of Hope Street, the cathedral, and the adjoining cemetery, and by the light of the moon hanging over the chimney pots of Toxteth, Phyllis could see that some of the shadowy people creeping about among the gravestones were wearing cloaks. She put their number at six. On the following morning, work-bound people taking a short cut through the cemetery saw that one of the tombs built into the sandstone walls had been opened, and whoever had broken into the Victorian sepulchre had been very determined and organised, because they had neatly removed huge blocks of stone to gain entry and they had even wrenched away the copings to allow the removal of wrought-iron railings that had guarded the place of rest for a century. A child's coffin lay three feet away from the desecrated tomb with its lead-lined lid prised open, revealing the lifelike open-eyed corpse of one Eliza Nicholson. Inside the open tomb, police found the nine other coffins of the Nicholson family, and some of the caskets had been 'interfered' with, according to later press reports. Some accounts say garlic bulbs were scattered about the tomb and white crosses had been daubed on the walls. Eliza's coffin was resealed and she was put back in the tomb, which was subsequently bricked up. Police blamed vandals – possibly thieves who wanted the lead from the coffins, but as the local Parks and Gardens Superintendent P. F. McCormack told reporters from *The Daily Mirror* and the *Liverpool Echo*: 'I don't think it was vandals or criminals. This was done with great precision and no lead or valuables were missing from the tomb. These people went to a great deal of trouble using crowbars and other tools to get into that tomb.'

All the same, the police staked out the cemetery on the nights after the incident and hid behind gravestones – but the criminals never returned to the scene of the crime. Fifteen years later, in 1967, a group of about sixty students were having a party at a house on Percy Street one summer evening, when a long-haired and bearded stranger in his early twenties gatecrashed the "shindig" and told the revellers that he had discovered the secret of eternal life. At this time, drug-taking was rife and young people were always looking for new kicks and ways to expand their minds, and interest in the Occult was at an all-time high, so most of the students at the party were absolutely transfixed by the claims of the hippy-like gatecrasher – who said his name was Adam. He told his mesmerised peers that there was a hole in the wall of a certain tomb in St James's Cemetery (which Adam called "that canyon graveyard down there" because it was a sunken cemetery over a hundred feet below street level), and that he had been told by a voice within the tomb to put his hand through the hole. Adam had then felt a slight pin-prick in his wrist. According to Adam, the being in the tomb was a man who called himself Chris the New Christ and he had been resurrected by Jesus, and he had chosen Liverpool to inaugurate his cult of the Undying Ones. Adam said he had been dying from a hole in his heart before he was 'reborn' and was now able to stay awake for weeks at a time.

One of the people at the party was a 20-year-old man named Graham, and although he was a little drunk and had been having a great time, he was also the nephew of a certain vicar, and he looked at himself as a lapsed Christian. He thought the claims of Adam about Chris the Christ sounded blasphemous and very shady, and he tried to talk his girlfriend Frieda from going down to the cemetery with a group of other people. Frieda called Graham a bore and said that if he didn't go with her she was leaving him. Graham marched out of the flat in a huff and when Frieda caught up with him he told her he was going to make a telephone call to his uncle because he suspected the hippy Adam of trying to recruit young people for a group of Satanists.

'Oh grow up you square!' countered Frieda, and she ran off to join the rest of her friends down in the cemetery.

Fifty of the students had eagerly followed Adam into St James's Cemetery and he led them to the tomb with the hole in its frontage.

'Shush! Shush, be quiet!' Adam told the excited young men and women gathered around the tomb. 'Let me talk to my master,' he said, and after the giggles and excited banter had died down, Adam brought his mouth close to the hole in the front of the walled-up tomb and in a soft voice he said: 'Chris – Chris the Christ, Redeemer of humankind, are you there my supreme master?'

There was no reply for about six seconds, and then a raspy voice hissed: 'Yes – did you bring any?'

'Yes, I brought many, master,' said Adam, 'and they are all young, and they all wish to live forever.'

'Are there any virgins among them?' Chris asked.

There was a wave of chuckles by the inane among the group of students.

'I doubt it, my Lord,' Adam said with a smile to the hole in the wall.

'No! Wait, I am!' said Frieda, fighting her way to get to the front of the crowd.

'Yes, master, there is one!' Chris said excitedly into the squarish hole in the tomb facade.

'And she has not been penetrated nor has she never received the seed of a man?' was the strange and rather rude question posed by the gravelly-voiced person hidden in the tomb.

'No, I have never been shagged,' said Frieda, slightly unsteady on her feet because of all the drinking, 'and I have most certainly never had any seed in me, man's or bird's,' she added, and everyone laughed, then some girl shouted: 'Pure as snow!'

'Adam,' said the unsettling sissing voice, 'bring the virgin to me last, after I have taken blood from all the others.'

'I will, master,' said Adam, nodding.

'What is the name of the virgin who will become my wife?' Chris then asked.

'What's your name, love?' Adam asked Frieda.

'Wife?' Frieda asked with great surprise, and she stumbled backwards and two men caught her and laughed. 'Who said anything about a frigging marriage?'

'Bring them to me, Adam,' said the voice from the tomb. 'Bring them to Chris the New Christ! I am the only way to everlasting life!' said Chris, a lot louder now, but one of the young men present, an Irishman named Barry, said, 'I don't know if this is just some stupid joke, but the voice of that Chris is making my skin crawl.'

Adam suddenly ran up to Barry and threw a powerful upper-cut punch to his pointed elfin jaw which knocked the young Irishman out cold. 'Blasphemer!' Adam roared, and he tried to stamp on Barry's head but several of the men pushed him back and dragged the unconscious lad out of harm's way.

Adam then told the volunteers for eternal life to queue up, and a young man forced his girlfriend to the front of the queue and Adam seized the girl and roughly bent her left arm up her back and forced her to shove her right arm into the hole. Her screams echoed throughout the cemetery, and she said she'd been bitten. 'It's sucking my blood! Stop it!' she cried, and fainted.

The line of people moved forward and the drunk and drugged put their hands into the hole and someone in the tomb seized their hands and wrists and they all felt sharp teeth sink into their wrists, followed by the sensation of blood being sucked out of their veins. After each man or woman was bitten, Adam said to them, 'Chris the Christ has received your wine. Welcome to eternal life!'

A few more people arrived in the cemetery, and Frieda started to feel very scared. Every time she tried to sneak away, Adam dragged her back. The ones who had been bitted drank the bottles of wine they had brought into the place of the dead, and some even played guitars and flutes. After about twenty minutes, when the last of the volunteers were offering their blood to the unseen Redeemer in the tomb, a nasty orgy broke out. Una, a diminutive, nervous and innocent girl of seventeen who had befriended Frieda at the party was carried off by four men against her wishes and laid out on an old toppled gravestone. She was stripped as she screamed for help...

Adam dragged Frieda to the tomb and told Chris: 'Master, your promised virgin is ready.'

'Keep her there and I will come out shortly,' came a reply that was barely a whisper.

'If you don't let me go I'll scream,' Frieda warned Adam, and the latter suddenly clamped his hand over her mouth and held her with her arm up her back.

It was around 4am, and starting to get light, and Frieda heard a commotion among the debauchees of the orgy. She saw two men on motorbikes approach, skilfully weaving their machines between the forest of gravestones. The two strangers were dressed in flamboyant, old-fashioned-looking clothes. They propped the motorcycles up against gravestones and came over to the tomb of Chris. The taller, stout one with a beard carried a green canvas bag and the other, a slightly younger man of about thirty years of age with long blond hair, carried what looked like a Gladstone bag. This latter man opened the Gladstone bag and took out a large golden cross embedded with pearls emeralds and rubies, while his companion opened a long green canvas bag and took out something that looked like a red metal watering can but he produced a lighter and lit a wick at the tip of the spout where the perforated nozzle would have been. He then pressed his finger on a small lever in the handle of the can and a jet of flame jumped into the air. The thing was some type of flame thrower.

Adam threw Frieda down onto the grass and lunged at the blond stranger who was carrying the elaborate cross, but the bearded man unleashed a roaring burst of flame which hit Adam in the face. Frieda screamed as she smelt the aroma of petrol and saw Adam instinctively throw his hands up to his face. The cross-toting blond kicked Adam hard in the testicles, and as the disciple of Chris bent over in agony, he received a powerful boot in the face from the elegantly-dressed blond. Another jet of flame jumped out of that odd-looking can and set Adam's hair ablaze. He screamed and tried to pat the fire out and Frieda saw the skin fall off Adam's face.

'Who *are* you?' Frieda asked the violent blond dandy, and without looking at her, he casually said, 'My name is Jonathan, and this gentleman here – ' and he indicated the bearded man with his thumb, 'is Charles. We are vampire-hunters.'

From the cavalier way Jonathan had answered her question, Frieda thought he was unbalanced – and frighteningly violent.

The two self-styled vampire hunters went to the tomb where Chris the vampiric being was hiding, and Jonathan said to Charles, 'So, this is his lair.'

Charles poked the spout of his flame thrower into the hole and shot a column of liquid fire into it.

The thing in there let out an unholy scream.

'What is it?' Frieda appeared at the side of Jonathan. 'The thing in there; what is it?'

'A vampire – what do you think?' Jonathan asked, and he took the flame thrower off Charles, and while his companion rummaged through the canvas bag, Jonathan smiled as he let loose more jets of cruel white flame.

Charles took out a huge crowbar and he began to lever the blocks of stone which formed the front of the tomb until five of them were loose. He then took out a massive hammer, almost as big and heavy as a sledge-hammer, and he belted the blocks so they fell into the tomb. The orgy had well and truly stopped now, and most of the ones who had shared their blood with Chris stood naked among the gravestones, watching the proceedings with blank, emotionless faces.

'Did he siphon off your blood? Did he bite you at all?' Jonathan asked Frieda and she shook her head and breathlessly told him: 'He wanted to marry me! And that brute held me here against my will,' she said, pointing to Adam, who was now shaking in agony from the severe burns to his face and hands. His bald head smouldered, and he was speaking jibberish.

'What's your name?' Jonathan asked Frieda.

She told him and, and then she asked him why he was dressed so outlandishly but he did not address her question.

'Frieda, get as far away from here as you can, and stay away from here for the rest of your life,' said Jonathan.

'What – you mean now?' she asked, and seemed surprised at the advice.

'Yes, now,' said Jonathan, 'and if any of your friends were bitten by the thing in that tomb, you must never associate with them again. They're as good as dead now.'

'Can't I stay and see what you're going to do?' Frieda asked. She was starting to fancy Jonathan.

'No you can't!' Jonathan told her, 'Now get out of here and leave by the gate to the south. Go!'

'Where's south?' she asked, disappointed at the order, and Jonathan pointed at the Upper Parliament side of the cemetery.

She looked over at poor Una. She sat propped up against an obelisk, and there was blood pouring from savage bite-marks all over her. The four men had had their fun with her and she looked as if she'd lost her mind. She was beyond help now. Frieda reluctantly hurried away, and when she looked back a minute later she could hear piercing screams and she saw flashes of light from that flamethrower.

When most of the blocks had been removed by the vampire killers, the crowd saw a tall greyish naked man with huge black eye sockets and a mouth of fangs cowering in a far corner of the tomb. Jonathan thrust the golden cross at the weird entity and it screamed and shielded its eyes.

'You're killing Christ!' screamed a naked girl who had been bitten by "Chris", but Jonathan replied, 'That is no more Christ than the man in the moon! It's a vampire! Get out of here!'

'I'm not a vampire!' said the monstrosity in the corner of the dank tomb. 'Please don't kill me! I'm not a vampire, I'm not!' It whined and got down on its knees, but as it grovelled, Jonathan could clearly see the entity's fanged teeth.

Charles fired the flamethrower at the kneeling grey figure and the fire was so intense, Jonathan backed out of the tomb and knocked over the damned nude girl who had tried to protect the thing which had condemned her to an awful end. Charles backed out of the tomb with smoke billowing around him, and then he turned and went to pick up the bags with Jonathan.

At the far end of the cemetery, Frieda bumped into her boyfriend Graham, and she tried to tell him what had happened, but he interrupted her, saying, 'I know, I know, Frieda – my uncle sent for them!'

'What?' Frieda was confused.

'My uncle – the reverend – he contacted them,' said Graham. 'I had my suspicions you see – I thought there was something very wrong about a thing promising eternal life in return for blood.'

'Who are they?' Frieda asked.

'I don't really know that much about them,' confessed Graham, 'they're from Huyton and everyone thinks they're eccentric crackpots.'

'I just want to go home now, ' said Frieda, and she seemed exhausted. As she and Graham walked up the gentle incline past the wooded area close to the old lodge, Frieda sniffled and wiped her eyes. 'Graham, that Jonathan fellow said that all those people who were bitten by that thing are as good as dead. Poor Una, she was like my kid sister.'

Graham looked shocked. 'He bit Tony Morrison – he's a good friend.'

'Well stay away from him now, Graham,' said Frieda, 'and maybe we should start going to church. I don't feel safe.'

'Whatever that thing was,' said Graham, looking towards the flickering light in the tomb and the resulting long shadows cast by the gravestones and obelisks, 'they've killed it now, so you'll be alright now, Frieda. And yes, I think we should start attending church.'

'Do you really think I'm safe now, Graham?' Frieda asked, and she squeezed his hand as they walked towards the south gate, which had been left wide open.

'I know you are, Frieda,' her boyfriend told her, 'good has triumphed over evil here this morning.'

The couple then heard a sniggering sound coming from the woods to the left, and Frieda yelped with shock.

'Bye bye Frieda!' said a hissing voice.

Moments later, Jonathan and Charles roared past the couple on their bikes and left through the gateway.

Graham and Frieda ran as fast as their legs could carry them out of the cemetery and they went to their flat on Huskisson Street where they hardly slept for the remainder of that morning. As the weeks went by, the couple noticed that all of the people they had known who had been bitten by that thing in the tomb had unaccountably gone missing, and none of them were ever heard from again. I assume the victims became night-roaming vampires themselves, which means that they may still be at large even now, as vampiric bodies do not age as human ones do.

In 1984, there was another case of a vampire attempting to start a cult, only this time it was in Wirral. That year, a 20-year-old woman named Natalie lost her beloved grandmother Susan to a long illness, and, against the wishes of "Nanny Sue" (as Natalie had always called her), Susan was cremated at the Landican Crematorium after the funeral service at St Hilary's Church in Wallasey. Nanny Sue had always told Natalie that she wanted to be buried because she believed that one day, Jesus would return and, as the Bible promised, all of the dead who had believed in Christ would be resurrected to be reborn in paradise. Nanny Sue was an ardent Christian fundamentalist and as such she believed there'd be nothing to resurrect if she was cremated. Natalie had told her father and mother about her Nan's wishes but they took no notice. Now Natalie kept the urn containing her Nan's ashes in her room, and her sister Abbey thought this was a barmy thing to do. Natalie identified with the burgeoning Goth movement and she slowly turned her back on Christianity and most of the organised religions. She painted the walls of her bedroom at her home on Harrow Road, Wallasey, a stark dark purple, installed red and blue spotlights in the matt black ceiling to cast a scarlet light on her bed and "Egyptian blue" on her bookcase and record player, and she also lit joss sticks to create a mystical atmosphere. Natalie also started to devour books on Black Magic – as well as lots of wine - and she toyed with the idea of forming her own coven. In the bedroom next door to hers, 17-year-old sister Abbey was the very antithesis of Natalie. Her walls were bright yellow and orange, and she listened to Buck's Fizz, Modern Romance and the likes of Duran Duran, whereas the music emanating from Natalie's "Sanctum" (as she called it), was usually the caterwauling voice of Siouxsie Sioux or something by The Cure. Then one evening as a thunderstorm raged over Wallasey, Natalie decided to try a spell for raising the dead from an old book on ritual magic that she'd bought in a jumble sale. The controversial spell required a fragment of bone from a dead person or the ashes of a person who had been cremated, and Natalie decided to use the ashes from her Nan's urn. She lodged a chair under the handle of the door in case anyone tried to enter, and then she started the long invocations as the thundering skies opened and pelted the roof with heavy rainfall. At the end of the ritual, nothing happened. Natalie swore – but then she noticed the shadow of a thin man on the door – which, being red, was the only thing a shadow could be visible upon in this room of black walls. She was stunned and a little afraid, but when the ghostly shadow vanished she told it to come back. That evening, Natalie went to bed at midnight, and she fell asleep. She had a vivid dream that the ghost of a naked young man had come into her room through the ceiling. He told her his name (it sounded like "Salin" – pronounced as Say Lin) and he said he had come to her because she had tried that rite to raise the dead and wanted to show her how to do it properly. Salin said he was from the "world beyond the grave" and that if Natalie did what he said, he'd give her eternal life and even reunite her with her deceased Nan.

'I am the only way to everlasting life,' he told Natalie, then explained: 'To give you eternal life, Natalie, I will have to make love to you and draw off just a little bit of your life-force and then I will breathe my life-force into your body and you shall be initiated into our way of life, the life everlasting.'

Around the time of this dream in the waking world, Natalie's sister Abbey was awakened from her sleep by the rhythmic sound of bed springs and a thumping of a headboard on her wall. She thought that Natalie – who was single – had brought some boy home, and the sound of lovemaking became so loud, Abbey's father got up, went to his daughter's bedroom door and knocked. There was no answer and he suddenly heard Natalie cry "You're killing me! Get off me!"

Abbey peeped from the doorway of her own room and saw that her father had now been joined by her mother. There was a scream, and Natalie's father burst in. He and his wife saw a shadowy figure fly up from his daughter's bed and pass through the ceiling. A naked Natalie got up, and wrapped a blanket about her body, and then, feeling something running down her cleavage, she discovered that she had blood trickling from a bite mark in her neck. Her father said he was going to burn all of her books on the Occult, as he believed that Natalie had conjured up something demonic with her cavalier dabbling, but at least once a night after that, the shadowy Salin would return – always after midnight - and assault Natalie in her bed and draw off blood from various parts of her body, including her feet. Abbey went to several priests and told them about the bloodthirsty 'ghost' but the holy men said it was more a case for a psychiatrist than a clergyman.

A young reverend in the area named Daniel heard about the vampiric attacks and visited the family at Harrow Road. He said he had heard of similar nocturnal assaults in the area and he told Natalie's parents that Salin was a real-life vampire who had been active since the 1930s. He had been a pillar of the community in Wallasey long ago, but behind closed doors he was an occultist who craved eternal life and he was an immoral man who would go to any length to stay young forever. He died from a disease of the lungs in his forties and was buried in a certain grave in the churchyard of St Hilary, and not long afterwards, dark rumours circulated about the late businessman. People claimed to see his dark vaporous ghost rise from his grave on some nights, and Daniel claimed that people were witnessing Salin going in search of "prana" – the life-force vampires feed off in human blood. Daniel eventually contained the vampire for a few weeks by burying an old Norse amulet with the potent "Gibu Auja" protection rune engraved upon it in Salin's grave, but after just a fortnight, the shadowy form of the vampire with a lust for the life-force *and* sex was seen drifting up from the cemetery and into the night skies of Wallasey.

Daniel and Abbey even staked out the cemetery and saw Salin rise from his grave with their own eyes, so Daniel planted a hawthorn bush on Salin's grave. Hawthorn is traditionally said to keep vampires at bay. However, in 2007 there were reports that Salin was active again in the Wallasey area, and I myself received reports from that area of Wirral concerning people who experienced paralysis after waking in the wee small hours of the morning before they were bitten by a silhouetted being that later disappeared. Across the globe there has been a dramatic increase in nocturnal visitations from so-called "Shadow People" – eerie figures in black or dark-coloured silhouetted form - and while a majority of these encounters have not resulted in any physical harm, there have been some cases where people have reported being bitten in places all over their body by the shadow-person whilst they have been unable to move in bed, and these bites might have been inflicted by a vampiric being. There doesn't seem to be much a potential victim can do to keep these things at bay either, especially if the prey is an atheist. Some keep a copy of the Bible or the Qur'an in their bedroom. Whatever your religion is – may your God protect you...

THE THING UNDER THE ROYAL COURT THEATRE

It's strange how coincidences strike in the world of showbusiness. Take for example, the prized framed print of a painting entitled *September 16th* which Marc Bolan had mounted on his living room wall. This print of the surrealist artist Rene Magritte featured a crescent moon above a huge tree situated in the middle of the picture, and Bolan was always asked what September 16 had to do with a tree. He later died on September 16 1977 when his car hit the type of tree depicted in the surrealist painting. Then we have the intriguing accounts of two future Doctor Whos – Jon Pertwee and Patrick Troughton – meeting monsters that could have come straight out of the episodes of the phenomenal time-travel serial. When Pertwee was a boy in the 1920s, he often went to stay with a well-to-do school-friend during the school holidays, and his friend lived in an Elizabethan manor house in Sussex. On this occasion, there were guests staying at the house and the only room Jon could sleep in was a dusty old bedroom off a minstrels' gallery, and on the first night at this bedroom, Jon awoke feeling ill, and threw up over the bedcover. It was all hours in the morning and Jon had to sneak to a toilet, fill a basin with water and clean the sick off the bedcover. On the second night at the old bedroom, Jon fell fast asleep, but in the wee small hours something woke the boy up. He was greeted by a hideous stench which he later compared to the aroma of a dead sheep he had once seen on a farm. Jon realised that this putrid smell had probably made him throw up in his sleep on the previous night. He sat up in bed and saw something standing at the foot of his bed; it was a thing he could only describe as looking like the trunk of a tree with a quivering mouth in it which was blowing out small bubbles. Jon was so scared, he wet the bed, and then the trunk-like entity came round the bed towards him, and he ran from the bedroom screaming for help. When the parents of Jon's friend heard about his account of the monster, they looked at one another and Jon could tell they knew something about the thing in that old bedroom but they said nothing more. Jon Pertwee later learned from his friend that many other people had seen the terrifying oddity in that room off the minstrels' gallery but no one knew what the thing was. Fifty years later, Jon Pertwee would tackle similar unearthly monsters as the cult Timelord Doctor Who, and his predecessor in the famous series, Patrick Troughton, also had a hair-raising encounter with a very strange being that would not have looked out of place in the long-running science fiction serial. The time was March 1946 and the place was Liverpool's Royal Court Theatre, and 26-year-old Patrick Troughton was to play the part of a messenger in Shakespeare's *Much Ado About Nothing*. Troughton was notorious as an actor who was not 'letter perfect' – he did not always follow the script to the word – he often improvised and added dialogue, but he knew that this was not possible with the lines of Shakespeare; to deviate from them was almost blasphemous in theatrical circles, so he attended a read-through of the play at the Royal Court one rainy afternoon when the theatre was closed and out of bounds to the public. During an interval in the rehearsal, an old stage hand named Billy, sat puffing on his pipe on the edge of the stage, and he suddenly said "Thingio's been larking about backstage. Not sure if you heard him, he caused a right racket, he did.'

'Thingio' is an old English slang substitute word for something unspecified whose name is either forgotten or not known (like thingamabob or thingamajig). Patrick Troughton was curious as to what Billy was referring to, and he asked, 'What's this thingio? Someone messing about?'

Billy smiled, looked at the floor sheepishly, and replied, 'Oh no, Patrick, not a person – a *thing*, and well, I better not say any more, and I shouldn't have mentioned it in the first place.'

Patrick was naturally curious as to what the stage hand was referring to, and he said: 'Oh come on Billy, you can't just intrigue me like that and leave me in suspense!'

'Well, you'll think I'm a crackpot if I tell you what the thingio is,' said the old sceneshifter and propman, and he fidgeted with his pipe, then let out a terrific sneeze.

'Bless you Billy! No I won't think you're a crackpot at all,' Troughton reassured him, 'so tell me – what *is* this thing larking about backstage?'

'Very well Patrick,' said Billy, and he pulled out a handkerchief, blew his nose hard into it, then puffed on his pipe, and when he spoke he spat blue smoke.

He said, 'this old theatre was built on the site of an old well, and they tried to fill it in but sometimes there's subsidence down there and water seeps up through the foundations. It's always been a worry for the management. A hole's appeared down there, and I know this is going to sound like a load of codswallop to you, but there's a thing that comes up out of that old well, and my old father first saw it when he was your age, and others have seen it too – '

'Seen what?' Troughton had to ask.

'Well, it's like nothing I've ever seen before, so it's hard to describe,' said Billy, looking up into the air, as if he was picturing the mysterious thing he'd seen. 'It's about – well, I'd say five feet and five inches – about my height, like, and – '

'Okay everybody, break's ended, back to rehearsals!' shouted the play's director.

Billy stopped talking and looked at Troughton with an awkward smile, and he complained of his cold and blew into the handkerchief again.

'It's okay, Billy carry on,' he told the stagehand with two brief nods, and then he shouted to the director, 'Be with you in a moment!'

The director sighed and walked with the other actors to the centre of the stage and as he flipped through the script, Troughton urged Billy to continue.

'Well, I'd be better drawing it, hang on,' Billy took a notebook out of his back pocket and pulled a tiny thin pencil out of a holder in the spine of the book. He drew the "thingio". It was a strange being indeed. It had a curved back with spines like a hedgehog, and it stood on two thin legs with three-toed feet. The face of this bizarre creature curved out into a beak, and that beak also had spines upon it, and the eyes were huge and black with concentric rings around them. The arms were spindly with hands of three fingers at the end of them.

'They say it's a boggart, an old Lancashire name for a mischievous spirit,' said Billy, 'but this thing's solid and looks real, it's no spirit. I forgot to tell you that it's green too.'

'Patrick?' the director shouted from centre stage.

'It squirts what looks like blood out of its eyes,' said Billy, and he looked deadly serious as he imparted this peculiar piece of information to the actor, and then he put notebook back in his pocket and said, 'but you probably think I've lost my marbles.'

'No, I don't Billy, I'm rather intrigued and I'd love to hear more but I'd better get back to work,' said Patrick.

'Yes, er, the play's the thing,' said Billy, and he gave a self conscious smile.

'It certainly is, bye for now,' Patrick went to the other actors.

On the following evening, Billy the stagehand was off sick because his cold had worsened, and when Patrick Troughton made his first stage exit, he walked in his 15th century costume to the back of the stage because he heard raised voices and people arguing (which was very unprofessional in a theatre with the Royal Court's reputation), and there seemed to be some commotion coming from the crossover – a glorified narrow passage actors used to access the wings of the theatre. Two young stagehands and an electrician had been spooked by something they'd only caught a fleeting glimpse of. It had been something *green*. It had shot along the crossover at a phenomenal speed without making a noise, and it had left a trail of water with strange prints in it. An electrician from the dimmer room had brushed past it and was so scared, he threatened to leave the theatre and had to be cajoled to stay on duty. The electrician said the thing had not looked human, and it had flitted towards the corridor leading to the stage door, but the stage door keeper was adamant that no one and nothing had passed him.

'That's that bloody Billy and his stupid stories that's caused this,' said the debonair-looking stage manager, 'putting things in people's brains, and superstitious sawdust brains at that!'

'Aye-aye, I haven't got a sawdust brain!' protested the electrician, and he threatened to leave unless he received and apology.

'Oh very well! I regret that little transgression, however deserved!' said the stage manager, and left the area.

Patrick Troughton followed the watery trail allegedly left by the 'thing' and thought he could discern footprints. The voices of the actors out front on the stage faded somewhat as Troughton came to a dark corner in that backstage area they called "the shop" where scenes and various large props were stored, and here he saw "thingio" standing in the shadows. He froze, and once he had gotten over the initial shock of encountering the thing, which looked as green and slimy as a slug with those huge black eyes Billy had sketched so accurately, Troughton wondered what to say to the creature, but the electrician suddenly came upon the scene and let out a scream. He picked up a fire bucket full of sand, and before he could even throw it, that creature sprinted away into the darkness of the storage area without a sound. The two stagehands, the director of the play, and the stage door keeper arrived to see what the scream and the loud racket was about, and they saw sand all over the floor from the hurled bucket. There was no sign of the "boggart", and Patrick Troughton did not say what he had seen, for in those days, people did not speak openly about things we would now class as paranormal, and if you did own up to seeing a ghost – or a "boggart", you'd earn the reputation of being mentally unstable and prone to "seeing things" – and any actor with such a reputation would find himself almost as good as blacklisted. The thing from the well was allegedly also seen by many people over the years, including several famous stars who appeared at the theatre, including a certain young thespian of great promise named Richard Burton, who first acted in public at the Royal Court in November 1925. The present Royal Court Theatre, built in the Art Deco style, dates from 1938, but it really began in the 1820s when a circus owner named John Cooke purchased the site – along with its ancient well – and the building erected there was known as Cooke's Royal Amphitheatre of Arts. I researched this early theatre and discovered that the black circus performer and circus proprietor William Darby – better known by his stage name as Pablo Fanque – often performed at the Royal Amphitheatre, along with an amazing gymnastic performer and trapeze artist named William Kite. Beatles fans might recognise the names Pablo Fanques and William Kite because John Lennon referenced them in a song on the *Sergeant Pepper* album called *Being for the Benefit of Mr Kite!* in 1967 after seeing their names on an old Victorian circus poster. The Royal Amphitheatre was redesigned in 1881 and reopened as the Royal Court, and during this time there were still rumours of the 'thing' which was said to come up from the well at night to roam the theatre's backstage area. The thing is said to have been seen in early February 1894 when the theatre put on the first-ever stage production Berlioz's *Faust* to a packed house. The famous work was performed by the Carl Rosa Opera Company and there was a band of sixty instrumentalists which played stirring music during the four-act performance and even mechanical horses which raced to Hell with an early form of moving back projection to give the illusion of a descent into the abyss. Sir Charles Halle conducted the musicians and enthralled concert-goers cheered as a full military procession took place on stage to the sounds of "The Hungarian March" – but backstage, as the audience were yelling "encore!" the slimy green entity came out of the woodwork and stood before two burly stagehands as they cranked a clockwork mechanism which moved the panorama on the stage. One of the stagehands was so terrified at the sight of the demonic being, he ran off, and the remaining stagehand cranked the wrong lever in shock – and the panorama reversed, which caused some amusement to the audience out front, for it now looked as if the coal-black steeds were riding backwards. Several critics noted this gaff and mentioned it in their otherwise positive newspaper reviews. The thing was then seen on various occasions – always behind the scenes at the theatre – including the aforementioned occasion when it was seen in 1946 during the production of *Much Ado About Nothing* - but there was much ado about the reputation the subterranean "boggart" was gaining for distracting actors by the 1960s. The comedian and celebrated compere Norman Vaughan had heard the strange stories about the supernatural nuisance at the theatre, and so, when he was due to appear at the Royal Court in May 1967 in a production of the classic farce *Boeing Boeing*, he went to the unusual length of insuring himself against forgetting his lines, but of course, he could not say why, and the Press thought it was a publicity stunt. Arthur Harrison, head of J. A. Harrison (Brokers) Ltd., of Birmingham – a firm that had extensive business dealings with stage personalities and entertainers – said: 'As far as I know, this is the first time I've heard of an actor taking out insurance in case he dries up or fluffs his lines; it really is quite extraordinary.' And Gerald Croasdell, the secretary of Equity, was also baffled by Norman Vaughan's insurance policy. He said, 'I have never heard of such a precaution before in all my years.'

The thing from the vestiges of the ancient well beneath the Royal Court Theatre is not as active as it used to be, but who knows, it may emerge from the murky depths one night and once again make a dramatic – and terrifying – entrance...

TATTOO JACK

A few years ago I wrote a book called *Beasts, Banshees and Bogeymen* which I had naively envisaged as being the last word on Liverpool bogeymen, but now I have gathered enough material to fill three such books, such is the rich folklore of this truly multicultural city. A glib sociologist will tell you that a bogeyman is a mythical creature dreamed up by adults to frighten children into good behaviour, but not all of the supernatural entities that have terrified children over the years were created by adults; they seem to have had lives of their own; a case in point being Tattoo Jack. He was allegedly encountered from 1961 to 1975 in places ranging from Walton to Huyton, and adults are also said to have seen him. At 7.30pm on the Sunday night of April 30, 1961 – Walpurgis night (one of the most important nights in the calendar of witches), a 16-year-old girl named Tina was left to mind a 5-year-old boy named Bobby at a terraced house on Walton's Lochinvar Street. A full moon shone brightly in the heavens that night, and Tina was sitting in the cosy armchair nearest to the television set watching *Danger Man* - an action adventure serial about a secret agent - as she ate crisps and sipped lemonade, when she heard a knock at the kitchen window. Little Bobby, the child Tina was minding, looked up from the book he was colouring in as he sat on the sofa and asked, 'Who's that? Is Daddy back?'

Tina didn't answer. She went into the kitchen, looked into the backyard and saw no one, but she did hear a voice that sounded like the puppet Punch. Whoever it was must have had a "swazzle" (two strips of metal and tape) in their mouth to create that harsh raspy voice. Tina assumed it was a mischievous boy who lived in the neighbourhood named Gary Hurst. He was always playing pranks on people and he also seemed to have a crush on Tina. The girl went back into the living room and sat next to Bobby. 'It was just a silly boy messing about Bobby.'

'When will my Mummy and Daddy come back?' the child asked.

'Later on tonight, when you're in bed, Bobby,' said Tina. 'Now, if you're a good boy I'll let you stay up till half-past eight and you can have some lemmo and a chocolate tea cake.'

'What's a tea cake?' Bobby wanted to know.

'It's a scrumptious marshmallow made out of chocolate and white fluffy stuff in it with a blob of raspberry jam in the middle, and there's like a biscuit at the bottom of it,' Tina told the lad. 'You'll like them.'

'Can I have a corned beef sarnie instead, Tina?' Bobby asked with pleading eyes.

Tina smirked. 'No, you can't, Bobby, you'll have indigestion when you go to bed.'

'What's interjeshon?' Bobby queried.

'Oh Bobby, just colour your book in will you? I'll go and get the lemmo and the tea cakes and we can have a picnic on the settee,' said Tina, and she got up and went to the kitchen, but there were three slow knock at the front door.

'That might be Mummy and Daddy!' Bobby

suggested, and he smiled, put down his coloured pencils and book and went to go to the door of the living room but Tina went after him and seized his wrist.

'No, Bobby, it's not your mam and dad, now go and sit there,' she told him, and tried to guide him to the sofa but he wouldn't sit down and she couldn't budge him.

Tina crept into the hallway but she never turned the light on out there. She looked at the two long rectangles of stippled-texture glass and she could see the shadow of someone blocking out the light from the lamp post in the street.

'Who is it?' Tina shouted, and she looked back and saw Bobby peeping round the doorway.

It was that bizarre voice again; the one that sounded like the voice of the street puppet Punch, only now it sounded more like Donald Duck – a way of speaking in a pseudovoice known as buccal speech. From the size and height of the huge silhouette, this obviously wasn't the schoolboy joker Gary Hurst – so who on earth was this adult caller, and why was he putting on such a ridiculous voice? Tina ached to know the answer and she shouted: 'Who is it? What do you want?'

The reply, in that daft voice, was: 'Tina! Tina! I want to show you something!'

'Donald Duck!' exclaimed Bobby, and he smiled and clapped his hands.

'Bobby, go back in there or you're going to bed,' Tina told him, and she went to the boy and had to drag him to the sofa as he put on a mock coughing type of sob. Tina then hurried back to the hallway and closed the living room door behind her. She couldn't help herself; she just had to know who the goofy caller was. She undid the catch on the Yale lock and opened the door.

A huge fat bald man with no clothes on stood there, and he had the weirdest smiling face Tina had ever seen. She tried to close the door on him but he stepped forward and a huge bare foot prevented the door from closing.

Tina backed away – and bumped into Bobby, who had come out of the living room to see who it was, and she hit him so hard with her backside she knocked the child over. He started to cry, but whether this was at the sight of the tall fat naked man, or whether the fall had winded him was hard to say, and Tina tried to pick the boy up and take him out of harm's way, but Bobby got to his feet and ran up the stairs.

'Hello Tina!' said the naked stranger in his creepy put-on voice. The light shining from the living room was now illuminating the body of the sinister visitor in the dark hallway, and Tina saw something very strange indeed. The towering hulk of the man was covered in tattoos of girls' pale faces with their eyes closed – as if they were asleep – or *dead*. Tina ran into the living room and she slammed the door on the naked spine-chilling pervert, and she leaned against that door with all of her might, but it steadily opened as the intruder came pushing his way in using just one arm. Tina fled to the kitchen and tried to find the cutlery drawer so she could grab a knife and defend herself. The corpulent crazed trespasser emitted an unnatural high-pitched laugh that sounded like that of a parrot, and Tina's hand grabbed a rolling pin. She swung it back, threateningly, but the twinkling smiling eyes of the potential rapist did not even react. She threw the rolling pin hard at the tubby tattooed intimidator – and it glanced off the side of his bald head and he merely closed one eye for a second and continued to advance towards the babysitter as if the rolling pin had been made of balsa.

Tina gave up the search for the knife and ran to the door which led to the backyard but of course, it was locked, and she had no idea where the key was. The only hope of escape now that Tina had in mind was a quick dash around the unclothed maniac, but he seemed to read her eyes and her thoughts and he stepped sideways, positioning himself so he blocked the kitchen doorway. And then, in that unsettling voice he said, 'Your sister!' and held out his left hand. On his palm was a tattooed picture of a face Tina recognised; her sister Joan – and that face, like the other ones inscribed upon the stranger's skin, had its eyes closed. Tina screamed, and the man lowered his hand, and then he turned around and walked out of the house without saying a word. Tina went to the front door, slammed it shut, and put the bolt on. She turned on the hallway light and she noticed Bobby sitting on the top step, sucking his thumb with a look of fear in his huge eyes.

Tina just wanted to grab Bobby and rush out of the house with him to her home a quarter of a mile away, but the girl was too scared to venture outside because she imagined that the hideous tattooed freak would still be prowling the moonlit streets. Tina was in a terrible state when Bobby's parents returned home just after 11pm. Bobby's mother thought the tattooed caller had been some escapee from a mental hospital but her husband seemed to think that Tina's story had been invented to cover up the visit of some amorous boyfriend who had perhaps wanted to go too far with her.

Three days later, Tina's sister Joan died of a brain haemorrhage as she was getting a bath. Tina immediately believed that the tattooed oddball who had called on her had been some omen of death. Tina's uncle said he had heard of the same weird man calling at other houses in Walton with a voice described as being like Donald Duck's, and her uncle said the weird caller probably did this to get young people to open the door to him. By the time the uncanny corpulent 'bogeyman' was seen in Huyton a month later, he was being called Tattoo Jack, and again the eerie story circulated about him having the faces of people who had died tattooed on his body, and the face of a person marked for death would always be displayed on his hand. Tina had nightmares about Tattoo Jack for months when she heard about the other visits he was paying, and her mother tried to reassure her teenage daughter that the whole affair had just been caused by some lunatic with a tattooed body taking his clothes off, and the rest was simply exaggeration and embellishments with each retelling of the tale.

One Sunday evening around 7.20pm in September 1968, a 13-year-old girl named Louise was sitting in on her own at her terraced home on Tuebrook's Sutton Street. Her parents, grandparents and two older brothers had all gone for a drink at the local pub and Louise was glad to have the place to herself for a few hours. She watched *The Forsyte Saga* on BBC1, and when it ended around a quarter past eight, she turned the telly off because there was nothing worth watching on any of its channels. At 8.30pm, Louise went into the kitchen to make herself a jam butty and she thought she saw a man's face looking in at her. By now it was getting dark outside, and in the brief moment Louise saw the face, she thought it was of a bald-headed man with wide staring eyes. He seemed to duck down incredibly fast when he noticed that she'd seen him. Louise was naturally startled by the possible Peeping Tom and she pretended she was not alone by talking to her father as if he was there, in case the man – who would have to be in the backyard – was still there and listening. Louise went upstairs to her brother's bedroom because the window in that room gave a good view of the backyard below, and she peeped through the gap between the curtains, but could see no one down there. The girl then went back downstairs, and as she reached the hallway, she heard the letterbox flap, as if someone was trying to post something. She could hear a shuffling noise on the front doorstep and she asked, 'Who's that?' There was no window in the door, so Louise could not see if the caller was that bald man who had peeped through the kitchen window.

'Hello?' a voice replied, and Louise thought it sounded as if it was a put-on voice – it did not sound natural.

'Who is it?' Louise asked, and she looked at the bolt at the bottom of the door and thought about putting it on.

'Are you Mary's daughter?' the unknown man asked.

'Yes, who are you?' Louise asked, and she felt a little better now because the caller was probably just someone who knew her mum.

The man outside told the teenager. 'Tell your mum there's a job going in Scott's supermarket and that Ronnie Jones has put a good word in for her so she'll get the job if she goes to Scott's in the morning.'

Louise's mother was currently out of work, so this was good news indeed.

'Okay, I'll tell her when she comes home,' said Louise, 'she's gone out with me dad and me brothers. Are *you* Ronnie Jones?'

'Yes, I went to school with your mother. Keep this door locked, love,' said Ronnie, 'there's a strange man knocking about, looking through windows.'

'Oh!' recoiled Louise, 'I've just seen him!' she said, excitedly.

'Well watch he doesn't get in, he can pick locks,' said Ronnie. 'Well, you sure you're alright kid?'

Louise opened the door as she said, 'He tried to get in here – '

And she went numb when she saw a huge naked man standing there, covered in tattoos of faces from his shins to his Adam's apple – and it was him – the baldy man she had caught peeping in through the kitchen window.

'Boo,' he said, and went to walk in, but Louise slammed the door shut and let out a scream. She ran to the kitchen, found the key to the kitchen door in a drawer, and she let herself out and ran down the backyard. The terrified girl ran down the alleyway with only moonlight to guide her, and she expected the naked tattooed man to jump out on her at the end of the entry, but she ran for almost a quarter of a mile to the pub where her parents, brothers and grandparents were drinking, and she was so exhausted when she got there, she could hardly speak. When she managed to tell her mother and father about the naked man, a few of the drinkers made jokes about the bizarre-sounding story, but the landlord said he had heard of "a man in the all together" with the tattoos and said he was a lunatic who was said to have killed mostly children over the years, but had been released because of friends he had in high places. The landlord advised Louise's parents to go home straight away while he called the police. 'Trust you to ruin a great night out,' moaned Louise's father, and he reluctantly left the pub with his wife and the rest of the family and headed for Sutton Street, moaning and swearing. Outside the front door of the family home there was a pool of urine, and there were imprints leading from this pool made by a pair of very large (possibly size 14) bare feet. The back kitchen door was unlocked the way Louise had left it when she fled, but there was no sign – beyond that pool outside the front door – of the weird naked tattooed man. Out of curiosity, Louise's mother went to Scott's supermarket on nearby West Derby Road and asked if a Ronnie Jones had put a word in for her about a job that was supposed to be going in the store, but a baffled employee there said there were no vacancies and he knew of no one named Ronnie Jones, which deepened the mystery. On this occasion Tattoo Jack – if that's who the naked caller was – did not give any portent of a forthcoming death with a face tattooed upon his hand, unless he didn't get the chance to issue an omen because of Louise's speedy exit from her home. When I mentioned this character on a show about the supernatural on BBC Radio Merseyside around 2010, I only got a few calls on air, but steadily over the months and years following the broadcast, I received the odd email and letter from listeners regarding Tattoo Jack and other 'bogeymen' of his kind, and they seemed to indicate that he was seen first in the north of the city in the early 1960s (and possibly the late 1950s), and then each year there would be a spate of encounters with Jack in locations that indicated he was moving further south as time went on. I got a letter from a man named Phil in Chester regarding Tattoo Jack. Phil had moved to Chester in the 1980s but he was born in Huyton, and in 1975 he was aged nine and living off Blue Bell Lane when he and his 11-year-old sister received a visit from Tattoo Jack one summer night. This was on the Wednesday night of August 27, 1975, just after 11pm. Phil's father had gone to bed full of 'medicinal' whiskey at 10pm because he'd come down with a bad case of summer flu, and his mother Julie was still next door, gossiping with her neighbour, so Phil and older sister Sarah had the house to themselves. Sarah was sat at the table in the kitchen making patterns with the popular geometric toy Spirograph, and Phil was eating half a jar of Cheddar Spread between two thick rounds of Sunblest bread as he watched *The Baron* - a TV serial about an American antiques dealer who also happens to be an undercover agent.

'Turn that down, Phil,' Sarah shouted to her brother from the kitchen. 'You'll wake me Dad up!'

Phil turned down the volume on the TV set and the two kids could now hear their father's distant sonorous snores upstairs and thought it was funny.

'Don't you eat any more of that Cheddar Spread or you'll be sick,' preachy Sarah was telling her brother when she heard a slow knocking at the front door. The girl sighed and dragged herself from the kitchen table. She assumed it'd be her mother, returning from next door, but when Sarah went into the hallway, she could see an unfamiliar silhouette of a bald bullet-headed man in the square window in the top half of the front door.

'Who's that?' Sarah asked.

'Open the door or I'll knock it down!' said someone in a weird-sounding voice which sounded to Sarah like a bad imitation of Donald Duck's trademark voice.

Sarah hurried into the living room and alerted Phil. 'Hey!' she shouted to him. 'There's some barmy man at the front door!'

Phil came out into the hall (carrying his butty) and he too saw the silhouette of the weird-sounding man. 'Beat it Kojak, or my Dad'll come down and thump you!' Phil shouted to the front door, and then he looked at Sarah, expecting her to be impressed with his macho threat. She just looked very nervous.

'Open the door or I'll break it down!' the stranger on the doorstep said in that silly yet disconcerting voice.

Phil looked at his older sister with a worried expression, as if she'd know what to do. 'Get me dad, Sarah,' he suggested.

'It's your Uncle Ronnie messing about,' the late-night caller suddenly said in a normal voice. 'Open the door; I've come to see your father.'

The children didn't believe him. As far as they knew, they had no Uncle Ronnie. It's curious to note that when Tattoo Jack gained entry to the house in Tuebrook in 1968, he did so by claiming to be a *Ronnie* Jones, and now he was claiming to be an Uncle Ronnie. This point may signify nothing, or it could be a clue to the identity of Tattoo Jack.

The letterbox flap swivelled open, startling Phil and Sarah, and they saw a pair of bulging, mad-looking eyes gaze through the letterbox. The night visitor said: 'It's your Uncle Ronnie, and I've got sweets for you.'

A scream outside made Phil and Sarah jump, and they both recognised the screamer – it was their mum.

'Oh my God! Oh!' she shrieked, and the children heard the caller say, 'Oh shut up!'

'Police!' cried Sarah's mum Julie. 'There's a man on my doorstep with no clothes on!' she yelled.

Sarah heard the voices of the next door neighbours followed by the sound of bare feet padding away.

Julie put the Yale key in her door a minute later and barged into the hall with the husband of her neighbour – a tall broad-shouldered man named Alf. 'Did he try to get in?' Julie asked Sarah, 'Did you open the door to him?'

'No, I didn't – who was he?' Sarah replied, 'He said he was our Uncle Ronnie; have we got an Uncle Ronnie?'

'No, there's no Uncle Ronnie,' Julie replied with a mystified look.

'Do you want me to go after him Julie, and give him a thump?' asked Alf.

Julie curled her arm around Phil, who started to eat his butty again, and told her hard-knock neighbour: 'No, don't do that Alf, he might have a knife. I think he was deranged by the look on his face. Oh God, I could have been molested!'

'Why didn't he have any clothes on?' Phil asked his mother with innocence in his eyes.

'He's a flasher,' Alf told Phil, all matter-of-fact.

Julie made eye-contact with Alf and shook her head as she put her hands over Phil's ears. 'Don't say that in front of him, he's only just turned nine,' she said to her neighbour. Then she said a curious thing which Phil recalls clearly. Julie said to Alf: 'Did you see all those tattoos on him? He had tattoos of girl's faces all over him. He's definitely escaped from a mental hospital. We should really get in touch with the police.'

Julie, Alf and the children then heard a loud thud. It came from the kitchen. Alf walked straight into the kitchen and said that the window was cracked. He told Julie to turn the light off in the kitchen and he looked through the cracked window. Alf said he could see someone at the end of the back garden, moving about in the shadows. 'It looks like *him* - he's in the garden Julie,' Alf said, his nose pressed against the window pane. 'He's just climbed over the fence! He can't half move for someone so fat.'

Julie and her kids hardly slept that night, and the littlest natural sound would startle them out of their snatches of light, restless sleep. They talked about the overweight pervert the next morning over breakfast, and Alf called round to say that the chubby tattooed flasher had been seen by two women on Rupert Road. Two men had chased the naked man but he literally seemed to vanish into the night. Phil, upon hearing this, asked his mum if the man had been a ghost.

'Nah, just a dirty old man,' she answered, adding: 'and he probably lives around there and knows the place well. Probably just hid or sneaked back to his house. Insane people are always cunning.'

'Funny he should ask if he was a ghost,' remarked Alf, looking at Phil, 'because my cousin Vera said the same fellah had been chased by two coppers down Green Way into that blind alley [which was probably Green Way Close] last year and there was no way he could have got out of there, yet they couldn't find him – he'd vanished.'

'Then he must live there,' reasoned Julie, and she looked at her spooked son and assured him, 'there're no such things as ghosts. People just make a mystery out of nothing.'

'Only telling you what Vera said, Julie,' said Alf, raising his eyebrows and shaking his head slightly. He looked as if he was sorry he'd mentioned the ghost theory.

Phil knew his mother was just trying to cover up the fact that this Tattoo Jack was not only a weird character, he also seemed to be something quite out the ordinary, and the lad would dare and scare himself each night by peeping out his window to see if the roly-poly streaking stalker was about, but thankfully, he never saw him again, but he heard of many alleged local visitations. After the Halloween of 1975 (when Jack, or someone pretending to be him was supposedly seen chasing kids up Jeffreys Crescent in Page Moss) Tattoo Jack vanished back into obscurity. He really is an enigma wrapped up in a supernatural mystery. What's his history? Was he a living person or something demonic? I lean towards the latter in my personal evaluation of the case but I'm not entirely sure. What do the tattoos of the dead girls mean? Was he a killer of young girls or was he someone who morbidly had the faces of girls (and only girls) who had died through disease and tragedy tattooed upon him for some warped reason? And why did he go about his business stark naked? The strange voices he put on only add to the menace. I have this horrible feeling that Tattoo Jack will return one day...

GLIMPSES OF STRANGE FUTURES

We assume we know what time is – until we have to define it. How long does "now" last, for example? A second? A microsecond? A femtosecond (one millionth of one billionth of a second)? According to modern science the shortest duration of time is known as Planck Time (named after Max Planck), which is the exact time required for light to travel in a vacuum a distance of 1 Planck length, which is approximately 5.39×10^{-44}s. However, there is a theory that now says that there are smaller durations than this too.

We soon see that "now" is too slippery to pin down, but we are given the impression that it's where the receding past and oncoming future meet – the 'present' in other words. If you are holding this page about a foot from your eyes it will take the image of these words a nanosecond to reach your eyes – about a billionth of a second, so you can never see things as they *are* – only as they *were* in the past. Even before we are born we are *defined* by time. When you were but a bump in your mum's tummy people would say, 'Mrs Jones is six months,' and long after the baby is born some might remark, 'He's a big lad for a two-year-old,' or 'She's clever for a three-year-old', and then the child is indoctrinated with time-telling (confusing algorithms concerning, minute hands, second fingers, hour hands) and the observation of birthdays. We then eat, sleep, study, work and take holidays by the clock, and some people even receive a gold clock on retirement – but very few of us ever wonder what time is; is it something measured by clocks or is it all in the mind? Throughout history there have been strange incidents that have made a mockery of our notion of time – and they are known as timeslips. Until a few years ago, slippages in time were found only in the realm of science fiction, but now they are accepted scientific fact. In June of 2017, physicists detected gravity waves generated by two black holes merging three billion light years from earth, and they actually measured the warping of the space-time continuum with ultra-sensitive laser interferometers in the US. Einstein had stated that time and space were warped by gravity, but now we have the proof, and that means that time travel is a step nearer, and may be achieved by using superdense materials and sophisticated electronics to distort time and provide portals into the past and future. But some force has been doing this for years, and it has subjected everyday people to mind-blowing experiences where they have literally found themselves in another time period. In Liverpool, I have catalogued a concentration of timeslips in the Bold Street area, and in Wirral, Grange Road – and Grange Road West in particular – there seem to be a high incidence of timewarps – and I am not sure if the geology of the area in Bold Street is a governing factor, as there are large subterranean deposits of quartz, and also a stream that runs parallel to the street. In recent years I have been investigating other timeslip hot-spots in Liverpool, and I noted that there is an intriguing locus of time slippages at Mitchell Place, a covered opening on Great Charlotte Street (located between

McDonalds and a pub) which leads into Back Lime Street. I mentioned a few strange time slips concerning Back Lime Street in *Haunted Liverpool 28* in a chapter entitled "Timeslips Galore", and they included, a man taking a short cut through Back Lime Street who walked into a type of Limbo, a girl almost being raped on the same backstreet when it shifted to some earlier time – possibly the 18th century – and a man who saw a futuristic monorail from the part of the narrow street that joins Elliot Street. I also related the strange account of two air-conditioning engineers who were working on a roof which afforded a view of Back Lime Street and Mitchell Place, when they saw weird figures in tight-fitting black costumes and balaclava-like coverings on their heads. These sinister figures flitted about at superhuman speed on the street and also on Mitchell Place, before vanishing. Many people who read of this latter account in my book contacted me and said they too had seen the exceedingly agile men in black suits (which many likened to the rubber wet suits worn by skin divers and scuba divers). However, one of the strangest stories regarding a timeslip incident at Mitchell Place came from a retired policeman. Years before I had heard the far-fetched story of a robot being arrested by two policemen in Liverpool in the 1970s, and how the thing fell apart before they got it to the station, and a few years back I even talked to people on a local radio show phone-in who said they had heard the weird tale from a friend or relative. Then, shortly after the publication of *Haunted Liverpool 28* in October 2017, I was contacted by a retired policeman named Geoff who actually told me he was one of the officers who actually apprehended what seems to have been either a humanoid robot made by some genius ahead of his or her time – or it was the work of some master-hoaxer. In November 1972, Geoff – then a 27-year-old constable, and his older colleague Mike, were on the beat in the city centre when they heard a disturbance on Great Charlotte Street, very close to the spot where the opening to Mitchell Place now exists. People were crowded round a tall bald-headed man in a green Army surplus jacket and jeans. The man was rotating at high speed like a human spinning-top near the Blacklers department store as the crowd, and the two coppers, looked on in utter disbelief. People said this man had just appeared out of thin air as he spun like a gyroscope. The man was not turning like those ballet dancers who perform pirouettes on their toes; this individual seemed to have the soles of his boots parallel to the ground, yet he was apparently hovering off the ground by a few inches, and he was turning faster than any ballet or ice-skating dancer. Geoff stated that the man was turning as if he was tied to the drill bit of a giant electric drill, so he was mostly a blur, and he was making a humming sound from the resulting air friction against his body and clothes. After about twenty seconds of this impossible high-speed rotation, the man came to a dead halt – and then he ran off at an incredible speed to the junction of Church Street and Lord Street, a quarter of a mile away. The man had a bald head that looked shiny and he had a well-defined jaw which led Geoff to believe that the man was in his early twenties or late teens. He was also very slim and moved faster than any athlete Geoff had seen on TV. Geoff and Mike and quite a few people chased after the young man. They all caught up with the agile stranger at the Church Street/Lord Street junction, where he exhibited rather bizarre behaviour, such as laughing and dancing around bemused shoppers, and right away, Geoff could discern at closer quarters that there was something *mechanical* about the movements of the man, who started grabbing at women of every age to hug and kiss them. The kisses weren't light pecks on the cheek either, but full-on passionate kisses which naturally left the females – some in their sixties and others in their teens – shocked and a little scared. There is a cognitive mechanism in the human mind which reacts to the so-called Uncanny Valley effect, which has been debated by psychologists for years. This is the feeling you get when you see something which just doesn't look right, be it a sophisticated humanoid robot with lifelike silicone flesh, or a special effect in a film; the mind just knows something is not quite true about the thing it is looking at. In Geoff's case, he just knew that the oddball he'd pursued to the top of Church Street was not a human, but something electro-mechanical masquerading as one, and he wondered who would have the technology to build such a sophisticated robot. He later discovered that his colleague Mike also believed that there was something 'off' about the man which he couldn't put his finger on. Geoff and Mike confronted the weird public nuisance, and he started to laugh and tried to knock their hats off. 'I'm arresting you for disturbing the peace and assault – ' Geoff was saying as he received a light, 'playful' slap across his face from the crazy man.

Each policeman grabbed one of the man's arms, but his head turned 180 degrees, and then they noticed he had black eyeballs with blue lights in them. Handcuffs were put on the young offender as he struggled to get free, and then the figure *removed his hands* one at a time at the wrists to slide each cuff off – and then he reattached the hands, which left the policemen dumbfounded. The strange man's skin looked reflective, as if it was plastic, and he started to speak unintelligible gibberish, which, to Geoff's ears, sounded just like the needle skipping on a badly scratched vinyl record. The artificial-looking man then told Geoff and Mike in a well-spoken voice: 'In the future, comedy is a big religion, and all the old comedians are saints. Many of them were from here.'

Mike, who was still in shock at the detachable hand 'trick', asked 'Is that so?' and then a number of "Smiley" badges on the artificial-looking man's coat lit up.

At this point, a middle-aged passerby with a cheap-looking camera took a picture of the unearthly man as he was flanked by the two officers. As the police were distracted by this man taking the snap, the arrested man of mystery bolted away from the policemen at such a speed, he knocked two men clean over as he departed – never to be seen again. Mike said he was just 'a double-jointed freak' but Geoff reminded him of the stranger's impossible neck-breaking head-twist and the removal and reattachment of his hands, and Mike said, 'Don't mention this to anyone, even your wife, mate, or they'll have us locked up.' Geoff and Mike said nothing about the strange incident to their families or colleagues back at the station, but the many witnesses in the street who saw the astonishing escapades of the 'robot' with their own eyes naturally talked about their experiences and so the story lived on, but was largely dismissed by most people (myself included) as a weird urban myth. Was it all a sophisticated hoax or did a future android visit us in 1972? I wonder if the photograph taken by that passerby is currently in someone's family album; it'd be very interesting to see what we could glean from that snap. And if that android – or possibly a cyborg – was indeed from the future, what was all of that talk from him about comedy being a 'big religion' with the comedians of old being regarded as saints? It does sound very surreal, but there are some cults which are just as surreal, and an example off the top of my head is the Prince Philip Movement, founded by the Kastom people on the southern island of Tanna, which is part of the Pacific island nation Vanuatu. The Kastom people truly believe that Prince Philip, the Duke of Edinburgh, is a divine being. No one knows why the natives of the island revere the Duke in this way, but a visit to the island by him (accompanied by the Queen) in 1974 probably reinforced the flaky credo of the Kastom. If a religion can be based on the Duke of Edinburgh, who knows? Perhaps a future religion based on comedy *will* become a reality. With the exception of Henri Bergson, philosophers have had little to say about humour and very few psychologists have conjectured on the future of comedy and the lack of humour in the Bible and other religious texts. There are still many unanswered questions regarding the android from a future age, and the most obvious one is: why did it come back to our era? Was it on some mission? That seems unlikely, considering its erratic behaviour (hugging and kissing women etc) so did someone send it back purely for amusement (and that would not seem too unusual if the person was a follower of a comedic religion). What seems to have been another timeslip also concerns a future age: a time in the not-too-distant future when someone from Liverpool will apparently become a gargantuan history-maker by unifying the nations of the world's second largest continent and creating a superpower in the process. The roots to this milestone in World History lay in Toxteth, if there is any truth in the following strange account, and I have no reason at all to doubt the testimony of the woman in it.

On the Saturday night of 11 September, 1965, Mary, a heavily-pregnant black woman in her early twenties, lay in her bed at her flat on Upper Parliament Street, Toxteth. Her husband – a heavy drinker and womaniser - had walked out on Mary eight months prior, and she had not got over this desertion. She felt as if she had lost the will to live, and unable to shake off the depression, she had locked herself away in her room, even though her mother and close friends had urged her to go to the maternity hospital on Oxford Street. Mary cried herself to sleep, feeling as if she had even been abandoned by God, but around four in the morning she awoke to see the room flooded with the soft diffused light from the full moon beyond the windows. What she witnessed next would haunt her for the rest of her life. Three figures in white suits stepped out of the facing wall. They were three black men, and they were all about six feet in height. The ghostly man on the right was bald, and in a very rich, well-spoken voice, he said: 'Mary, you are about to give birth to the woman who will be the mother of the man who will unite all of Afri.'

Mary froze in terror, thinking the men were ghosts, but when the bald man gave a reassuring smile, she felt as if the trio was more like angels. The smiling bald visitor said: 'Your life is hard, Mary, but don't despair, it will get better, and you will go down in history because your grandson will be the first president of all Afri,' and as he said these words, a partially transparent globe of the world appeared in mid air in front of the speaker, and it presented the African continent to her. The bald man then said: 'All of the countries of Afri will unite because of your grandson and it shall become a superpower. We hail him.'

The three mysterious men simultaneously clenched their fists and placed them against their chests and said something that sounded like 'Hail Rob.'

The room then filled with blinding white light and Mary passed out. She awoke in Oxford Street Maternity Hospital and shortly afterwards she gave birth to a girl. A nurse told Mary that three men, all dressed in immaculate white suits, had brought her in, and then they had left. The only trace of the trinity's passing were flowers and a huge expensive-looking box of rum-flavoured chocolates. Mary asked the nurse if the three men were black and the nurse nodded and assumed they were relatives. Mary told a priest about the visitation in the middle of the night, and the open-minded holy man carefully considered Mary's account before stating that he believed that those three men had come from the future on some pilgrimage to help the grandmother of a leader who really had united Africa. What became of Mary after that is unknown; perhaps her grandson will indeed unite the 54 countries of Africa. Liverpudlians have been founding fathers to many nations, and a case in point is scouser Robert Morris, a signatory of the American Declaration of Independence, financier of the American Revolution, and the first person to use the dollar sign!

In my search for timeslips evidence I have explored the possibility that this present era might be receiving visitors from the future, not only in solid form but also in a nonphysical form, similar to a hologram. By a hologram I mean a true three-dimensional image, rather like the one we see of Princess Leia in *Star Wars* when she's projected from R2D2. This fictional hologram is the type scientists are currently working towards, and you'd be able to walk around such a hologram and view it from all angles. The 'hologram' of Tupac Shakur which appeared onstage with Snoop Dogg and Dr. Dre at the Coachella festival 2012 may have looked three-dimensional to the audience but the whole effect was just a modern reworking of the Victorian "Pepper's Ghost" illusion technique which dates back to 1862. The same technology was used to resurrect Michael Jackson as a realistic onstage projection for the 2014 Billboard Music Awards, but again, it was all done with reflective semi-transparent foil and overhead projectors; you would not have been able to see Michael Jackson or Tupac Shakur side-on if you'd have looked at their images from the wings of the theatre. A true hologram is an image you can walk around and look at from any angle, and you can see such a hologram if you wear a Virtual Reality helmet or goggles (similar to products like the Oculus Rift Virtual Reality Headset), but that type of hologram has to be programmed into a computer, whereas the true hologram would be viewed with the naked eye without the need to wear any special goggles. The technology to produce such a true hologram is very close, and I have no doubt that when time travel is cracked, scientists will project realistic holograms of people and objects into the past to provoke reactions and even change the outcome of the future. If a hologram of an armed policeman for example, was sent back in time to distract Mark Chapman from shooting John Lennon in December 1980, this could change our history or shift the timeline to a parallel one where Lennon lived on after that wintry Monday evening in December when he had originally been blasted with four bullets.

The possibility of sending three-dimensional projections back in time would throw some light on the following story. In August 1968, a glowing blue disembodied head began to haunt the office of a city centre DIY hardware store. The building only dated back to the 1950s, although Victorian shops had existed upon the site until they were destroyed by enemy bombing in World War Two. A female employee at the store named Hazel was the first to see the glowing head of a smiling man one afternoon as it hovered in the air in a stockroom. She'd noticed the light emanating from this startling apparition shining under the stockroom door and went to see what it was. She ran away screaming and returned with a work colleague named Tony Faye, but he saw nothing. On the following day, however, Hazel and a man delivering work tools entered the same stockroom around ten in the morning, and both saw the sudden materialization of a man's head. It was made up of blue light and seemed partially transparent. Hazel backed out of the stockroom in fear but the delivery man was more fascinated by the ghostly head, and he stood his ground. The face of the ghost smiled and then it shimmered and vanished. The delivery man swiped the air where the head had been suspended with his hand, and then he left the stockroom and told Mike Johnson, the part-owner of the store, what he and Hazel had seen, but Johnson did not believe in the stories of the ghost, and said it had probably been a reflection. That evening, Mike Johnson stayed late at the office as he carried out a periodic inventory, and around 8pm, he decided he'd call it a day and telephone his wife Frances to see if she fancied going to eat out in town. Johnson tried to telephone his wife, but instead, the line started to buzz and a well-spoken voice behind him said, 'Hello, I'm Uri – how can I help you?'

Johnson swung around in his chair and saw the radiant blue head of a smiling man floating in mid-air. He immediately realised he was seeing the ghost Hazel and the delivery man had mentioned.

'What in God's name are you?' Johnson asked, and the apparition said: 'I am Uri,' and what sounded like "Universal Resources Interface", followed by 'What do you wish to know?'

Johnson asked the weird manifestation if he was a ghost.

'No, I am not a ghost, I am a hologram,' said the detached shining head.

'I don't understand – I – I can't take this in – ' Mike Johnson struggled to get his words out. He was not scared of the thing – more confused and baffled.

'What aspect of Uri do you not understand?' Uri asked. He had a friendly face, Johnson thought, but the store owner was lost for words for a moment, and then he thought of an obvious question.

'Why are you haunting here, Uri?' Johnson asked.

'I am not haunting this place,' said Uri, in a reassuring voice, 'I am here because you called me on your phone.'

'I never called you at all,' said Johnson, astonished at the thing's assertion. 'I was calling my wife.'

Johnson had a lengthy conversation with the levitating head and soon discovered that Uri had the answer to almost anything ranging from weather predictions, football results to future stock market data. 'Who made you, Uri?' Johnson asked, intrigued by the origin of the eldritch intelligence, and the cryptic reply he received sounded like "Em-Zee created me."

'Could you explain who or what that is?' Johnson asked, and the apparition became distorted, turned into a ghostly double image and vanished but reappeared about half an hour later, and again Johnson posed many probing questions – and discovered that Uri was actually in the 21st Century, but had visited him through some fault.

'Who's the prime minister, Uri?' Johnson asked.

'James Harold Wilson,' came the instant answer from Uri.

'No, I mean who's the prime minister in *your* time?' Johnson asked and wondered if this was all some elaborate hoax along the lines of the highly popular *Candid Camera* television show where unsuspecting people are set up in staged and often embarrassing situations while they are secretly filmed.

Uri told Johnson who the prime minister was, but it was a very unusual name and a strange-sounding one to Mike Johnson's ears. It sounded as if it was an Indian name, and Uri showed a hologram of this politician's head. He was bald and looked Asian.

'Uri, if you're in the future, would it be possible for you to tell me when I will die?' Johnson asked, and he thought it was a morbid and frightening question, but he had to ask it.

'I can tell you exactly when you die if you wish Mr Johnson,' the simulated human head replied. Johnson felt perspiration form on his forehead, and it was not because of the warm August evening either. He backed out of hearing anymore and said, 'Don't tell me when I'm going to die, Uri.'

Uri then went out like a bulb being turned off, and he left a brief after-image in Mike Johnson's eyes. The telephone started to ring, and Johnson answered it. It was his wife Frances; she wanted to know why he'd been detained so late at the office.

'You'd never believe me,' Mike told her, 'but I'll tell you over dinner if you fancy coming into town.'

'You've left it a bit late, Mike,' complained Frances, 'I'd have to get ready and what about booking a table and that?'

'I have a friend who runs that hotel off Hanover Street – Tony Cromwell – he'll find a table for us at the grill,' said Mike, 'so do you think you can get here by nine?'

'Yeah, okay,' said Frances, 'but can you tell me what I wouldn't believe?'

'No, I'll tell you over some good food and wine.

Ciao!'

Mike hung up and looked at the spot in the air where the ethereal mine of information had conversed with him. He lit a cigar and pondered on the strange visitor, and he hoped he'd see Uri again. After all, if he knew about the future, Uri would be able to give some sterling investment advice, and he had even given stocks and shares figures when Mike had tried to catch him out. This Uri was a big nugget of opportunity, and Mike was excited at the prospect of seeing him again. At 9pm, Frances turned up at the store and Mike drove her to his friend's hotel, where the couple were given a seat in a corner. When Mike told Frances about Uri, he expected her to disbelieve him, but instead she questioned the state of his mind. 'My Uncle George thought overwork was healthy,' she told her husband, 'and he started seeing this black spidery thing in his bedroom, and his doctor told him it was caused by sleep deprivation.'

'This is *not* sleep deprivation, Frances,' said Mike, gruffly, and he rolled his eyes up to the ceiling.

'He died, Mike, through overwork,' said Frances, grasping Mike's clenched fist on the tablecloth. 'And what would I do if you went and died on me, eh?'

Mike sighed loudly. 'Frances, I was *not* seeing things, and this Uri thing was seen by Hazel and a delivery man and I believe a few customers saw the thing as well.'

'But it doesn't make sense,' Frances reasoned, 'why would it come back in time to a hardware shop and tell you things?'

'I haven't a clue,' admitted Mike, 'but I don't think the penny has dropped with you yet, has it?'

'How do you mean?' Frances asked him.

Mike excitedly explained what he was driving at. 'Information about the future can translate into riches, Frances. If a person knows about the future state of the stock market and what companies are going to do well, it's as good as money in the bank.' Mike then glanced around the restaurant in case anyone was listening in and he whispered to Frances: 'And then there are inventions Uri will know about; gizmos that no one has even dreamed of yet – and I could manufacture them.'

Frances didn't look convinced. 'Mike, are you sure this Uri thing isn't some clever joker just playing a big prank on you?'

Mike gave a faint smile, closed his eyes and shook his head. 'No, Frances, no one could pull off something like that, even that magician, what's his name? David Nixon – even he couldn't project a glowing head into mid-air and show me the things Uri showed me. We are going to be rich, Frances. I can actually smell that rosy aroma – what do they call it – the sweet smell of success.'

But unfortunately for Mike Johnson, he never saw or heard from "Uri" again, and as time went on, people continually told him that the floating head had just been some hallucination caused by overwork. Mike was that desperate to contact Uri again to get his money-spinning programme into operation, he even resorted to using alleged mediums (most of them fraudulent) and the Ouija board, but he was unable to contact the talking head from the future.

Could Uri be some advanced descendant of Apple's Siri, the artificial intelligence-powered personal assistant accessed by iPhones? Siri can understand spoken questions and will answer most of them with his own voice as well as by displaying text and graphics on the iPhone. Is it such a stretch of the imagination to visualise a future Siri who can appear as a disembodied head floating in mid-air as a hologram? But how and why would such an advanced personal assistant appear to someone back in the age of analogue telephones with dials on? Well, Uri said it had visited Mike Johnson through some 'fault'. Was this a fault in Uri's programming code, or a hardware malfunction, or can the scientists of a certain era in the future send holograms back in time, and if so, was Uri sent back too far by mistake? We may know more one day; and perhaps sooner than we think, in this century of exciting technological progress. If the following timeslip account is to be believed, then there are going to be some very frightening military vehicles and lethal hardware in the wars of the future.

In 2005, a woman visited me at the studios of BBC Radio Merseyside to tell me how her late husband Jim had been haunted by a very strange incident which had taken place at Charing Cross, Birkenhead in the 1950s when he was a young policeman. There had already been a terrible accident involving a police motorcyclist which had left Jim traumatised, and now, on this particular night, a dense fog had invaded Wirral and yet some idiotic motorists were still speeding towards the busy roundabout at Charing Cross where five roads converge. A lorry had 'conked out' with the cold and Jim directed traffic in the thick fog around it, and visibility became so bad, he could hardly see anything beyond twelve feet. A man on a bicycle ran into him at one point, and then the rush hour began with dusk gathering, making the driving conditions even more treacherous. As Jim was directing the traffic at one point, everything went as silent as the grave, and the policeman could hardly see his gloved hand in front of his face because of the opaque fog. He could see no headlamps nor hear any engines – and then the policeman heard a low rumbling which shook the road and made Jim's teeth chatter. Whatever the thing was, it was coming his way – and then he saw its ghostly outline as it came from the direction of Grange Road West. It resembled a military tank – but it was like no tank he had ever seen before. It was enormous – as big as a house - and beams of red light shone from a dome on top of the weird vehicle that dazzled the shocked policeman. He bolted to the left just in time, or he would have been crushed to pulp under the colossal caterpillar tracks of the unknown armoured vehicle, but then he saw something even more terrifying and inexplicable – a towering robotic figure about 20 feet in height – was marching towards him. It was a grey silhouette in the greenish-grey void of fog, and something distant was backlighting the striking object, but as it approached, it slowed down and stooped – and a massive metallic hand made a grabbing motion towards Jim. He ran off, and saw other similar giant robotic figures in the distance and heard terrible screams, but Jim then experienced what he could only describe as an explosion of traffic sound, and as the fog thinned, he found himself near the familiar Martins Bank building. There was no sign of any gigantic tank or that mechanical goliath. Jim told no one about his frightening experience, and only told his wife about the incident many years later. Military research is constant in this violent world of ours, and it's known that the superpowers are all developing drones and humanoid robots that will one day result in a virtually inexhaustible army of armoured androids that will have all sorts of terrifying weapons at their disposal, and it is known that there are designs on drawing boards in military research facilities across the world for gigantic armoured personnel carriers able to transport over a thousand troops through any wartorn environment. I think that the timeslipped policeman in 1950s Birkenhead somehow glimpsed one of these troop carriers. What war was he witnessing though? Hopefully it's a conflict that's a long way off.

I always find it particularly satisfying when two timeslips, often experienced by two separate people sometimes days, months, or even years apart, seem to agree in their version of future events. The following is a good example of two timeslip cases which seem to be glimpses of the very same future – in this case, the totalitarian future of England. Early in 1974, a secretary we shall call Jane (not her real name) was hard at work in her office at Ocean Transport & Trading Limited, a major company dealing in the cargo liner trade with a vast network of freight distribution that encompassed the world. The Ocean group included the Blue Funnel and Glen Lines (serving the Far East and South-East Asia), the famous Elder Dempster Lines (which served West Africa), Ocean Titan (which served the globe with tankers and bulk carriers), and ten other major global companies. The headquarters of Ocean Transport & Trading Ltd was at India Buildings, down in Water Street, and upon this afternoon in the spring of 1974, the aforementioned secretary Jane was surprised to see a man in her office. He had a shaved head, and he was of what we would now call mixed race, but in those times the man was described as being half-caste. He wore a jacket which was originally a shade of yellow (described by Jane as gamboges), and the trousers of the stranger were dark brown, but as Jane looked on, the jacket changed from yellow to this shade of brown, and this naturally astonished the secretary. The man stood there, looking a bit nervous, and in a well-spoken non-Liverpudlian accent he said: 'I'd like to apply for an exit permit again. I was refused three months ago but I have to visit my brother who's seriously ill in Sydney.'

'I'm sorry, but you're in the wrong part of the building. We have nothing to do with passports and that,' Jane told him, 'you'd need to go to the fifth floor and ask for – '

The man interrupted her and said, 'I could pay you a lot – in gold – please help me. I'm suicidal.' He leaned across the desk and looked into Jane's face with tears in his eyes, and she pushed herself away from him so hard, thinking he was unbalanced, her wheeled chair backed into a filing cabinet. And then she suddenly saw that the office was empty; the man had vanished into thin air. Three days later, what seems to have been the same man appeared in another part of India Buildings, and this time he got speaking to an American visitor to the shipping company named Doug. The unknown man never identified himself, but told Doug he was lucky to be able to go back to the United States, as he had been trying for almost a year to get out of "The State" – a term he kept using to describe England. The intrigued American asked the odd stranger what material his clothes were made from, as they were changing colour. The conspicuous man ignored the question and asked the same question he had asked the secretary Jane three days before, with a slight variation: 'I'd like to apply for an exit permit again. I was refused three months ago but since then my circumstances have changed; my brother is seriously ill over in Sydney and I need to visit him before it's too late. Can you please use your influence, because if I don't get out of the State soon, I might as well end my life.'

'I'm a bit confused,' said Doug, 'but when you say an "exit permit" do you mean a visa or passport? What you're saying doesn't make much sense.'

The stranger answered in an excited manner, poking Doug in the chest with his index finger as he emphasised certain words. 'They won't let people leave the State, it's like the way it was in old Russia, where they wouldn't let people leave the country, only in the State they sometimes shoot people trying to emigrate or throw them in the chemical prisons where the food is laced with downer depressants.'

'Look, bud, I think you need to leave, okay?' said Doug, pushing against the demented man. 'You'd better leave before they call the cops.'

'So that's it? No exit permit?' said the man perceived to be some trespasser by Doug. 'Well then I better go and kill myself.'

'By all means, do what you need to do, but do it somewhere else, come on, out you go pal!' Doug opened the door and shoved the manic man into the corridor. Doug looked to his left first, to see if there was a security guard about, and then he turned right – and saw that the corridor was empty. There was no sign of the strange man. Thinking he might have slipped back into the office, Doug went in there and looked about, but it was plain to see that there was no sign of the kook anywhere. It was only some days later that Doug learned of Jane's encounter with the same man with the colour-changing attire and his excessively eager wish for that bizarre exit permit so he could leave the "State". That is not the end of strange matter. In 2009 I was on a radio station on Liverpool one Halloween, and the presenter asked me to explain timeslips to the audience and after the brief explanation a listener named Guy telephoned the radio station and he was put through to me. Guy related a very strange experience and I subsequently checked many of the details referenced in his story and found them to be true. One February evening in the year 2000, when Guy was fourteen, he and a gang of lads from the Halewood area of Liverpool were trespassing on land close to the runways of what was then Speke Airport; a year later in 2001 the airport would be renamed Liverpool John Lennon Airport. Guy had a harebrained plan to rob cargo off the planes at Speke but instead he and his gang were spotted by security men and chased. At one point in the chase when it looked as if the security men would have the gang cornered by a chain-link fence, there was a flash of light, a bit like the glare of a camera's flashgun, only the light was blue. The guards were now nowhere to be seen, but Guy and his gang didn't realise that something very strange had happened. The gang hid in long grass they had not noticed before and when they were certain the guards had somehow passed them by, the young men got to their feet and saw a massive plane silhouetted against the actinic lights of the airport. Guy then noticed a man, aged about forty-five perhaps, crouched in the grass, and with him were three young children, aged about ten or twelve, and there was also a woman hiding with them.

'Go away! You'll attract them to us!' the man whispered to Guy, who was standing nearest to the people crouching in the grass.

'Who are you hiding from?' Guy asked, and the five other gang members gathered around the man and woman in the grass with the children.

A blinding beam of light shone down from above, and Guy saw that the powerful beam was coming from something that looked like a helicopter, only this helicopter made no noise whatsoever. It came down and hovered about six feet off the ground some fifty feet away, and three men who looked like soldiers jumped from the silent craft. They ran past Guy and the gang and pointed handguns at the couple and the children hiding in the grass.

'We've got exit permits, it's all above board,' said the man, rising slowly to a standing position with his arms raised.

One of the armed men fired at the man at almost point-blank range and the blast knocked him backwards into the grass. The children screamed in terror and the woman gathered them with her arms as another one of the men, who was of soldierly appearance, pointed a gun at her.

The man lying on his back in the grass started to move, and sat up, as if he had been stunned by whatever was fired at him. He received a boot in the face, and Guy decided to make a break for it. Once he ran off, the other lads followed him, and they expected the men from that silent helicopter to fire upon them, but they never did. When Guy looked back less than a minute later, he saw that the three military men had vanished, and so had the helicopter, the couple and their children, and even the long grass. Now it was just tarmac. Guy and the gang ran straight into the security men, who detained them till the police had arrived. Each member of the gang was interviewed by the police and each of them told the same story about the men from the weird helicopter shooting the man who had claimed to have something called an "exit permit". Police visited the scene of the alleged shooting and found no evidence of the incident described by Guy and his gang. The security guards who had pursued Guy and the other would-be robbers that evening said that at one point they had seen a flash of light in the vicinity during the chase, and afterwards they saw that the gang had somehow vanished, yet there was no place to hide. The ground was flat there and there were no trees of any objects to hide behind.

All of the members of the gang had distinctly heard the man who was subsequently shot mention the words "exit permit" – the very same words the mysterious visitor to India Buildings mentioned. The man in India Buildings vanished into thin air on two occasions, and that's exactly what happened to the dramatis personae on the periphery of Speke Airport – they vanished, along with that *futuristic* helicopter – or whatever it was. So, are the incidents at India Buildings and Speke Airport some glimpse of a future totalitarian state that will exist in England at some point in the 21st Century? If we are headed for such an Orwellian dystopia, how did things get so bad in the future? Surely in a coveted democracy like ours, such an unthinkable state of affairs is impossible? Beijing now has around 500,000 closed-circuit television (CCTV) cameras which cover every corner of its city; there is nowhere to avoid the gaze of the electronic eyes, except by going indoors. After Beijing, London has the most CCTV cameras, with around 450,000 of them watching the citizens of the capital. The excuse for such saturation of cameras is 'to tackle the crime rate' but in recent years the crime rate in London has risen to new heights, and there are now more murders in London than in New York City. In the entire UK there are around six million CCTV cameras watching us in shops, supermarkets, at filling stations, in bars, in the street and even on the highways. In short, outside of China, Britain is the most spied upon nation on earth, and long ago, George Orwell warned us that the Big Brother Society was coming but many mistook his novel as an allegorical work attacking Russia. Now the state is fighting terrorism, so it claims it has a legitimate and moral right to keep the country under the ever watchful eye of the CCTV camera, and there are even sophisticated voice-recognition computers than can listen in for specific words on telephone and mobile conversations. The UK now also has the biggest DNA database in the world – but there are thousands of samples of DNA taken from innocent people. Are we sleepwalking into the "State" mentioned by that possible time-walker seeking an exit permit in the India Buildings in 1974? Most civil liberties groups would say we are heading towards Orwell's *1984*, and groups like the Electronic Frontier Foundation, based in San Francisco, also believe that governments should keep their noses out of the internet – another area that is being increasingly monitored by the authorities.

Of course, another ominous scene often glimpsed in the many timeslips reported to me is one of utter devastation of the land – be it by nuclear holocaust, asteroid bombardment or some ecological extermination. The firepower of the world's nuclear weapons is one thing, but Mother Nature can put our power of destruction to shame if she wants. The 1883 eruption of the volcano on the island of Krakatoa, Indonesia, killed over 36,000 people with the eruption and tsunamis, and the earthquakes it produced were even felt in Australia. The blast was equal to thousands of nuclear megatons. There are supervolcanoes rumbling away now that could cause just as much devastation, like the Yellowstone Caldera in north-west Wyoming, which measures 34 by 45 miles. This volcano could erupt at any moment with consequences too horrific to imagine. The last time it erupted was 640,000 years ago, and an incredible 240 cubic miles of rock were blown into the upper atmosphere. As I write, this American supervolcano is being monitored by geologists because a geyser that sits on top of the volcano has started to emit jets of steam. This volcano is also 'provoked' by regular earthquakes. Similar apocalyptic supervolcanoes exist in Japan, New Zealand and Italy.

Then we have the controversy concerning Global Warming: the increasing rise in the temperature of the earth. Many independent lines of scientific enquiry have established beyond a shadow of a doubt that the emissions produced by civilization's industry and even the aerosols and other chemicals the individual uses are having a detrimental effect on the planet's delicate ecosystem. In a nutshell, we are treating the earth like dirt, and if nothing is done to halt and reverse the abuse of the planet, our descendants will inherit a drowned world of rising sea levels (and Liverpool would be one of the first cities to go under, being around fifty feet above sea level with the hills of Everton being the highest points of salvation at 220 feet), a choking atmosphere full of carbon dioxide, unbearable high temperatures from the Greenhouse Effect, and a very violent climate of hurricanes. It might already be too late to do anything about it now unless our technology advances dramatically and some geniuses produce an undreamt of antidote to all of the damage inflicted upon this precious world.

A most intriguing - albeit frightening – timeslip, which might have given a 20th century man a preview of some future catastrophe was reported to me by a retired policeman in his mid-seventies named Ken, who now lives in Liverpool's Garston district. In January 1973, Ken, like every other police officer in the Wallasey area of Wirral, was on the lookout for a very mysterious and brutal maniac with a hammer who had just killed a 37-year-old woman on Gorsedale Road. The same murderer was thought to be behind two previous attacks on young women at Matthew Street and Clarendon Road (and after the latter attack the victim died). Photographs of the type of hammer used were put up on hoardings by the police and there were door to door enquiries. Ken was on his beat up at New Brighton around this time, when he suffered "a funny turn" on the Marine Promenade. Everything went completely silent, and he could not even feel the sharp coastal January wind. Then suddenly, the grey oppressive clouds of New Brighton were instantly replaced with a clear blue canopy of sky with a scorching, blinding sun beating down. This sudden change in the weather was confusing enough to the policeman, but as he took this in and regained his hearing, he was shocked to see that the Mersey and Liverpool Bay resembled the sand plains of the Australian Outback. Ken looked to his left and saw the lighthouse standing in this surreal arid landscape, and it had sustained serious structural damage, was heavily pockmarked and missing most of its white paint – and then Ken noticed the huge rusted hulk of a cargo ship lying stranded further out on the dried seabed of Liverpool Bay, lying on its side as it shimmered in the tropical heat. About fifty yards from Ken was the sun-bleached shell of a bus with windows begrimed with sand-dust, and near it were human remains – white skulls and rib cages and bones. Ken swore, and he tried to radio HQ to tell them what he was seeing, but all he could hear was white noise on the VHF band. No one answered, and he felt intensely alone. The backs of his hands turned red in the savage searing sunlight, and he began to hyperventilate. He felt as if he'd strolled into the aftermath of a nuclear war. Ken negotiated mountains of rubble and one of the few landmarks he could recognise was St James' Church on Victoria Road, although the building's steeple was blackened as if it had been burned. Inside the church,

Ken was shocked to see hundreds of skeletons in tattered clothes, many of them kneeling in the pews. 'Oh my dear God,' he gasped to himself, 'what's happened? What has happened?'

He turned and ran outside, and had another "funny turn". He felt as if he was falling, and experienced butterflies in his stomach. 'Oh!' he cried out, and then he found himself among the familiar traffic noise. He was back among the living on Victoria Road, and the landscape of desolation and the baking sun had gone. He decided he could tell no one about his unearthly experience. Ken went back to the station and said he didn't feel well, and the desk sergeant said, 'Hey Ken, what's wrong with your face?'

Ken's face was red and the skin was peeling, and skin on the back of his hands was also raw. This was proof that Ken had not hallucinated his inexplicable short-lived trip into some nightmarish future. On the following day the policeman suffered intense headaches and a doctor diagnosed something he found unbelievable – sunstroke in January. Had Ken walked through some ecological disaster, or as he suspected, the aftermath of World War Three? Let us hope that all of these futures of holocaust, catastrophe and dystopia can be avoided. Perhaps they are just warnings of a future that will result if we don't nip certain problems in the bud today. So, be careful who you vote for, and be mindful of the environment...

THE ENCOURAGER

It was Saturday, 14 February 1970 – Valentine's Day, and two memorable things happened that morning. The postman delivered a pale pink envelope through the door of a semi on Gateacre's Lulworth Road – home of a 41-year-old divorcee named Jo. It was also the day the ghost of Lydia arrived at the said house. The time was 8.15am and Jo had been in the kitchen, having her cornflakes breakfast with a towel wound around her wet hair as she looked through her Green Shield Stamps saver book when she heard the letterbox flap clank. She'd expected it to be the gas bill, and being between jobs in the aftermath of the divorce, Jo was relying on her savings to make ends meet. She went into the hallway, and immediately noticed the pinkness of the envelope on the mat, and then she realised it was Valentine's Day. With a bemused look, the housewife picked it up and saw just her first name, followed by the address, so whoever had sent it had not known her surname. She took the envelope to the breakfast table as her oldest daughter, 19-year-old Harriet came almost sleepwalking into the kitchen behind her. The teen was working at a newsagent's on Renshaw Street, and her mother had called her half an hour ago to no avail. 'What's that?'

Harriet asked, noticing the pink envelop propped up against the cereal box. 'Never mind, Speedy Gonzales, get your breakfast down you and get to that job,' said Jo, bringing the girl's cereal bowl and spoon to the table. In a stern voice she told Harriet: 'Mr Higgins has already cautioned you about rolling in late, and we need the money now your father's gone.'

'It's a Valentine, isn't it?' Harriet realised with a grin, and she wiped the sleep from her eyes and tried to grab the envelope but her mum was too quick and swiped it from her reach. 'You're blushing! Ha!' Harriet noted.

'I am not – I'm having a tropical – just a flush,' Jo told her. 'Now come on Harriet, get fed and get your make-up on and get through that door.'

'Bet it's from Mr Jones from across the road,' said Harriet, going to the other side of the kitchen; she wanted toast instead of cornflakes. 'He's always gawping at you – and he looks like Norman Bates.'

'Will you get a move on?' Jo looked up at the clock, and then she hid the envelope in a drawer. At 8.40am, Harriet finally left the house, bound for the bus stop, and Jo opened the envelope. It said, *'Jo, this is from someone who has fallen in love with you, and I know I'm not supposed to give my name, but it's Charlie x'*

'Charlie?' Jo said to herself, 'I don't know a Charlie – do I?' She made herself a coffee and sat at the kitchen table, trying to think of any males named Charlie. The train of thought was interrupted by Jo's mother ringing her to suggest two jobs that had been advertised in the *Echo* the night before: a shop assistant needed at Sturlas and a demonstrator at Blacklers. 'Mum, I appreciate you thinking of me but I'll find my own jobs thank you!' Jo snapped, and hung up.

'Excuse me,' said a feminine voice to Jo's left. Jo slowly turned to see who it was. It was a woman around Jo's age, maybe a little younger, but much smaller (about 5ft 2) and she wore an old fashioned bonnet and an elegant outfit which, in the eyes of Jo, dated her to the days of Jane Austen. She really did look as if she'd stepped out of one of those BBC Regency dramas. In a split second, Jo realised she was looking at a ghost. It stood there, framed in the kitchen doorway, and its light-green eyes did not look real somehow – they looked like the inanimate eyes of a doll.

Over the years I've seen people react in different ways to ghosts; some run and some stay put. Without appearing sexist, I would say that women tend to accept visitors from the hereafter and remain calm, whereas men tend to recoil and either flee or go on the defensive. Jo asked an obvious question: 'Who are you?'

The ghost bowed her head slightly, and whispered 'Lydia.' Her accent was not a local one, and she was very well-spoken.

'Lydia, why are you haunting me? Do you need help or a prayer?' said Jo, and she looked the ghost up and down, noting the fine silky long dress that went almost to the floor, where a pair of off-white court shoes could just be seen.

'I lived at Lee Hall,' said Lydia, speaking so softly, and she now glanced up to make eye contact with Jo. 'I knew your grandmother – mention me to her.'

'Which one – I have two?' Jo asked, and inched further towards Lydia. She felt so sorry for the forlorn-looking ghost, sensing somehow that she was lonely.

'Mary,' Lydia replied, and she turned in an odd way as if she was on a turntable – and then she walked silently into the kitchen – and Jo followed her rather tentatively. The ghost fidgeted with her hands, and said, 'Charlie – the man who sent that Valentine missive to you – loves you dearly and needs your love as you need him, Josephine.'

Jo smiled; it was an age since anyone had called her Josephine – and then she looked at the Valentine's Day card, realising what Lydia was referring to. At this point, Jo detected a lovely scent of patchouli. 'I don't know anyone named Charlie;' Jo admitted, then wondered: 'why are you playing Cupid, Lydia?'

The ghost rambled on about Lee Hall, and a family named the Okills who owned that stately pile of bricks, and how she was abandoned by a certain aristocrat there – and she talked as if the desertion had happened only last week. 'Everyone deserves love,' said Lydia, and she produced a silk handkerchief, dabbed those long-dead eyes, and said, 'Charlie is the one you have seen walking his dog.'

And then – Lydia was no longer there, and the scent of patchouli quickly faded.

Jo dried her hair and drove to see her 90-year-old Nan, Mary, a fiercely independent lady who lived in Woolton. She only looked about 70, yet she had only recently given up cigarettes. When Jo mentioned the ghost named Lydia, Mary seemed flabbergasted and she fell backwards into her fireside chair. Mary said that Lee Hall had once stood where Lee Park Golf Course now existed, and that when it had been demolished around 1956, Lydia had visited her in tears one morning and had told her that her home had been torn down. Mary was naturally shocked by the ghost, and for some reason no one else could see her – but she eventually got used to the phantom from what seemed to be the Georgian era. That ghost always gave Mary accurate warnings and steered her from danger. 'If she advises you to go with this Charlie fellah – perhaps you should,' was Mary's advice.

'I think he's about sixty though,' said Lydia, recalling the debonair, well-dressed man she would often see walking his dog near her home. She saw him on the following day, a Sunday, and he seemed so shy. She asked him if he had sent the Valentine and he blushed, and nodded, and looked so scared. Jo said she had never received a Valentine before, and they got talking. He was a bachelor, and was very introverted, but Jo asked him if he'd like to go out on a date, 'Just to see how it goes.'

They went to a restaurant, and Charlie came out of his shell. What a raconteur he was, a font of funny stories, and afterwards they went to a beautiful old pub, where he actually danced – ballroom style – as people laughed and clapped. That night, as he took Lydia to her door, they kissed, and he said a strange thing. 'Did Lydia put a word in for me?' he asked.

Jo was stunned, and she slowly nodded. 'You've seen her too?' she asked.

Charlie smiled and said: 'She persecuted me to ask you out.'

'Can we do this again, Charlie? On Saturday?' Jo asked, and Charlie kissed her knuckle and said, 'I'd love to – yes.'

They were married by July, and Lydia often popped

in to act as some ethereal marriage guidance counsellor on the rare occasions when the couple had silly rows. Jo and Charlie have sadly left this world themselves now, and I wonder if Lydia is still playing matchmaker somewhere in her locality today...

THE STRANGE WORLD OF WARNING DREAMS

In the lifetime of a person who has lived an average lifespan, he or she will spend about 230,000 hours asleep, which means you spend approximately a third of your life in that mysterious realm of dreams and altered consciousness which has confounded scientists for centuries. Joseph, in the Bible's Book of Genesis was deemed to be a great prophet because he was able to decode the strange worrying dream of the Pharaoh of Egypt concerning seven fat cows and seven lean ones. The Pharaoh's magicians and high priests could not unravel the meaning of the dream, but Joseph said the dream meant that Egypt would enjoy seven bountiful harvests followed by seven years of famine and drought, so the Pharaoh immediately ordered his farmers to stockpile grain and create a spare reservoir of water in preparation for the hard times envisaged. After this famous dream interpretation, Joseph was elevated to become a vizier – the highest official in Egypt to serve the Pharaoh. Thousands of years later, Sigmund Freud was elevated from a neurologist to an international star when he practically invented psychoanalysis in the 1890s and became an official (and an exceedingly well-paid) dream interpreter. Despite scientific analysis, the dreaming mind continues to defy the laws of physics. How, for example, can people dream of future events or of incidents in the present happening miles away? A case in point is mentioned in a press report for June 10, 1935. On the death of their mother, a brother and sister in Bebington quarrelled and the brother went abroad. Months later, the sister had a dream on a Friday evening in which her deceased mother appeared to her in a strange azure satin dress and said: 'Go to my grave and you will meet your brother – go tomorrow – you must talk to him again!'

The sister went to the grave in Bebington Cemetery – and there was her brother at the graveside. He told her he was there because of a strange dream he'd had on Friday night: 'Mother appeared in the dream in a pale blue dress, and she said: "Go to my grave and you will meet your sister – go tomorrow – you must talk to her again."'

Brother and sister made up and remained close for the rest of their lives, and all because of a dream.

Dreams of death are one of the most commonly reported ones that come my way. In 2016, a 44-year-old Tuebrook woman named Leanne returned from her shift at a school canteen one Friday afternoon, and although she was feeling rather tired and worn out with being on her feet in the school kitchen all day, she had to put the tea on. Her husband and two sons were due home in an hour's time and Leanne always enjoyed serving them their meals when they came home. However, on this particular afternoon, Leanne sat on the sofa and her tiredness overcame her. She drifted off, and had a very disturbing dream. She found herself walking down Church Street, and she turned left into Primark, when she almost collided with a workmate she had not seen in years – a 33-year-old woman named Clare, and at first, Leanne thought she was carrying a child – but as Clare got nearer, Leanne saw to her horror that her former workmate was carrying a little coffin.

Leanne awoke with a start and saw that she'd only dozed off for about five minutes, and she got up and went into the kitchen to make herself a strong coffee. As she put the tea on, she thought about the short nightmare, and wondered where shocking imagery like that had come from. Leanne never even watched the most dated and innocuous horror films on the TV; she preferred romantic films and comedies.

She told her husband about the strange dream, and he didn't even seem to listen to a word she said. The very next day, which was a Saturday, Leanne went to the city centre to do a bit of shopping with her friend Joanne. Leanne preferred ordering clothes and goods online, but Joanne had persuaded her to go to town so they could have a drink and a meal after they'd been around the shops. Leanne found herself heading towards Primark on Church Street, and she was filled with an intense sensation of *déjà vu* – she just knew she was going to see her old mate Clare, and she slowed down and looked at Joanne.

'What's to do, Lee?' Joanne asked her friend, noticing that she seemed worried about something.

'Nothing,' came a reply from Leanne that was almost whispered.

The two women walked into the popular Irish-owned store – and there was Clare; she was walking towards a thunderstruck Leanne. In her arms, Clare carried her three-year-old son. Clare and Leanne said their hellos and Leanne asked Clare to come and have a drink with her and Joanne, but Clare said she couldn't. She had promised her husband she'd be home soon because it was their anniversary and they were going for a meal. Clare said goodbye and Leanne asked Joanne if they could go for a drink first because she'd just had a shock. Joanne thought her friend was pulling her leg at first, but Leanne insisted on going to a nearby pub on Hanover Street. The two ladies went there and Leanne told her friend about the dream she'd had about Clare carrying the little coffin and Joanne said it had just been a nightmare, and that she was reading too much into it. Leanne said she just knew something was going to happen to Clare's son.

A week later, Joanne called Leanne on her mobile and said, 'Where are you?'

'At home, why?' Leanne replied, wondering why Joanne had asked her that question.

'Are you sitting down?' a sombre-voiced Joanne asked.

'Standing up – why? What are you asking me daft questions for?' Leanne replied, getting a bit irritated by Joanne.

'Sit down, Leanne,' said Joanne, 'Clare's son passed away last night. I only heard about it about ten minutes ago.'

'What?' Leanne felt her stomach drop through the floor.

'He had an allergic reaction to something and stopped breathing,' Joanne told her. 'The paramedics were called out but they couldn't revive him or something.'

'Oh my God,' said Leanne, over and over as she felt her blood run cold. 'Maybe that dream was a warning and I should have told Clare,' Leanne reasoned, and she started to cry. 'I should have told her – it must have been a warning and I didn't do anything about it.'

'Leanne! Stop it! You couldn't have done anything about it. I'll come and see you in a minute, love,' said Joanne, and she came over and comforted her friend.

Another dream concerning a warning from beyond occurred at Birkenhead in 1960. A midwife named Christine was asleep at her home on Portland Street when she had a vivid dream about her late mother, Winifred – a Liverpool woman who had also been a midwife. Christine's mother told her to go at once to a girl who was in labour at a house on Grange Road West, and she kept emphasising the number of this house and warning Christine that there'd be a death if she didn't go. Christine awoke and told her husband about the realistic dream but he just said, 'Ah, you had cheese on toast for supper; that's caused it. Go back to sleep will you? I've got to be up at five.'

The same dream played in Christine's mind two more times and her mother was livid at her for not doing what she was told. Christine felt that her mother had really visited her somehow, and so at 3.15am she sneaked out her bed and drove in her Morris Minor to the address she'd dreamt of on Grange Road West, and a young girl named Susan answered the door with tears in her eyes. She thought it was her father calling. She explained that her older sister, Patricia, who was just sixteen, was upstairs – about to have a baby - with no one to attend her. She'd run away from her Liverpool home months ago after getting "into trouble" with a boy. Christine went upstairs and with the help of Susan, she delivered Patricia's baby boy and convinced the girl to go to hospital. Christine's husband was dumfounded when he realised his late mother-in-law apparently *had* contacted Christine in a dream.

One of the most surreal types of warning that can come in sleep is the well-documented 'backwards dream' – and the following account is an excellent example of this type of dream. A 50-year-old Tuebrook man named Roy Horner had a series of recurring dreams over one month in 1982. The dreams were very strange because everything happened backwards in them. Roy was the only person in the dream who could move forwards, and the dreams always began with him standing on the corner of Maiden Lane and Finvoy Road, and the opening scene was always the same eerie one. He was looking down Maiden Lane towards the Knoclaid Road end when he'd see the slow-motion reversal of a weird black car. This turned out to be a limousine full of mourners, and there were six more limos travelling backwards up Maiden Lane behind it. The funeral cortege would reverse around the corner where Roy was standing and travel backwards into Finvoy Road, with the hearse being the rear car. The procession of ominous black cars would then all swing left into Isabel Grove, and it was easy for Roy to run to this street to see where they were going because the whole world was moving so slow, but he could move at a normal speed. Upon reaching Isabel Grove, the funeral hearse stopped at a certain terraced house where all of the windows were covered with white blinds. The pall bearers then removed the coffin from the hearse and walked backwards into the house, and Roy went in with them, but they didn't seem to notice him. The six men walked backwards through the hall into the little front parlour, and as they put the coffin on a stand, a spectacled woman said to the man next to her, 'Checked heart bleeding his get and go to him told Stan.'

The lid of the coffin was then pushed off by the body inside it, which sat up and reached out for the woman. The 'dead' man was baldy but had tufts of red hair on either side of his head. He was in tears, and the shock of a dead man merging from a coffin would always wake Roy at that point.

Roy had this dream almost every night, for a month, and then they stopped. A few weeks later, Roy was visiting a friend on Portrush Street, and he had to take a shortcut down Isabel Grove, so imagine the shock he got when he not only recognised the street in the dream, he also saw a hearse, followed by a train of black limousines pull up. The hearse was outside the very house he had seen on so many nights in that scary backwards dream. He mingled with the crowds outside the neighbouring houses and he saw the very same spectacled woman come out of the house after the pallbearers had carried the coffin into the hearse. To some man, the woman with the glasses on said: 'Stan told him to go and get his bleeding heart checked.'

Roy went cold in the pit of his stomach, because he realised now that he had heard the woman say those very words – in reverse – in those ghastly morbid dreams. Roy did not know the man who had died and he was baffled as to why he had experienced so many dreams about him. Thinking it might be a warning, Roy visited his doctor and lied about having chest pains. The doctor eventually referred Roy to a heart specialist – who discovered that Roy had a dangerously enlarged heart, and Roy had to have heart valve surgery. Roy stopped smoking and made a full recovery and he is still alive today, and he thinks those strange dreams somehow served as a warning – a warning which saved his life.

The most chilling case of a psychic dream concerns a 40-year-old Birkenhead woman named Celia, who woke up screaming one night in 1968 and almost throttled her milkman husband Brian, who was trying to get some precious sleep before his working day started – at 3.30am. Celia said that she had seen a ghastly murder in a dream in which a smart-suited man with red hair had strangled and raped a woman. The whole thing was too realistic to have been a dream, Celia maintained, and she'd had these dream warnings before. The dreams went on, night after night, and Celia, who was very good at drawing, sketched a picture of the red-headed murderer in his black suit, white shirt and royal blue tie. 'He's got a Scottish accent,' Celia told her bemused husband, 'and Brian, he knows I've seen him in the dreams because he's psychic too and he's come down here to look for me.'

'What? All the way from Scotland? You're going worse, you are,' Brian told her. 'It's all in the mind – all these crime series you're watching on the telly and that.' However, on the following morning, Brian saw a red-haired man with a blue tie and black suit standing outside his home on Price Street, and he looked like the man Celia had sketched. 'Nice morning isn't it? The stranger said to Brian in a Scottish accent. He was also seen following Celia to the shops and after a week of this, Brian reported the Scotsman to the police. A policeman who looked at the sketch of the stalker remarked that he looked like the identikit picture of "Bible John" – a mysterious religiously-motivated serial strangler and rapist wanted in Scotland. A policeman followed Celia whenever she went out the house, and he too saw the red-haired man when Celia pointed him out, but this man ran off and he never stalked Celia again. Bible John was never captured...

THE GRAVE WORMS

One warm Saturday night in 1981, two 18-year-old girls – Michelle and Lisa – were walking up Priory Road on their way to the house of a friend of theirs named Jenny who lived on Winslow Street. The girls were gabbing away about boys as they walked past the railings of Stanley Park. There was a full moon hanging low in the sky, and its silvery light was falling on the dark green expanses of the park. 'We should be out tonight instead of going to Jenny's,' said Michelle, 'hate having no money.'

'I want to meet some rich fellah,' yearned Lisa, 'get married to him and just go out every single night, clubbing it.'

Michelle suddenly let out a shriek. She'd been walking on the left side of Lisa, so she was nearest to the park railings, and she jumped sideways, recoiling in fright at something. Lisa looked down and saw something that looked halfway between a giant slug and a snake. It had slid out of the park through the railings, and it was green and slimy and it had open jaws which snapped. Michelle swore and ran off up Priory Road, and as she did the snakelike creature attacked Lisa's feet, which had flip flops on. Lisa ran off, and screamed when she realised that the thing was chasing her at some speed. As the unidentified creature chased the girls, it made a clicking sound, a bit like the noise a dog makes when its claws tap against the pavement as it trots along. Lisa could hardly run because she had flip flops on, and she thought she felt the thing pinch her left ankle as she ran. At one point in the 400-yard dash to Walton Lane, Lisa halted for a few heart-stopping moments, took off her flip flops and ran barefoot with Michelle. They passed two bemused lads around their age, and one of them said, 'What's up with you two?' to Michelle and Lisa.

'There's some snake thing after us,' Lisa answered, and she turned and saw nothing.

'A snake?' asked the lad. 'Have you two been sniffing glue or somethin'?'

Two dark serpentine shapes darted out from the railings just to the left of the sandstone gateposts of the park, and the Lisa jumped behind the lads. Michelle ran off across Walton Lane and came close to being run over.

The two wormy creatures were greenish and their skin had thousands of yellowish bubble-like domes, but they possessed no visible limbs or eyes, and the most terrifying things were the jaws of the creatures; they snapped loudly and when the jaws were fully open, the three terrified teenagers caught a glimpse of a ring of sharp yellowish-white teeth. Lisa was that scared when she saw the hissing slithering creatures inch nearer and raise their heads, she became dizzy and unsteady on her feet, as if she was going to pass out.

'What are they?' one of the lads said, and he spat at the thing nearest to him as it snaked forward, and it drew back, but then leaped about two feet forward, and Lisa let out a scream. All three teenagers ran off across the road and joined a hysterical Michelle.

This was one of the first reports of the cryptids (unknown creatures whose existence is unproven) known as grave worms. They have allegedly been seen in many of the major cities in the vicinity of graveyards, and the theory is that with the increasing popularity of cremation, the worms can no longer feed on the flesh of corpses and so they are leaving graveyards in search of living flesh to feast upon. But what are they? They might be descendants of the bristle worm, an ancient aggressive worm which is the ancestor of the common earthworm, or they may be a mutated species of toothed worm that has grown stronger from imbibing the blood and flesh from corpses buried in cemeteries. They may even be the European cousin of the Mongolian Death Worm, which is said to exist in the Gobi Desert. A policeman once told me how, in the 1970s a gang of children ran up to him on Smithdown Road one evening and said and old man had been murdered in the local graveyard – Toxteth Park Cemetery, The kids led the policeman to a body sitting up against a gravestone. The constable clicked on his torch and saw the corpse was the body of a vagrant with a bottle of half-empty purple methylated spirits still in his hand, but there was a gaping hole where his left eye had been. As the policeman shone the torch close to this hole, the children all let out a chorus of 'Eww!'

And then the children screamed when something popped its head out of that gaping hole in the tramp's face. It was a red shiny wormlike creature, about three inches in diameter, and it had jaws arranged in a circular pattern around the O-shaped lips of a mouth that opened and closed rapidly. The children withdrew to a distance of about twelve feet, and the policeman also stepped back, unsure what the thing was. He knew that the rest of the bizarre creature was still inside the dead tramp's head. The overgrown 'worm' shout out of the hole, fell, bounced off the left shoulder of the corpse, and landed in the grass. The policeman searched for the thing with his torch but it was nowhere to be seen. The post-mortem on the vagrant did not mention what seems to have been some flesh-eating worm; instead, the cause of death was said to be natural causes and the hole in the face was assumed to have been caused by rats and even crows that had pecked out the eye of the dead man. One evening around 11.40pm in September 1990, a woman named Muriel was travelling home to Lordens Road, Huyton after spending an evening with her mother at her house on Stonebridge Lane. The hackney cab was travelling along Finch Lane when the cabby noticed what he thought were rats swarming across the road, from Yewtree Cemetery's gates towards Finch Dene.

'Look at this!' the taxi driver shouted to Muriel.

Muriel leaned forward a little, partially restrained by her seatbelt, and looked at the road ahead, bathed in the soft orange light of a sodium street lamp. She thought she could see something moving up there, but her eyesight was terrible.

'See them?' The cabby slowed the hackney so it was inching towards the exodus of the little creatures as they poured out of the cemetery.

'What are they?' Muriel asked, thinning her eyes.

'Rats!' said the cabby, 'loads of them, all coming out

the boneyard on the right.'

'Ooh!' Muriel shuddered. 'Can't you go round them?'

'Nah, they'll scarper when I beep the horn,' said the taxi driver, and he drove forward and sounded his horn five times.

The things sweeping out from the cemetery now curved – and headed for the hackney cab. In seconds they were climbing all over the vehicle, and by then, the horrified taxi driver realised they were not rats, but huge greenish-gray snakes about three feet in length with jaws that clicked against the windscreen.

'They're not rats! What are they!' yelled Muriel, and the cab-driver turned on his windscreen wipers in an effort to try and knock the terrifying creatures off. Some of them were dislodged by the wipers, but others stuck to the side windows of the cab, tapping their teeth hard against the glass. Muriel started to scream, and then she saw that these things were squirting what seemed to be blood out of their open mouths at the windows of the cab. Eventually the last of the anguine monstrosities fell off the window, and the cab driver kept swearing and saying he wished a car wash was open because that'd get them off his taxi. The cabby, in his panic, had driven half a mile past Lordens Road, and so he turned his vehicle around, and headed for Muriel's home, and he kept asking her if she was alright because he could see she'd been pretty shook-up by the hideous attack of those giant worms with jaws.

'I've never seen anything like *them* before,' she told the driver, and she asked how near her home was now.

'Nearly there now love,' said the cabby. 'They must have been brought into the country from Africa or something. They don't belong here, obviously.'

At last the cab pulled up in front of Muriel's house on Lordens Road, and the woman tried to pay the cabby but he refused to take the money. 'No, it's alright, keep it love,' he insisted, 'you've had a horrible ordeal tonight. Just get safely indoors, go on, I'll watch you go in.'

Muriel thanked the cabby and got out the hackney. She had to walk across a grass verge to reach her home, and after she had crossed this she heard a thump behind her. The cabby had left his vehicle and he was running towards her.

'I'm quite alright, driver,' she said with a smile, 'you get back to your taxi.'

'Take your coat off love,' said the cabby in a stern manner.

'Sorry?' Muriel queried.

The cabby began to take her coat off by pulling at her left sleeve and dragging the collar of the coat back.

'What *are* you doing?' she asked, a little afraid of his actions.

'One of them's on the back of your coat!' he said, 'Take it off, quick!'

Muriel screamed as the coat was whipped away from her. The cabby threw it on the grass verge, and there was a particularly bloated version of one of those repulsive long writhing creatures. It crawled off the coat and shot forward, snapping its jaws at Muriel and the cabby.

'Get in, quick!' the taxi driver almost pushed Muriel over as he tried to shove her towards the gate of her terraced house. He then dashed back to his cab, and returned with an old lug wrench that he kept under his seat in case a customer ever tried to rob or attack him.

He lifted the wrench high above his head and tried to smash it down on the puffed up snaky little brute, but he missed it, and the thing shot forward and its jaws tried to bite into the toe of his boot, and this really frightened the cabby. He kicked the thing into the grass, and he was so scared, he ran back to his car and drove off at high speed. He called on Muriel the next day and asked her if she'd seen any more of that weird creature. She said she hadn't. That taxi driver always avoided Finch Lane if he could after that night, and he has no idea what those creatures were, but it's highly probable that they were grave worms. There are many unidentified species roaming the British Isles today, from strange 'big cats' to huge flying bats which are alleged to bite victims and suck blood. We also have creatures such as the Beast of Dean, which resembles a giant boar with massive tusks, and even a gigantic shrimp-like creature with teeth which has been seen coming ashore at Hoylake. I have an old story in my files about a girl named Pauline who found a doll with no clothes on in Grant Avenue, Wavertree, in the 1960s. She brought it home and told her mother the doll belonged to her friend Elsie, and Pauline was allowed to take the doll to bed. During the night, Pauline's mother looked in on her daughter, and saw to her horror that a long red worm was writhing across her sleeping daughter's face. One end of this worm had gone up Pauline's nose and the other end was still in the doll and had emerged from a small round hold in the doll's back. Pauline's mother rushed to her husband and told him what she'd seen and the husband carefully pulled the worm out of his daughter's nostril – and he saw that it had a small mouth with a jaw, which was quite unlike any worm he had ever seen. He put the doll and the worm in a bucket and he took it into the backyard and poured kettles of boiling water over the weird worm. It writhed in agony then died, and the water turned red from the blood of the worm, which was about fifteen inches long. A friend of the family who saw the dead worm said: 'That's a grave worm that; it's probably come from the Holy Trinity Churchyard.'

The churchyard in question was less than a hundred yards away from the house, and close to the spot where Pauline found that doll.

BOGEYMAN FROM ABOVE

There are certain paranormal entities which are very difficult to categorize, and a case in point is the strange being which is alleged to have attacked three teenagers in Halewood on Boxing Day, 2010. The three teens were Dylan, Rory and Jack, all aged 13, and on the Sunday morning of 26 December, 2010 – Boxing Day - at around 7am, Jack left his home on Halewood's Rutland Avenue and walked up Church Road, where he met his friends Rory and Dylan at the Okell Drive/Cambridge Lane roundabout. Jack slowly trudged through crispy frozen snow texting his friends, and as he passed the graveyard of St Nicholas – Halewood Parish Church – he heard someone whistling an eerie echoing tune. The teenager looked about but saw no one. The sun had not yet risen but the predawn light was bright enough to show Jack that no one was around. He heard the weird whistling sound again, and this time, Jack thought that the whistler was above him, and he gingerly looked up. A waning gibbous moon hung above, and a bright point of light – the planet Venus - was hanging in the eastern sky. Jack had been certain that the whistling sound had come from up in the sky, which, of course, seemed impossible. The teen felt very uneasy as the whistled melody came to an abrupt end, and he was only too glad when he saw Dylan and Rory in the distance, about 150 yards away, heading in his direction. When the lads met, Rory said he had lost his remote-control plane. The whole reason the boys had arranged to meet so early on such a wintry morning was to fly an old remote-control model airplane belonging to Rory over some farmland near the roundabout. A rocket that had been saved from Guy Fawkes Night had been taped to the plane, and the plan was to light the fuse of the rocket and then fly it as far up into the air as possible before the rocket would hopefully boost it to a high altitude. Instead, the rocket had not gone off and the plane had flown across the farmland and had been lost to sight somewhere in the direction of Gerrard's Lane, where it had gone out of range of the radio controller. 'I thought you were going to wait till I got there?' Jack moaned to Rory, when suddenly, the teenaged trio heard what they would later describe as mad laughter. Rory glanced up and said, 'Look!'

Jack and Dylan followed the line of his gaze and also looked heavenwards, and they could not believe their eyes. The figure of a man in a brown tight-fitting suit was descending rapidly, and the first thing Jack thought of was that the man had jumped out of a plane and his parachute had failed to open. The figure slowed down though, whereas a doomed parachutist would continue to accelerate due to gravity as each second passed. Thinking the falling man would land on them, the three teens scattered, but because the ground was so slippery with the snow and ice, Jack and Rory fell over, whereas Dylan literally dived through the thick spiny hedge bordering the cemetery of the parish church. Dylan expected to hear the body impacting into the ground but all he heard was screaming laughter and the cries of Rory. Jack got to his feet and witnessed a terrifying sight: the man in that brown suit was hovering a few feet over Rory and he was making grabbing motions at the lad's mop of curly hair. Rory's nickname was ketwig because his hair was so overgrown and unruly, and this weird hovering man was trying to grab at his hair, but Rory kept batting his hands away as he tried to get up off the ground. The face of the levitating man looked very sinister; it was as white as the snow lying about, and he had black swept-back eyebrows, large almond-shaped eyes, a sharp, pointed nose, and a large grinning mouth with vivid red lips and jagged long teeth. Dylan said the man also wore black calf-length boots and that his one-piece brown suit was similar to a boiler suit.

One second the figure was attacking Rory, and then in a flash the thing seemed to fly up into the air to an estimated altitude of about 300 feet or more. It hovered, stationary, and then the three terrified lads heard distant screams of laughter, and the unearthly entity swooped down at them again. Dylan told Jack and Rory to come through the hedge to hide from the nightmarish being, and they did as he suggested and the three of them took shelter under a tree. A Hackney cab came down the road and Rory ran out from the hedge to flag it down. The cab stopped and the driver naturally eyed him suspiciously. Rory begged the cabby to take him and his two friends – who scrambled out from the cover of the hedge – to his home on Clifton Avenue. 'Get in,' said the taxi driver, and he asked the three young teenagers what they were doing out so early on Boxing Day and on such an inclement morning. Rory told him about the weird figure which had swooped down and attacked him and his friends. As the cabby smiled at Rory's seemingly far-fetched story, everyone in the cab heard someone whistling loud – and it seemed to be coming from somewhere near. Something thumped the top of the cab hard three times, and the cabby caught sight of something brown flitting upwards and to the right in his right wing mirror. He slowed the cab, wound down the window, stuck his head out, trying to see what the thing was, but Rory became hysterical and told the driver not to stop. Jack and Dylan had to calm their friend down because he became so panic-stricken, he started to hyperventilate. No one believed the weird account given by the three teens, but I heard about the incident a few years later, and it reminded me of a similar report found in my files dated Boxing Day, 1970, only this time the victims were two teenaged girls (aged 14 and 15) and the venue was Spencer's Lane, Aintree. On this occasion the incident happened on a snowy Saturday evening, and the girls - on their way to meet two boys - said a man in black came screaming down out of the night sky and had tried to grab them, but the teens screamed and ran home after escaping from the clutches of the airborne assailant. I wonder if the entity which attacked them – described as having a very pale face – was the very same one which attached the teens in 2010 – and if so, what on earth is it?

MR FORGETTABLE

Frankie Rome sat in the corner of the Sandown pub on Wavertree's High Street that evening in 1961 and awaited a double fate. Two interested parties would be coming through that door soon – Big Johnny to knock his block off because Frankie had been seeing his wife behind his back – and a certain detective – a jack named McDonald – would arrest him for Frankie's part in a botched warehouse robbery in Bootle. An old black man came in with a suitcase full of fancy ties and tried to sell one to Frankie. 'I'm not interested mate, sorry,' said the two-bit crook.

'Don't brush me off mate,' said the tie seller, 'you'll like this. Now, ever notice how some people are just forgettable?'

'What do you mean?' Frankie grimaced as he looked at the pub door tensely for a moment. The tie seller said, 'Look, kid, I know you have problems, and I have just the thing for you. Wear this brown tie with the embroidered gold F letter and people will forget you. You might owe a lot of money, but the creditors will forget you as soon as you put this on. You might be public enemy number one, but if you wear this tie, you won't even make the back pages of the local paper; the police will forget you as if you'd never existed.'

'Do I look as if I've just come over on the banana boat, eh?' Frankie asked, but then he saw something in the tie-seller's eyes; a warm benevolence, as if he really was trying to help him somehow.

'I know you haven't,' said the ballyhoo street salesman, 'I'm just trying to get you out of a pickle.'

'With a tie,' Frankie chuckled, and wearily smiled. 'How much?' he asked.

'A quid,' said the hawker.

'Beat it!' said Frankie, and he folded his arms and rocked back and forth on the upholstered pub seat. 'What's it made out of? The Queen's knickers? A quid!'

'It's no ordinary tie,' said the man, his eyebrows raised and his eyes wide to convey the strange truth of what he was asserting. 'It's a hoodoo tie. Pure mulberry silk, quality interlining to keep a pristine shape, invisible seam and an indestructible keeper loop. The monogram is made from real Egyptian gold thread.'

'Hoodoo tie,' Frankie wheezed as he laughed, and he never thought he'd laugh on a day like this. 'Alright, I'll try it on first – giz it!' he said, reaching for the tie. He went to look in the mirror behind the bar, took his drab olive tie off, and put this dark brown one on with its silly gold letter "F" embroidered into it. Frankie adjusted it, and the barman, who was winding a linen cloth around the inside of a pint glass, smiled and quipped: 'Got a date, Frankie? Lucky woman!'

'Okay you robbing bastard, I'll take it – ' Frankie said – to an empty seat reflected in the mirror. The tie-peddler had gone. Frankie turned around to make sure; yes, the seat was empty, and the pub door wasn't even still closing. He swung around and asked the barman: 'Where did that black man go?'

'What black man?' the barman asked without taking his eyes off the glass he was cleaning.

'The one who was selling ties you docile get,' said Frankie, 'he was sitting at that table over there with me.'

'You're seeing things Frankie,' said the bar tender, 'you were sat there on your own with a face as long as Lime Street, as you always are nowadays.'

'Was he a ghost?' Frankie whispered to himself, and he asked for a double scotch, neat.

Big Johnny never came in, nor did Detective McDonald, and Frankie Rome was forced to consider the possibility that the tie really did make people forget about him. Or it was all a coincidence.

On the following day Frankie was walking up Picton Road when he encountered Big Johnny, and the latter should have punched Frankie to pulp for screwing his wife behind his back, but instead the goliath took him into the Wellington pub and bought him a pint and never mentioned the adulterous affair.

Oh my God, thought Frankie, he *has* forgotten the affair – the tie colporteur was telling the truth!

A few days later, Frankie, realising the slate had been supernaturally wiped clean, did not turn over a new leaf; he saw the tie as an ally in a new chapter in his life of crime. He recruited a gang to rob an Aigburth mansion but someone grassed on the gang – and not one member of that gang could remember Frankie Rome's name or even describe him when police grilled them – because he wore that tie. On the one hand he was upset at the gang being busted, but he was confident he could use his hoodoo tie on another, bigger job. He always thought better when he was drinking in the city centre 'dive' pubs, mixing with the lowest of the low and the real characters of the Liverpool underworld. While in town, Frankie met the woman of his dreams – a stunning aristocratic lady named Cordelia. Her Bentley had a flat tyre on Whitechapel and he replaced it, and something just clicked between them. He was from the gutter and she was from the stratosphere of high society, but there was some indefinable thing they had in common. He'd just had his hair cut, was dressed in a decent Burton's suit and looked presentable enough, and he tried to put on an accent but it kept slipping back into the vernacular scouse. Cordelia seemed both amused and yet smitten by Frankie. He took her for a drink in the Cross Keys pub and they really hit it off like a house on fire. She suggested meeting again – nearer her home in Chester, and a date was arranged. When Frankie walked home, he did something he hadn't done since he was eleven – he started to cry. He had long given up on finding true love back in his teens, and he just knew that this was the real thing. At last his girl had come, and now he intended to keep hold of her, and he knew it meant giving up his life of crime. It would be the greatest crime of all if he let Cordelia slip out of his hands. He took out his handkerchief and dabbed his eyes, and he hailed a taxi to take him home. All night his dreams were haunted by the beautiful smiling face of Cordelia.

When he went on that date to meet his love, she

wasn't there at the agreed rendezvous – the archway under the Eastgate Clock, and at first he just thought she was late – women were expected to be late on dates, but half an hour elapsed and she didn't show. He was baffled; had she come to her senses and decided not to go with him? No, she had been ever so eager to see him again. Then a mounting sense of horror rose up from the pit of his stomach and dried his choked-up throat as he recalled to his horror that she'd *forgotten* him – because he'd worn that accursed brown tie when he had met her. He went in search of her, just in case she was out, but he couldn't find her. He made enquiries in the pubs of Chester and someone told Frankie Cordelia's unusual surname. He found it in the phone book and called her. She answered and told him she had never met him. She admitted to being in Liverpool on the day Frankie mentioned but she had no recollection of meeting him. He started to cry and said, 'Please, Cordelia, can we meet up again? I love you!'

'If you don't leave me alone I shall inform the police!' she warned him, and hung up.

Days of drinking followed to numb the pain, and more out of spite than necessity, Frankie decided he'd go and rob a garage in Speke with his old mate Freddie. Frankie put on the brown tie and knew he wouldn't even need a mask, because no one would even remember him. They'd probably remember Freddie and he'd go down for the crime but so what? Frankie was sick of caring for other people in the light of all that heartbreak regarding the lost Cordelia. He went home after the job and threw the wad of money onto his bed and said, 'Crime does pay! Love's a load of rubbish!'

He looked in the mirror and saw that the brown tie he had on was *not* the one with golden "F" motif. His accomplice Freddie had innocently borrowed it before the garage hold-up, and when the police caught Frankie Rome and asked him who his partner in crime was, Frankie genuinely couldn't remember.

Printed in Great Britain
by Amazon